Accelerating AIX

Performance Tuning for
Programmers and System Administrators

Accelerating AIX

Performance Tuning for
Programmers and System Administrators

Rudy Chukran

ADDISON–WESLEY

An Imprint of Addison Wesley Longman, Inc.

Reading, Massachusetts • Harlow, England • Menlo Park, California
Berkeley, California • Don Mills, Ontario • Sydney
Bonn • Amsterdam • Tokyo • Mexico City

The publisher offers discounts of this book when ordered in quantity for special sales. For more information, please contact:

>Computer and Engineering Publishing Group
>Addison Wesley Longman, Inc.
>One Jacob Way
>Reading, Massachusetts 01867

Library of Congress Cataloging-in-Publication Data

Chukran, Rudy, 1952–
    Accelerating AIX : performance tuning for programmers and system
administrators / Rudy Chukran.
        p.   cm.
    Includes bibliographical references and index.
    ISBN 0-201-63382-5
    1. AIX (Computer file)   2. Operating systems (Computers)
I. Title.
QA76.76.063C495   1998
005.4'469—dc21   97–46800
                                                      CIP

Text printed on recycled paper
ISBN 0-201-63382-5
1 2 3 4 5 6 7 8 9—MA—0201009998
First printing, March 1998

Contents

Appendix   **197**

List of Figures

List of Tables

Preface

This book is intended for computer professionals who need to understand and control the factors that affect performance of their AIX compatible system. I learned the techniques and system background as a result of helping customers solve performance problems on their own systems for their own environments. The material in this book is an outgrowth of AIX performance-tuning seminars presented at conferences and customer sites. You will likewise learn methods of performance problem solving: which commands are easiest, which are most informative, which data is important and which is not, when you should stop tuning, and when you don't have sufficient data even to tackle the problem.

Who Should Buy This Book?

This is an intermediate book on AIX performance analysis for system administrators and programmers. AIX is a UNIX derivative. Previous experience with UNIX tasks such as editing files, manipulating files and directories, and shell programming is assumed. System administrators will find Chapters 1, 2, 3, 4, 5, and 8 most useful. Programmers will find Chapters 1, 2, 3, 6, 7, and 8 most useful. If you already have a firm basis in UNIX performance analysis, you can easily skip Chapter 1. Except for reading the material in Chapter 3, you can skip chapters and jump right to the topics that interest you.

Chapter Summaries

Chapter 1 is a basic overview of the concepts of performance analysis. This chapter discusses a general methodology that applies to any computer system.

Chapter 2 is a brief tutorial of the design of the AIX operating system. Design concepts such as virtual memory management, filesystems, and scheduling are covered. Emphasis is on the parts of the AIX design that offer some degree of tuning.

Chapter 3 covers the more rudimentary performance monitoring tools and techniques that perform the most crucial part of performance problem isolation. These tools allow you to determine whether it's the system or the application program that needs tuning. Both programmers and administrators can benefit from Chapter 3.

Chapter 4 covers remedies involving CPU, disk I/O, and memory bottlenecks. The emphasis in this chapter is on remedies that a system administrator would make to the system configuration, such as disk configurations and virtual memory settings.

Chapter 5 covers remedies involving local area networking bottlenecks. The emphasis is on network settings for TCP/IP and NFS that a system administrator would perform.

Chapter 6 covers performance tools that apply primarily to application program tuning. Programming tools such as compilers, linkers, and profilers are discussed. The emphasis is on compiler flags and techniques for implementing shared libraries.

Chapter 7 covers AIX system call programming. The emphasis in this chapter is on programming interfaces for interprocess communications and shared memory.

Chapter 8 is a summary of the entire book. This is the chapter in which the commands and techniques are reviewed for applicability. This is the "what do I use when" chapter.

Which Systems Are Covered?

AIX runs on several hardware platforms. IBM sells the RS/6000 line of products that use the PowerPC chip in their systems; Motorola sells the Power Stack line of systems; Bull sells Escala and Estrella; and Apple sells Network Server. All of these require the AIX version 4.1 or AIX Version 4.2 operating system. The techniques in this book apply to all of these systems and to both versions of AIX.

At the time of writing, AIX 4.2.1 was the most current version of the operating system. The material in this book works on AIX 4.1 and AIX 4.2 system levels as well.

AIX Version 3.2 is not specifically covered in this book; however, a great many of the techniques covered in this book also apply to AIX 3.2. Since AIX 3.2 is no longer serviced or sold, obtaining performance software for these systems is difficult, and the percentage of systems running AIX 3.2 should diminish to obscurity by the time you read this book.

Acknowledgments

Thanks to the reviewers of early drafts: Matt Accapadi, IBM; C. Schauble; Wayne Huang; Lee Cheng; Robert Boyce, American Express, TRS; James W. DeRoest, Computing & Communications, University of Washington; Jim Fox, University of Washington; and Bill Mansfield, CIBER. Also thanks go to Dave Robertson, my immediate manager at IBM, who gave me permission to use IBM equipment to test programs and generate figures.

Special thanks go to my wife, Bobbi, an experienced author herself, who was the major source of inspiration for creating this book. She offered invaluable advice on how to cure writer's block when I was stuck on Chapter 1. Her insistent reminders of "Don't you have a book to write?" when I wasn't actually writing kept me chugging down the track to the first draft. And she often did the dishes out of turn so that I could work on the book.

About the Author

I started in the computer industry in 1972, doing assembly programming on IBM mainframes. Fast forward through several years of languages, operating systems, and commercial products with IBM to 1983. That was the year AIX was born in Austin, Texas. I, like lots of my colleagues screamed, "Eunuchs! Isn't that who's entrusted to guard the harem?"

After an initial culture shock, I learned to like UNIX and AIX. I liked them so much I spent four years as a kernel developer. In 1987, I left the coding tablet behind to work with customers and IBM salespeople who didn't know how to spell AIX, let alone how to use and sell it. The past ten years have been spent consulting and teaching customers about AIX. A lot of that consultation has been about performance topics. On a number of occasions the effort results in a sales win or an appreciative word about the helpful information. I usually learn something new with every customer encounter, and I learned a lot in the process of writing this book. Hopefully you will be able to walk away with a lot of that information when you're done.

I welcome any constructive criticism about this book. Send e-mail to chukran@awl.com.

1

Introduction to Tuning Concepts

This first chapter introduces you to very basic concepts of performance analysis and tuning on any computer system. Hopefully this discussion is a review of material you are comfortable with; however, stating these basic concepts will set the stage for the rest of the book. By the end of this chapter you should have a good notion of what the rest of the book will cover. You should understand the general method of analysis and tuning, and you should be aware of the issues that computer system analysts encounter when they tackle performance problems.

1.1   Why Consider Tuning?

Presumably you are reading this book because you have an AIX system that somehow doesn't perform to your expectations. With the correct configuration changes, you could improve performance on the order of 50% to 200%. Now that I have your attention with this titillating claim, I must add that this magnitude of speedup is not typical, but it certainly is possible. I will show in Chapters 3 and 4 that speedups in the range of 50% are easily within grasp. Considering that the alternative may be shelling out big bucks for a "new and improved" faster system, learning how to use the system you already have more efficiently should be appealing.

What if you don't own an AIX system, but instead you have written an application for an AIX system and it isn't performing to your expectations? You know that it isn't possible simply to go and buy a faster version of your application. And you probably don't have the power (or courage) to tell the customer using your application that faster hardware is all that is required to get satisfaction. With the right analysis and a few coding corrections, you could be improving the speed of your applications by as much as ten times.

1

Before you become too excited, be sure you have read the warning in the preceding paragraph. I have personally observed 500% speedups with something as simple as inverting the indexes of a two-dimensional do-loop, and I have observed 100% speedups simply by recompiling with the right flags.

1.2   What Can I Tune?

Performance tuning is succinctly described as "resource management." The hardware resources on any computer system are limited in both speed and capacity. The only way to speed things up is either to use fewer resources or to get more resources. The emphasis of tuning is to change the environment to use fewer resources.

Following are most of the important computer resources listed roughly in order of importance:

- CPU
- Memory
- Peripherals
    - Hard disk drives
    - Network interface adapters
    - Graphics adapters
    - CD-ROM drivers
    - Magnetic tape drives
    - Asynchronous line devices

The CPU resource is probably the easiest to grasp, especially in the current age in which CPU speeds double every year or two. A given CPU can process instructions at a fixed speed. Adding more CPU resources means either getting a faster-speed CPU or adding more CPUs, and adding more CPUs makes sense in the context of a symmetric multiprocessor-based system (SMP). Using fewer CPU resources means eliminating CPU work load or using more efficient programming. Chapter 3 will give you insights on what sort of load you have. See Chapters 6 and 7 for some specific programming remedies that can allow programs to use fewer CPU resources.

Memory resource tuning quite often offers the most attractive payback in terms of performance improvement. Virtual memory allows a computer system to appear to have more memory than it physically has by using hard disk space to simulate real memory. Since real memory is 10,000 times faster than disk drive access, overuse of virtual memory can have a drastic negative impact on performance. Adding more memory resources is a very effective means to solve memory resource problems because modern computer systems are designed to add memory easily. Because of relatively inexpensive real memory chips, the cost-benefit of adding memory is usually very good. I will cover how to examine memory usage in Chapter 2 and how to reduce memory usage in applications in Chapter 7.

Hard disk resource is probably the hardest to optimize. The first consideration in choosing disk drives is capacity of data storage; the second consideration is disk speed: Buy the fastest disk drives you can afford. In Chapter 4 I will show how adding more drives can really speed up a system by increasing aggregate system disk bandwidth. You will also learn how to effectively "speed up" the disks you have by minimizing the number of seek operations by careful data placement.

Network resources do not affect all programs as do CPU, memory, and disk. But network resource problems can impact performance greatly since network speeds are on the order of 100 times slower than disk speeds. I am going to consider only TCP/IP networks on local area networks such as Ethernet. Faster network media such as optical, Fast Ethernet, ATM, and the like are important, but I don't have access to these types of networks. Therefore I can't give practical advice on them. The techniques I show are directly applicable to faster networks. You just have to crank the numbers up a bit.

Graphics resource optimization is not covered in this book, but graphics performance of certain kinds of applications can be a significant issue. All of the optimization would be at the programming level, so I suggest consulting graphics programming texts if you are interested in this topic.

I consider the remaining peripherals in the resource list to be of minor importance, so I do not cover tuning for them in this book.

1.3   What Are Your Performance Objectives?

This may sound like a trivial question, but do you know why you are considering tuning your AIX system? In other words, what problem are you trying to solve? Quite often the "performance problem" is vague and difficult to tackle—and I don't mean just difficult to isolate from a technical point of view. Perhaps some simple scenarios will illustrate my point.

A disgruntled customer calls you and says that the performance of his AIX system (that you manage) has been horrendous lately. At this point, you would interview him to find out what "horrendous" and "lately" mean. After a few minutes you find out that certain responses in his favorite application are taking 30 seconds. He is used to responses being 2 seconds at the most. Your interview process transformed an initial complaint of "horrendous performance" into a performance objective of "improve response time from 30 seconds to 2 seconds." This objective seems reasonable mainly because it was an expectation based on past system performance. You now agree to help your customer attain this objective. Sometimes the expectation is not so reasonable, as I illustrate in the next scenario.

Another customer complains that her system is performing abysmally right now. She was forced to move her application build environment onto a different AIX system. The marketing department wanted her system for a trade show, and she was forced to use another system that had previously been idle. Compile and link times are four times longer that she had experienced before the switch to the new system. You use your vast store of experience and intuition about why marketing might want the first system and why no one wants the second one.

A single phone call informs you that the first system is a brand-new system that arrived a few weeks ago. It is a fast, technologically desirable box. The cast-off system is a six-year-old bolt bucket that still runs but not quickly by today's standards. You consult your archived literature on these models and find that the newer model is rated four times faster than the older model simply because of new technology. Your user's expectation of improving performance fourfold is not reasonable or likely achievable. You then tell your customer to get on marketing's case to return the fast system "tout de suite." By the way, this little anecdote did really happen to me. I spiced up the scenario a bit, but the person who called me really was comparing two very incomparable systems and wondering why performance wasn't up to her expectations.

My point in the second anecdote is the importance of consciously evaluating the performance objective. This evaluation would entail determining the performance objective, analyzing how the objective was formed, analyzing all the various performance expectations, and then deciding how hard you want to work on the various aspects of the problem.

1.4   Methodology

Now that the discussion of resources and objectives is out of the way, let's see how they fit into a performance-tuning methodology. Any performance-tuning exercise can be broken down into the following rudimentary steps:

1. Establish performance objectives.

2. Measure system performance and determine the system resources in greatest demand.

3. Change something: increase system resources or use fewer resources.

4. Evaluate new performance against your performance objectives.

5. Repeat steps 2–4 until your performance objectives are met.

Step 1 has been discussed as much as I can discuss it. Performance objectives tend to be nontechnical issues anyway. Enough said. Step 2 is discussed in much greater detail in Chapters 3, 5, and 6; step 3 is discussed in greater detail in Chapters 4, 5, and 7.

1.5   Roles of the Performance Analyst

The previous section used the role of a technical support analyst to illustrate different performance objectives. There are a few more roles that performance analysts could potentially play. The following list illustrates which chapters would be most useful to which particular role.

Competitive benchmarking analyst—Chapters 3, 4, 5

Capacity planning analyst—Chapters 3, 4, 5

Technical support-system administrator—Chapters 2, 3, 4, 5, 8

Application programmer—Chapters 3, 6, 7

A competitive benchmarking analyst would be responsible for running, optimizing, and evaluating performance benchmarks for the purpose of comparing competitive equipment. An analyst running benchmarks on an AIX system and interested in tuning the system presumably has some ulterior motive in making the system perform well—the sale of some system and perhaps a sales commission are at stake. The rules for such a scenario typically are that anything on the system may be changed, including adding more hardware. However, changing the code of application programs is usually verboten. Typically time is of the essence, so concentrating on the essentials is important. Understanding the performance objective is crucial. Quite often, the benchmark competition is blind; that is, no one knows the results of the competitors until the competition is over. This rule makes for a vague objective: Make it run as fast as possible. Sometimes the competitor's performance is known ahead of time, and all you have to do is beat the competition. Chapters 3, 4, and 5 would be of most benefit.

A capacity planning analyst would be responsible for planning the configurations for new systems to be purchased or for upgrades to existing systems. Predicting the future is a tough job. Just ask any stockbroker. Likewise, it's a tough job planning for workload increases for the future. The job usually entails estimating a system configuration to accommodate a specific work environment. For example, the planning objective might be to estimate computer resources for a small bank that needs more up-to-date computer equipment. Chapters 3, 4, and 5 would be most useful to capacity planners.

Technical support analysts most often help other professionals troubleshoot problems. They need a very general background and good problem-solving skills. Theory behind how the system operates makes a firm foundation for this general background. Chapters 2, 3, 4, 5, and 8 would be most useful to technical support analysts.

Application programmers are usually very specialized in their field of discipline. They tend to concentrate on program design and debugging issues. Chapters 3, 6, and 7 would be most useful to them.

2

AIX System Design

In this chapter you will learn basic design points about the AIX that affect system performance. The topics you will study are virtual memory, the program loader, the filesystem, process scheduler, and the network subsystem. After reading this chapter, you will understand why simply adding real memory can drastically speed up both program execution and program I/O efficiency. You will understand why programs linked with shared libraries can save lots of virtual memory in some cases yet not save any virtual memory in others. You will also learn how processes are chosen for dispatching and why your favorite application processes may not be so favored as far as the system scheduler is concerned.

Before you can begin to adapt and optimize a computer system to perform at its fullest advantage, it is helpful to learn how the system is put together. You don't need to know minute details as well as the developer who wrote the code, but the more you know, the more effective you will be at tuning your system. I will use an analogy that compares cars to computers.

The computer system user is like a passenger in an automobile. It requires very little understanding of how the car is designed in order to be a passenger. If you know how the door works and how the seat belt buckles, you have the passenger skills licked. If you want to be the chauffeur or a system administrator, you need more design knowledge. The chauffeur needs to understand how to steer and accelerate. Some basic engine and braking design must be understood so that the brake and accelerator are not depressed at the same time. Likewise, the system administrator must not attempt to configure the system to perform conflicting tasks. However, if you want to be a mechanic to fix problems with a sputtering engine, you will need a much more complete understanding of the design of the car. The better you understand the overall engine design, the more effective mechanic you will be. And the better you understand the design of AIX, the better you will be at being an AIX performance mechanic.

First, I'll assume that you already have a basic background on how a generic computer system works. That is, you have already taken Introduction to Computers 101, and you already know what binary arithmetic is about. I will also assume you are familiar with UNIX in general and know some of the basic design concepts. For example, you should know what virtual memory is and why it is useful, what UNIX filesystems are, and what the basic commands are that UNIX users must know to manipulate the system.

In order to understand the finer points of the AIX design, we will describe some scenarios that you know and show a little bit of what is going on behind the scenes. To do this, we will take a tour of the guts of the AIX operating system when you execute a command. We will see the interesting things that happen until the program you want to run receives control at its first statement in the main subroutine. Once our sample program gets control and begins executing, we will follow its execution path, that is, the system subroutines.

2.1   General AIX Design Goals

The AIX operating system kernel was one of the first UNIX kernels to be designed with modularity and extendibility in mind. Several design factors contribute to these goals:

> Loadable device drivers
>
> Pageable kernels
>
> Dynamically growing kernel tables

Device driver support is not built into the core kernel. Instead, kernel device drivers are dynamically loaded and unloaded at runtime. This technique contrasts with the old way of needing to relink the kernel whenever new device support is required. AIX handles this by packaging the device driver with installation methods that load the driver and all the configuration data. This means that adding a new device driver for an existing device does not require a reboot.

The AIX kernel is mostly pageable. Except for device interrupt handlers that must be pinned into memory, most of the kernel is pageable. This allows the kernel to take a much smaller real memory footprint than it would if it were not pageable.

As a result of the kernel being pageable, kernel tables are able to grow on demand. Tables such as the process table are memory mapped; then entire large tables are assigned a virtual address range. The virtual entries are assigned to real memory as they are referenced. When a new entry of the process table is referenced, a page fault occurs, and a new virtual page is allocated. All of the kernel tables are allocated this way. They are mapped into virtual memory with a very large size and paged in as needed. For example, the process table is allocated with 131,071 (2^{17}-1) entries. Neither virtual memory nor real memory is used until the entry is really needed. The end result of this dynamic table allocation is that the AIX kernel does not need to be recompiled to make tables larger as is the case with other UNIX kernels.

2.2   Program Loading

The first order of business is to examine how programs are loaded in a virtual memory space and how control is given to the first executable statement. You start the whole process by typing a command at the shell prompt. The shell forks a child process, which then passes the string as an argument to the `exec` system call. The exec system call switches to the kernel system call handler that ends up calling the kernel loader. The loader is responsible for loading programs into virtual memory and resolving the various symbolic references into virtual addresses. This symbol resolution is done at the time the program is being loaded and will be finished by the time the exec system call is complete. This concept of resolving symbols at the time of the exec system call (which I call exec time for short) is called *dynamic loading*.

Dynamic loading is important because it enables you to write programs that can use less memory as compared with programs that do not use this facility. (We will get into more detail on symbol resolution in Chapter 6 when we talk about writing programs to take advantage of dynamic symbol resolution.) The loader locates the instruction portion of the executable and maps it to the text segment. The act of mapping is just a way of associating a part of a disk file to a portion of virtual memory; no copying of the executable text portion is done.

The text portion is not read into storage by the loader. This feature is useful for very large programs because the time is not wasted waiting for the whole program to be read in. As the pages in the address range are referenced, the corresponding page of the executable file is paged in. This technique is referred to as *demand paging*. If sections of code are never executed, then the time to read this code into virtual memory is not wasted, nor is the real memory used to hold this code wasted.

The most obvious mapping assignment that the loader needs to make is the text mapping. For AIX, text is mapped into a hardware segment. AIX implementations on Power and PowerPC rely on the fact that these architectures are segmented in which the 32-bit virtual address space is divided into 16 segments of 256 megabytes each. Each of these segments can be assigned its own protection domain. Text is mapped into its own read-only segment.

However, there are other segment assignments that the loader needs to make. See Figure 2.1. Segment 0 is always mapped to the kernel instructions and data. While the process is running in the user mode, as opposed to the kernel mode, the kernel segment is assigned read-only protection. User code actually requires the ability to read the kernel because user programs can execute code in the kernel while in user mode. Segment 1 is assigned the process main text segment. This is the part of a program that is executed and contains a main statement. Segment 2 is assigned to the private data segment. This segment is subdivided into program initialized data, program uninitialized data, program stack, and kernel stack. Segment 13 is assigned to shared library text; segment 15 is assigned to shared library data. This leaves several segments unassigned. The unassigned segments, 3 through 12, are available for use as auxiliary data segments, shared data segments between processes, or segments in which to map files.

At this point, the loader has mapped text and data into the proper portions of the executable file. The symbol resolution occurs after the text and data segments have been

Segment	Start Address		End Address
0	00000000	Kernel Segment	0 FFFFFFF
1	10000000	Program Text Segment	1 FFFFFFF
2	20000000	Program Data/Stack Segment	2 FFFFFFF
3-C	30000000	Available as Shared Memory Segments or Extended Program Data Segments F	CFFFFFF
D	D0000000	Shared Library Text Segment	DFFFFFFF
E	E0000000		EFFFFFFF
F	F0000000	Shared Library Data Segment	FFFFFFFF

Figure 2.1   Hardware segment assignments

mapped. Symbol resolution assigns to each symbol in a program an address in the virtual address space of the process that is about to execute. The loader reads a portion of the executable called the loader section. This portion is a list of all of the symbols that must be assigned addresses. Once this address assignment is complete, the program is ready to run. All that is necessary is to initialize the program counter to point to the first instruction in the program. Program counter initialization is accomplished in quite a sneaky way. When the exec system call returns, it returns to the new program at the first instruction rather than return to the point of invocation, as most other system calls do. The loader's job is done once the new program counter is initialized, and this signifies completion of the exec system call.

It is interesting to review which parts of the executable have actually been copied from the image on disk to the image in memory. These are only the executable header and the symbol dictionary. The header is a kind of road map that tells the loader where the various parts of the executable are located, and the symbol dictionary maps symbols into addresses. Once these two parts have been read and their use is complete, they are discarded. The actual code that is about to run has not been touched at all.

2.3   Virtual Memory Overview

When the first address is first touched, a *page fault* occurs. Page faults drive the virtual memory system to perform on demand. It is probably a good time to examine the virtual memory manager (VMM) at this point, because that will prepare us for the read and write system calls that most programs perform. A simple way to describe the effect of the virtual memory manager is to say that as the data is needed, it is fetched on demand. This concept is called *demand paging.*

2.3.1   Page Faults

Let's look at this concept of fetching data from disk on demand, the basis of how virtual memory is managed on AIX. First, let's review some terminology. Data is organized in units of pages that are 4096 bytes in size for the Power and PowerPC architectures. All fetching is done in units of pages. When these pages reside in real memory, they are capable of being addressed by the CPU. These pages can also reside on disk but are obviously not addressable by the CPU when they are there. We said that a page fault causes data to be fetched into memory. More specifically, a page fault is a detection, accomplished by a hardware interrupt, that a virtual page cannot be addressed. This means that the page is not in real memory, and the virtual memory address cannot be translated into a real-memory address.

When this interrupt occurs, the VMM looks to see if there is any room in real memory in which to copy the data from the disk. In a moment, we will investigate how the VMM page stealer creates room in real memory, but for now, let's assume that there is enough room. The VMM examines the page to see if it has ever existed in the context of this process. If not, this is called an initial page fault for that page. An initial fault causes the VMM to allocate two different pages. One page is the real address in RAM where the page is to reside; the other page is the backing page on disk where the page will be saved if the page ever has to be removed temporarily from RAM. The concept of allocating only when the virtual page is first referenced is called *late page space allocation.* Later, we will contrast this with *early* page space allocation.

If the page has previously existed, that is, if it has an image of it somewhere on disk, the event is called a *repage* fault. The VMM looks up the disk address of this page in the external page table, finds its disk address, and schedules I/O for that page to be read from page space into RAM. The act of resolving a repage fault by copying the page from page space into RAM is called *page in.* The process that is blocked while waiting for a page in to complete is said to be in *page wait* state.

Now let's talk about that most larcenous of AIX system components—the page stealer. The job of the page stealer is to ensure that there is a small supply of free RAM pages available when an initial page fault occurs. When the number of free RAM pages dips below a certain value, the page stealer goes into action and attempts to steal pages to add to the free-page list. The page stealer stops when the number of free pages exceeds a different value. The certain value that spurs the page stealer into action is the minimum free-page number. The value that causes the page stealer to stop stealing is the maximum free-page number.

The page stealer really gets a bad rap. It should more properly be called a page bor-
rower. The RAM pages are borrowed, or replaced, by selecting the stalest, or the *least*
recently used (LRU), pages and somehow getting rid of them temporarily. One possibility
is that a page is copied to page space if the page in RAM has been modified since it was
last paged in. In that case, the page is called *dirty* and is *paged out* to page space. The other
possibility is that the page is clean, which means that the copy in RAM matches exactly
the copy in page space. A clean page does not need to be paged out and is simply purged.

I mentioned stealing pages to page space as the target *backing store* because page
space is what is first associated with paging. Backing store is where dirty pages go when
pages are stolen. There are two types of backing store: page space is backing store for
working, or nonpersistent, pages, and a file system is backing store for persistent, or file,
pages. To put it more simply, files page to and from filesystems, and everything else pages
to page space.

Just to make sure you understand the performance burden of paging, let me summarize. Page faults do not necessarily cause disk I/O. Only repage faults cause page-in I/O.
Page-out I/O occurs only when there is a shortage of free RAM pages and the page des-
tined to be replaced is dirty. Thus we might consider that page-out I/O is the most direct
measure of how constrained real memory is at a particular moment. Page-in I/O is a
valid but less direct measure of constrained memory. Also note that a low amount of free
memory is not an indication that memory is constrained. The system could quite happily
run with free memory hovering just above the minimum free-page value. In fact, the system could be experiencing some initial page faults that could be resolved by stealing
pages that are stale but clean, thus resulting in memory allocation activity with no accom-
panying I/O. In summary, nonzero paging rates are not good, but low (almost zero) free
RAM is not necessarily bad. Later I will discuss the VMM role in filesystem I/O and will
explain why free RAM pages tend to hover around a few hundred (this is what I mean by
"almost" zero).

2.3.2   Late Page Space Allocation

Late allocation of the backing page is a unique feature of AIX. Let's contrast early and late
page space allocation in order to understand the advantages of each. Let's say you wrote
a program that dynamically allocated a very large array in storage and accessed elements
of that array in a random fashion. Let's also assume that the data the program encoun-
tered today caused only 1% of the elements to be used. Early allocation would allocate
100% of the array on backing store, even though the program needed only 1% of that
today. Late allocation would allocate only the 1% of the array on backing store as each
page is needed. This might be compared to the old saying: Eat all you want, but take only
what you can eat. That way there are no wasted "bytes"—either on your plate or on page
space.

There is a trade-off to late allocation. It is possible that when it is time to allocate a
backing page there is none to be had. AIX does a pretty ugly deed when there is a shortage of page space. It kills processes in an attempt to free up page space so that the system
can continue to run. This is the "sacrifice of the few for the good of the many" approach,
which is not always fair or wise. When page space first begins running low, a warning is

issued two ways. First, a message is posted to the system error log warning that a low condition has been reached. Then a message is posted to the system console warning that page space is low and processes should be terminated. If free-page space continues to decline, a kernel process is dispatched to conduct a "which" hunt. This kernel process scans the kernel process table looking for *which* process could be the best one to dispose of for the good of the system. The process that is chosen is not always the first process to encounter shortages, nor is it necessarily the process using the most storage. The victim is the youngest process. The chosen process is first sent a SIGDANGER signal. If this process did not take steps to catch SIGDANGER, then the process dies immediately. If the process does catch SIGDANGER, then the process can take remedial action. The best action is to save work and exit. If page space consumption continues beyond a level called the *page space kill* value, the hunter kernel process will issue a SIGKILL signal to the victim process. SIGKILL cannot be caught, and the victim process meets a grisly death.

Your first reaction to this severe action to page space shortage might be to gag in horror. How crude of AIX to kill processes indiscriminately. That isn't standard UNIX behavior. You would be partially right. The POSIX 1003.1 standard implies that malloc memory allocation system call should guarantee that storage be committed if the malloc call returns successfully. And, indeed, customers complained that this behavior did not comply with the standard. The POSIX standards body agreed with the customers and declared that AIX did not conform with the intent of the standard, even though AIX passed all the compliance tests.

In order to make AIX POSIX compliant to customers' satisfaction, the AIX developers fixed the behavior of the page space shortage algorithm. First, the default behavior is as previously described. If you want different behavior, you have to take explicit action. The action you take is to set the PSALLOC environment variable. Using Bourne shell syntax, this would look like

```
PSALLOC=early
```

If the variable is set to early, the process behavior is different. Most important, early page space allocation will occur for that process. The malloc call will return success and will have committed all the page space pages before returning to the caller. Furthermore, the process will be immune to the SIGDANGER and SIGKILL signals, so it cannot be killed for its page space usage sins.

You may be tempted to have the entire system use the POSIX behavior by setting PSALLOC in the /etc/environment file. Or you might set it in your shell *.profile* so that just your process hierarchy uses this behavior. I strongly recommend that you do not do this. There are many programs that greedily allocate much more storage than they actually use. The AIX X Window server is a good example of a program that allocates a 256-megabyte segment, but it typically uses 1% to 10% of that. Thus if you set PSALLOC in your .profile file, X Window would refuse to run; it could not satisfy its memory allocation because the free-page space was too small.

Even though paging space configuration is an important issue, tuning the amount of page space is never a performance issue. Stated another way, choosing too much or too little page space will not make your program run either faster or slower. However, too little page space may prevent your program from running at all.

2.3.3 Filesystem Caching

I mentioned earlier that the VMM plays a major part in the operation of the AIX file-system. Since the VMM manages all virtual memory, the VMM also manages memory on behalf of the filesystem. All of RAM is shared among file pages and nonfile pages, and the VMM decides which pages occupy RAM at any given time.

Recall that the page stealer replaces pages in RAM based on an LRU algorithm. Until now we had been considering pages without regard to type of pages; however, it is useful to know that virtual pages are classified into three types, based on the location of backing store of the page. See Figure 2.2 for an illustration of this concept.

Pages are collected into a virtual segment that can be of one of three types: persistent, working, or client. Persistent segments represent a file in a filesystem and, therefore, can be backed by a filesystem. In other words, the pages are paged in and out of the file-system. Working segments are backed by page space. Client segments represent a file in a mounted NFS filesystem and are, therefore, backed by a filesystem on an NFS server somewhere across the network. Since persistent segments and client segments are both a kind of filesystem-backed segment, it is also useful to think of segments as members of two broader categories: file segments and nonfile segments.

The VMM page stealer treats all three types of pages equally when things are quiet on the page-stealing front. I'll call this *quiet* condition the normal LRU page replacement situation, but increased paging activity causes the page stealer to treat file pages differently than nonfile pages. There are two situations involving nonquiet paging conditions. I'll call the *louder* case the "file pages only" LRU page replacement. In this case, file pages exceed a value called the maxperm threshold. (AIX uses this unfortunately inconsistent term to mean maximum file page limit. I suppose maxperm is short for maximum per-manent.) When the number of occupied file pages exceeds this value, the page stealer chooses only file pages as replacement victims. This bias toward selecting file page vic-tims is an attempt to limit the number of file pages. Note that this threshold is not a hard limit because it is possible for the number of file pages to drift beyond the threshold before the page stealer can be called into action.

The second *nonquiet* situation is when the number of file pages is below the maxperm value but above the minperm (minimum number of file pages) value. In this case the page stealer chooses which kind of page to steal by examining two other statistics. The VMM keeps count of repage rates for both file and nonfile pages. The page stealer will chose file pages if the file repage rate is greater than the nonfile repage rate. Otherwise the page stealer will treat file and nonfile pages equally.

The reason for all these decisions is that a system that experiences a lot of file I/O may tend to push out nonfile pages such as program text and data images. Program text images are persistent segments but are treated as nonfile segments for LRU purposes. It might sometimes improve overall system performance by limiting the amount of RAM that file pages occupy, thus keeping room for executable images. Otherwise the file page's greediness for memory could induce excessive page-in activity when the executable images are needed. In Chapter 4 I will discuss how you can change the minperm and maxperm values.

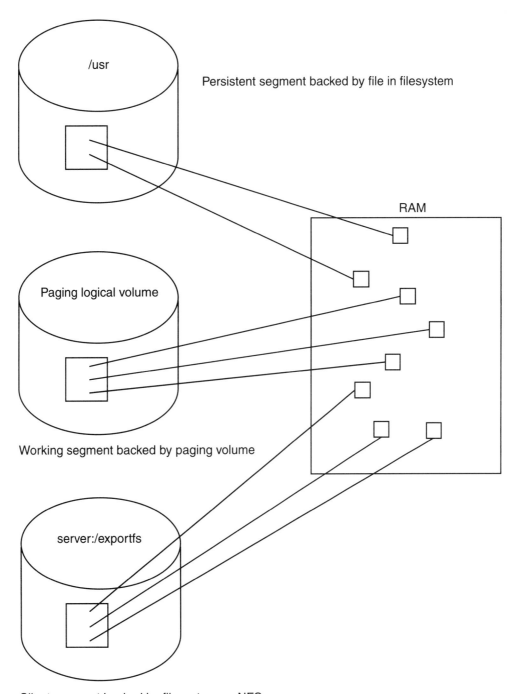

Figure 2.2 Virtual segment types

2.4   I/O Overview

A unique AIX feature contributing to AIX as an industrial-strength operating system is the Journal Filesystem (JFS). AIX was probably the first UNIX operating system to possess this feature, and others have recently followed. Let's discuss how the filesystem itself intertwines with the VMM and other system components.

2.4.1   Layers for File I/O

It is useful to view file I/O as four distinct layers. See Figure 2.3. It is useful to understand these layers because one of the performance statistics gathering tools that we will learn about in Chapter 3 tells how these layers are performing. The first layer is the *logical file*. Each read system call your program does is a logical read. However, each logical read does not necessarily result in a physical read. If the data desired is already contained in the VMM file cache, the VMM has no need to fetch the data from the disk, thus avoiding a physical read. The VMM manages the virtual segment layer. The next layer is managed by the logical volume manager (LVM), the genie of UNIX system administrators that responds to: I wish it was easy to partition disks for filesystems. LVM allows filesystems to span multiple disks and is responsible for translating file I/O requests into individual disk requests. The last layer is the physical volume layer, or device layer. This layer is managed by the disk device driver.

2.4.2   JFS Log

In a nutshell, JFS employs a journaling technique similar to a database in order to ensure consistency of the data making up the structure of the filesystem. This technique involves duplicating the meta-data transactions to the filesystem logical volume and to the journal. Filesystem meta-data is the data that makes up the structure of the filesystem itself, namely superblock, directories, inodes, and indirect data pointers. The journal, sometimes called the log, is another logical volume separate from the filesystem logical volume. It is used as a circular list in which to store the duplicate transactions. The journal is written to the disk before the filesystem meta-data is; thus the journal can be used to reconstruct the meta-data transactions if some of the transactions fail to complete. Frequent meta-data corruption would cause filesystems to become unusable in the days before journaled filesystems. This frequent corruption gave UNIX filesystems the reputation for lacking industrial strength.

Let's use an example to see in detail how the journal works on the JFS so you will appreciate what value it adds. Assume you wanted to create a new file.

```
ps -ef >> ps.out
```

The system actions are

shell opens ps.out file

ps writes one new block at the end of the file

shell closes ps.out file

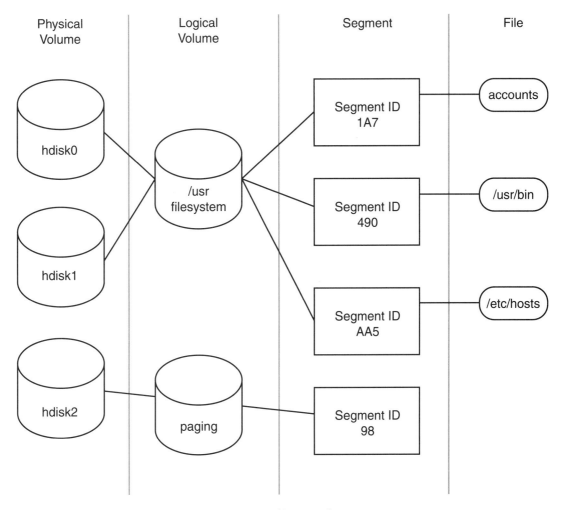

Figure 2.3 I/O system layers

After this command executes, the following meta-data is changed:

Current directory data is changed to add new entry for ps.out file.

Inode for current directory is changed to update modified time.

New inode created for file.

Free list changed to contain one less block.

These filesystem changes are performed twice. First the changes are recorded in the log by writing them in memory. The real data is recorded in the various memory structures that represent the disk meta-data. Figure 2.4 represents the state of the log after it has been written to disk. The state of the filesystem meta-data is shown after it was modified in memory but before it was written to disk. By using AIX kernel lock synchronization, log data is guaranteed to be written to disk before the filesystem meta-data. This data is written in one atomic chunk in a compact contiguous spot on the disk; the filesystem meta-data is written in several chunks across the disk. When the meta-data is confirmed to be completely written, a pointer residing in the log header is updated to point after the end of the corresponding log data. Figure 2.5 represents the state of the journal and meta-data after the meta-data is written to disk. Note that the sync point has moved to signify that the meta-data has been committed to disk and that the corresponding portion of the log can be forgotten and is available to be written over.

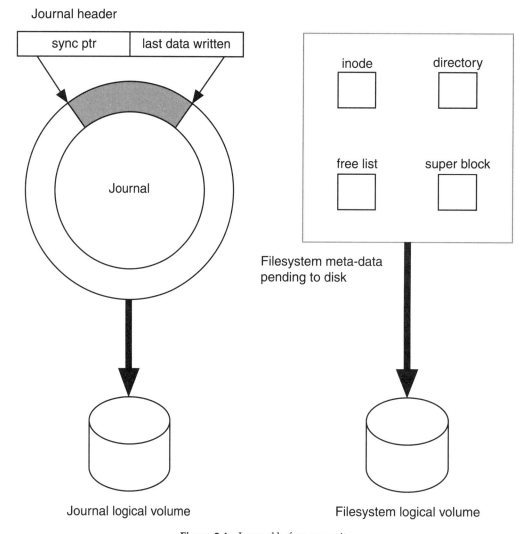

Figure 2.4 Journal before commit

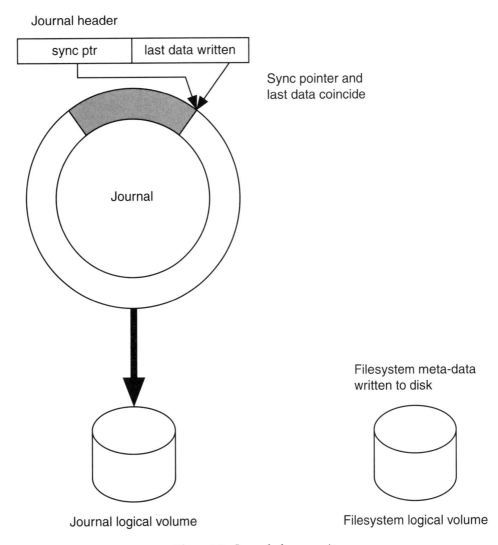

Journal header

sync ptr | last data written

Sync pointer and
last data coincide

Journal

Filesystem meta-data
written to disk

Journal logical volume   Filesystem logical volume

Figure 2.5   Journal after commit

If the system crashes between the times represented in Figures 2.4 and 2.5, the filesystem can be restored to a consistent state. When the system reboots, a program called *logredo* is run. It replays the journals to reconstruct the various corrupt filesystems. The logredo is run before the filesystems are mounted and takes the place of the archaic *fsck.* program.

The point of describing the journal mechanism is not to have you understand how the recovery works, but rather to show that extra disk I/O is being done to the journal. Usually this extra I/O is not noticed due to the low frequency. Note that the journal is not written if a file is read because the filesystem is not changing. Note, too, that the journal is not written if a file is being updated without appending new data.

2.4.3   Sequential Read-Ahead and Write-Behind

Programs that read files in a sequential manner can achieve greater throughput compared with performing the same amount of I/O in a random manner. This is due to a VMM feature called *read-ahead*. The VMM notices that a program has read two pages consecutively and anticipates that the program will continue to read consecutive pages. The anticipation results in VMM reading the pages before the program asks for them. When the program does read the pages, they will already be in RAM, and the program does not need to wait, thus reading more data more quickly.

The VMM performs this anticipation of sequential reading with the help of two thresholds—a starting read-ahead value (`minpgahead`) and an ending read-ahead value (`maxpgahead`). Upon detecting that two pages were read consecutively, the VMM will start by reading an additional number of pages specified by the `minpgahead` value. If the program continues to read sequentially, the VMM will keep doubling the read-ahead amount until the `maxpgahead` value limits the read-ahead size. If the program performs an *lseek* to the file to cause pages to be skipped, then read-ahead mode is canceled. Future detection of read-ahead mode on the same file would start from scratch. The defaults for `minpgahead` and `maxpgahead` are 2 and 8, respectively.

Where there is sequential reading going on, there is probably writing going on as well, and sequential writing throughput can be improved by some special processing. When a program writes data to a file, the modified pages will tend to sit in memory until a sync call by the sync daemon flushes the pages to the filesystem. However, if sequential writing is detected, flushing the dirty pages will happen early. This action is called *write-behind*. This detection is more primitive than that of read-ahead detection. When a program modifies all four pages of a 16K chunk and then proceeds to modify the next page, the previous four pages will be flushed to disk.

In Chapter 4 you will learn how to use vmtune to tune read-ahead and write-behind.

2.4.4   Logical Volume Manager

AIX has a unique feature of allowing filesystems to be managed dynamically without requiring the filesystem to be taken off-line. The AIX component that accomplishes this is called the Logical Volume Manager (LVM); it allows you to assign filesystems to chunks of disk called logical volumes. The LVM is implemented as a device layer between the VMM and the disk device driver. See Figure 2.6 for a conceptual picture of how the LVM fits into AIX.

The LVM itself does not affect disk I/O performance to any large extent. In fact, the extra layer probably adds a bit of overhead that is imperceptible in the overall scheme of things. However, to the system administrator seeking to optimize the system, the power of the LVM is in the flexibility and ease with which you can assign your data. On most UNIX systems, moving data from one disk to another or to another place on the same disk entails many hours of backing up, taking the system down to move disk partitions, rebooting, and copying backups to their new locations. On AIX, similar tasks involve changing some disk configuration parameters and telling the system to move the data for you.

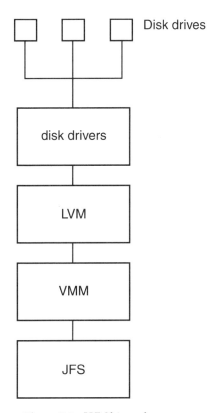

Figure 2.6   LVM hierarchy

I'll review some LVM terminology that is important to understand optimum data placement on disk. In Chapter 4, I'll discuss how to apply these concepts to learn how to control where your data goes.

See Figure 2.7 for a picture of the hierarchy of disk management objects. A disk (one that you could hold in your hand, if you knew how to extract it from your system) is called a physical volume (PV). A volume group (VG) is a collection of one or more PVs. A PV is divided into contiguous chunks called a physical partition (PP); each PP is nominally 4 megabytes but can vary from 1 to 256 megabytes. A VG can be grouped into several logical volumes (LV) that are divided into logical partitions (LP) that are the same size as the PPs. Logical volumes can span physical volumes, but they cannot span different volume groups.

When you create a logical volume (if you are creating a filesystem, a logical volume with sufficient size to contain the filesystem you specify is created for you), you must specify the volume group in which to place the logical volume. This specification limits which physical volumes the files can be on. Furthermore, you can specify that the logical volume be allocated in one of five bands on the disk. See Figure 2.8 for a picture of how these bands are laid out on a physical disk. The total number of cylinders is divided into five equal-sized bands of 20% each. From the center axle, the bands are called *inner edge*,

PHYSICAL   PHYSICAL
VOLUMES   PARTITIONS

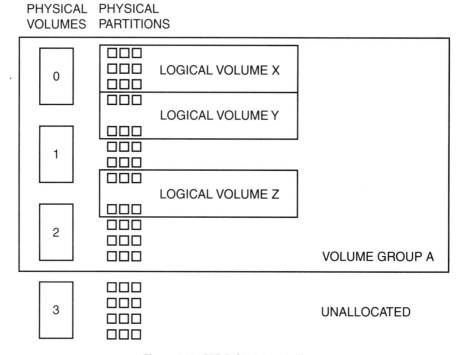

Figure 2.7   LVM object terminology

inner middle, center, outer middle, and outer edge. The band of optimum seek time is the center. A file residing on the center cylinder will have an average seek distance of one-half the total number of cylinders. All other file positions will have average seek distances greater than one-half.

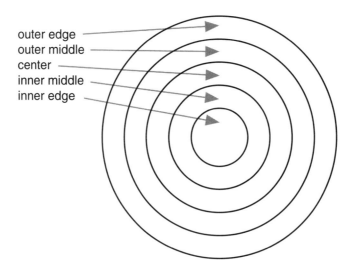

Figure 2.8   Disk allocation bands

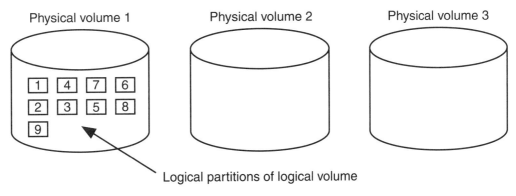

Figure 2.9   Minimum volume allocation for multivolume group

Since a logical volume can exist in a volume group that contains more than one physical volume, there is an LVM rule that decides how many physical volumes to use when allocating the partitions for the logical volume. The default is *minimum*, which tries to use the least number of volumes. Figure 2.9 shows how this would look for an LV with nine partitions. The alternative allocation, *maximum*, is to spread the logical partitions across as many physical volumes as possible. This arrangement, shown in Figure 2.10, might be advantageous on a system where there are many independent processes accessing the same filesystem. Since different physical disks can be executing their seek operations in parallel, there is more opportunity for parallel I/O operations with maximum. However, for a single process accessing a filesystem, maximum and minimum are about the same. The single process would block if one of the disks needed to be read with no opportunity to put the other physical volumes to work. With an ordinary JFS filesystem, it takes multiple processes to put multiple disks to work. However, a single process can put multiple disks to work concurrently if it is performing sequential I/O on a striped filesystem. We will investigate striped filesystems in Chapter 4.

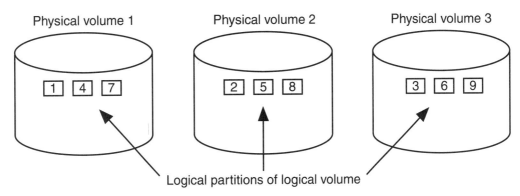

Figure 2.10   Maximum volume allocation

2.5   CPU Scheduling Overview

Effective use of the hardware CPUs (remember that a system may have one or more CPUs) is a job for the AIX scheduler. There are two situations to understand: The first is normal thread scheduling which governs how work is handled in most situations; the second is when memory usage is abnormally high and the system is virtual memory thrashing.

2.5.1   Scheduling Threads

Before I discuss how the CPU (or CPUs in the case of multiprocessor hardware) is managed by the AIX kernel, I had better define a *thread*, which is the scheduling entity for AIX Version 4. For AIX Version 3, the scheduling entity is the process which the `fork` system call creates. After a fork, parent and child processes share a copy of the program-executable text, but they receive their own copy of the program data. Therefore parent and child cannot communicate by modifying variables in the data segment but must resort to some interprocess communication means. New to Version 4 is the concept of threads, which is different from a process in that a child thread does not get a new copy of the data and therefore can communicate with the parent thread by modifying program variables. There are other subtle differences between threads and processes, but I won't discuss them here. I suggest you consult *Pthreads Programming* by Bradford Nichols and others for more information about threads.

If you are using an AIX Version 3 system, you can substitute *process* for *thread*, and the meaning will be the same.

Since there are many more threads than there are CPUs to run them on, the operating system decides which thread at any moment can use the CPU. The AIX scheduler is the component burdened with this task—so many threads and so little CPU time. The scheduler chooses the thread from a list of eligible threads that wait in the run queue. The run queue is sorted in priority order, and the top priority runnable threads get to use the CPUs. You may not be accustomed to thinking of more than one CPU, but a multiple CPU configuration is the most general case.

Figure 2.11 illustrates one run queue serving multiple CPUs. A process is placed on the run queue at the level that corresponds to the thread priority, once the thread is awakened from sleeping on an event. Unlike the grocery checkout queue, where breaking into the middle of the queue is met with looks that would melt the offender's ice cream carton, breaking into the middle of the queue on AIX is normal and quite civilized. The new run queue entrant thread jumps to its rightful place in line, using its priority number like a special pass. Every thread has a priority number, ranging from 0 to 127. The best priority is 0, while the worst is 127. Because the adjectives "high" and "low" get confusing, I will consistently use "better" and "worse" to describe priority goodness.

Thread priorities can be either fixed forever or changed as a function of time spent using the CPU. Most user processes have changing priorities, while most system kernel processes have fixed priorities. Threads that use the CPU are penalized by changing their priority to be worse; threads that are waiting to use the CPU are rewarded by changing their priority to be better. Let's examine exactly how this happens in detail, because in Chapter 4 you will learn how to affect the priority calculation.

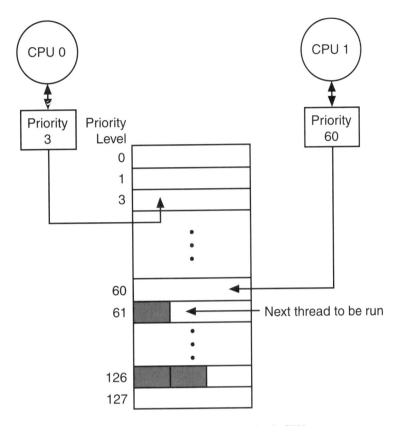

Figure 2.11   Single run queue serving multiple CPUs

The threads that are running on the CPU get a new priority calculation 100 times per second, based on the system 100 Hz clock interrupt. This can be expressed in the following formula:

    CPUnew = min (CPU old +1, 120)

CPUnew is the new value of the CPU penalty value that is calculated by adding 1 to the old CPU penalty. The CPU penalty cannot exceed 120. Loosely interpreted, this formula says that the running thread has its CPU penalty increase until the maximum of 120 is reached. If the penalty is zero, it would take 1.2 seconds until the CPU penalty reached the maximum.

Once every second, all threads, including those that are asleep, have their CPU penalty calculated with the following formula:

    CPUnew = CPUold*D/32   where D=16 by default

D is the CPU penalty decay factor. If we use the default value of 16 for D, then the CPU penalty value will be halved every second. If the penalty value were 120, it would take seven seconds for the value to be degraded to zero.

The priority that the scheduler uses is calculated with the following formula:

```
P = 40 + N + (CPUnew * R)/32   where R=16 by default
```

P is the priority value; N is the nice value. It is set typically to 20 and can be changed with the nice command. C will eventually grow to the maximum value of 120; R is a weighting factor and is defaulted to 16.

Let me summarize these formulas. While a thread executes, its CPU penalty increases; therefore its priority increases or becomes worse. The thread is penalized for running. While a thread sleeps, its CPU penalty decreases; therefore its priority decreases or becomes better. A thread is rewarded for sleeping. When the sleeping thread wakes up, it is put on the run queue with the same priority that was computed while it was sleeping.

Competing threads on the run queue get a fair opportunity to run because the priority of a running thread increases while the priority of a runnable, but not running, thread decreases. Every T ticks. Where T is typically one, the scheduler compares priorities of the running threads against those in the run queue and preempts them if a waiting runnable thread has a priority greater than that of the running thread.

Preemptive dispatching could be compared to a car repair shop with one mechanic, the owner. You bring your car (process) into the garage for a valve job. This takes a very long time to complete. The mechanic works on the car for an hour or so; another customer comes in for an oil change and wants to wait. The mechanic considers this job a high priority task (interactive job). He suspends the valve job and begins work on the oil change, completing it in 30 minutes. After the customer with the oil change leaves, the mechanic returns to the valve job.

2.5.2 Memory Overcommitment

The AIX scheduler gets called into action once again when processes are using too much virtual memory. This overcommitment of virtual memory is measured by the amount of paging that occurs. When paging exceeds a certain threshold, processes are suspended in an attempt to throttle back the memory load. (I know I said earlier that threads are equivalent to processes, but in this case I mean processes and all the threads contained therein.) While processes are suspended, no new forks can occur. When the paging situation returns to normal, suspended processes are reactivated. Once reactivated, a process is exempt from being suspended for a short time. Certain other processes such as kernel processes and fixed priority processes are always exempt from suspension.

Please understand that if there is no paging activity there is no problem. If there is a lot of paging, programs near and dear to you may stop executing.

Let's examine just what I mean by "a lot of paging." Imagine a page getting paged out by the page stealer and immediately being needed by some process. Imagine this happening with every page that gets paged out. If paging was ever this bad, the VMM would spend all the CPU time trying to resolve page faults of pages just paged out. The system going over the edge of sanity and spending more time paging than doing anything else is called *thrashing*. Let's come up with a formula that quantifies how much thrashing is tolerable.

I said earlier that page stealing does not always result in a page out. With luck, the page is not dirty, and stealing it means simply reusing the page. With no luck at all, every page would be dirty, and every page steal would result in a page out. Let's now define a thrashing severity ratio

    T = O/S

where S is the number of page steals in the last second and O is the number of page outs to page space in the last second. T cannot be larger than 1, and 0 is ideal. However, a value of 1 would mean a useless system. There is a value of T that when $T > H$, the AIX scheduler blows the whistle and considers putting processes into the penalty box. In this case the penalty box is a thrashing suspension queue. You can tune the value of H, which has been empirically set to 1/6 by default. You can adjust H to suit your opinion of when thrashing is bad enough to suspend processes.

Now that we know when thrashing occurs, we need to know which processes are chosen as suspension victims. If a process appears to be the main cause of all this paging, it should be suspended. Every process has statistics recording how many page faults it incurred in the last second, and of those faults, how many were repage faults. In the AIX justice system, suspicion of wrongdoing is grounds for conviction. Consider the ratio

    X = R/F

where R is repage faults by a certain process in the past second, and F is the total faults in the last second. When $X > P$, that process is sentenced for some time in the penalty queue. P has a default value of 1/4.

Once processes are suspended, the time during which the thrashing severity must return to normal is the value w, which has the default value of 1. The default value of m is 2. If there are less than m processes, suspension will not occur. Once a process is reactivated, it will be given a grace period in which it is exempt from suspension. This grace period, e, has a default value of two seconds.

In Chapter 4 you will learn to tune values of p and h, reciprocals of P and H, respectively, and e, m, and w.

2.6   Facts of Life about Disk Hardware

In order to understand how to maximize general system I/O performance, it is necessary to understand the limitations of random access SCSI hard disk technology. The disks of today are made of pizza-like platters spinning at 3000 to 8000 rpm. The data is read from a magnetic device on the end of a set of mechanical arms that move from outside edge to inside edge of the platter. These disks can deliver data to RAM in a typical time of 10 to 50 milliseconds. On the other hand, the CPU can access data in RAM in an average time of 20 to 70 nanoseconds. To put it another way, disks are 1000 times slower than RAM. There are things that can be done to reduce the access time of the disk to 10 milliseconds.

There are four components of this access time. The largest component is the time required to move the mechanical arm from where it is to where the desired data is. This component is called *seek latency*. Seek latency for modern disk technology is somewhere between 10 ms and 100 ms. Once the arm has moved to the desired spot, the next largest time component comes into play. *Rotational latency* is the time required for the desired data to pass under the mechanical arm. A typical disk spins at the rate of 7600 rpm. Thus a worst-case rotational latency would be 60/7600, or about 8 ms. Once the data passes under the magnetic head, it must be copied from the bits on the magnetic platter onto the wires attaching the disk to the SCSI controller card, which in turn attaches to the system I/O bus. This is expressed as the disk transfer rate. Disk transfer rates are between 1 and 10 MB per second. For a typical disk transfer of 4K on a disk with a transfer rate of 4 MB per second, the transfer latency would be 1 ms. After the data gets on the disk cable, it is transferred through the SCSI adapter through the system bus into RAM. This component is called the SCSI controller transfer rate. The rate for SCSI-2 is on the order of 10 MB per second; for SCSI Fast-and-Wide adapters, this rate is about 20 MB per second.

It is important to note that mechanical latency components are serial in nature. This means that seek latency cannot be overlapped with rotational latency. Nor can either of these be overlapped with disk transfer latency. While the disk is seeking to the next spot, that same disk obviously cannot be transferring any data. Since the disk platter spins at constant speed, the disk mechanism cannot even begin to wait for the platter to be positioned at the correct spot until the arm is done moving. Thus all the mechanical latencies are additive on the same disk. The SCSI controller transfer and the disk transfer can be overlapped up to the point where the SCSI transfer rate (more properly called bandwidth, but for our purposes I will declare them synonyms) is being exceeded. For example, it works fine to hook up two disks, each having a transfer rate of 3 MB per second, to an SCSI controller that has a transfer rate of 10 MB per second. However, connecting four such disks to the same controller is likely to induce a bottleneck, especially if the disks are actually approaching their maximum transfer rate for extended periods.

For some modern disks, the outer tracks have more sectors (a sector is the smallest unit of data that can be read from the disk) per track than the inner sectors. This is just a geometric fact that is exploited to increase the capacity of the disk. To us performance analysts, this is interesting because the more sectors per unit area, potentially the more bytes per second flying past the read head. And, empirical measurements show that the outer tracks on a variable density disk have a 15% to 30% improved transfer rate under optimum conditions.

The way to minimize the latency for one disk is to try to minimize each component. The only components that can be minimized are seek latency, rotational latency, and disk transfer latency, which is accomplished by judicious or lucky placement of your data on the disk. The SCSI controller transfer rates are fixed and cannot be changed. However, you can add additional SCSI controllers to boost total SCSI bandwidth to match the total bandwidth of the disks you have. We will revisit latency and transfer rates in Chapter 4 when we discuss how to optimize data placement.

2.7   Summary

The following are the most important points covered in this chapter:

1.   The AIX kernel tables do not need to be tuned by recompiling the kernel. The kernel dynamically allocates internal kernel data structures that require no tuning.

2. The AIX program loader gets a program started by resolving symbolic addresses, mapping the portions of the program into its virtual memory space, and transferring control to the program. A knowledge of the program loader will enable you to understand how to optimize virtual memory usage.

3. The AIX VMM maps a program's virtual memory in the system's real memory. It handles page in and page out of files, program data, and program code. A working knowledge of the VMM will enable you to optimize disk I/O performance and virtual memory usage.

4. The AIX Journal Filesystem (JFS) is the subsystem that interacts closely with the VMM in performing file I/O. Knowledge of the inner secrets of the filesystem operation will enable you to optimize disk I/O performance.

5. The AIX CPU scheduler controls which threads run on the various CPUs of the system. Understanding of the scheduling rules will enable you to optimize thread contention for the CPU in CPU-bound situations.

6. Understanding the realities of current magnetic disk technology will enable you to place data on disks to optimize performance and to make configuration choices that perform efficiently.

3

Tools for the System Administrator

In this chapter, I discuss a collection of AIX performance statistical monitoring tools that should be useful to a wide range of AIX performance analysts. Those of you who are analyzing system configurations will learn which tools to use to find bottlenecks that can be eliminated by changing the configuration of your system. Those of you who are analyzing your application program performance will be able to use the same tools to gain a better understanding of how your application program interacts with the AIX operating system. You may then change the coding of your application to ease performance bottlenecks.

Before we learn about specific analysis tools, it would be appropriate to look at the kinds of tools at our disposal. When you walk into an unfamiliar bookstore, you probably see a directory that classifies the kinds of books and their location in the store. Likewise, a directory of the kinds of tools and when you use them will help you to devise a methodical approach to solving your performance problems.

I use the analogy that AIX performance tools are like optical instruments that can illuminate details about some scene. When you are first alerted to a performance problem, you want to learn some initial details, but you don't need to learn too much detail. To illustrate the analogy, assume you are walking in the woods to gather wild exotic plants for dinner. You come upon some strange plant you don't recognize. You pick up a specimen, put on your reading glasses, and quickly determine that it is a mushroom. At this point, if you hated eating mushrooms, you wouldn't need any more information about this plant. However, let's assume you love mushrooms, and you want to determine if it is a poisonous type. You extract your magnifying glass and examine the plant structure more closely to identify the plant further. You narrow the identification to one species that has several related plants. Most of them are benign, but one is deathly poisonous. As a favor to your dinner guests, you want to be certain you don't harvest the poisonous variety.

You take your microscope from your field case, prepare a slide, examine the cellular structure, and determine that this specimen is definitely the poisonous variety. You silently congratulate yourself, knowing you have potentially avoided a nasty lawsuit; you've also avoided losing several good friends.

Now your appetite is, for certain, whetted for mushrooms. You need to find a better habitat for the kinds of edible mushrooms, so you climb to the top of the hill, take out your telescope, and scan the distant forest for more suitable terrain. You spot some better habitat, walk there, and go through the same identification process as before. This time, the mushrooms are edible, so you collect three pounds. Triumphantly you trudge back to camp, lugging your three pounds of mushrooms and twenty pounds of optical gear.

The first point of this analogy is that you used several kinds of optical tools for specific situations. You used your reading glasses, not the microscope, to make the first examination. Using the microscope would have worked, but it would have provided too much, possible irrelevant, information. You did not use the magnifying glass to examine the cellular structure because it is incapable of providing enough detail.

The second point of this analogy is that you have four distinct phases to your examination. The first is an initial, cursory examination (reading glass). This first phase is looking at systemwide statistics. The second phase is a more detailed examination (magnifying glass) that is done only if the initial examination indicates it is necessary. The second phase examines statistics specific to a particular process. The third phase is a minutely detailed examination (microscope) of a process that is typically needed only by programmers or analysts capable of understanding application design. The fourth phase is a long-distance examination (telescope) typically used by system administrators as a preventive measure.

Keeping this classification in mind as you learn the tools will enable you to choose which tool to use for a particular situation. But don't get hung up on my names for these tools types; these names are only a learning aid. This chapter will discuss reading glass, magnifying glass, and telescope types of tools. Chapter 5 will discuss the microscope types of tools.

Now we are ready to get to the real business at hand—collecting and analyzing data on a real system. The examples I use are only to generate an interesting work load and subsequently to capture performance statistics, which I will explain. I urge you either to create your own test scenarios to run or, better yet, to analyze a real system running a real-world problem.

3.1   Vmstat: **CPU and Virtual Memory Utilization**

The most frequently used reading glass type of tool is vmstat. Vmstat first appeared on BSD UNIX systems and on AIX version 3.1. Vmstat monitors CPU usage and virtual memory usage for the system as a whole. It calculates statistics averages by reading an AIX kernel structure from kernel memory at each sample. This structure contains statistics counters that continually increase with system age. Vmstat calculates the difference between two counter samples and comes up with an average over the sampling interval. It is typically run in a separate xterm window in the foreground with the output going to the terminal. It can also be run in the background while redirecting output to a file. The primary argument is the sample interval expressed in seconds. The second optional argument is the number of samples to capture. The most common way to use vmstat is to omit the second argument, in which case vmstat will run and sample until interrupted. All the following examples assume vmstat is running in its forever mode. Please note that the first capture of vmstat should be ignored; it is incorrectly computed due to the lack of a preceding capture with which to calculate statistics counter differences. See Figure 3.1 for a sample vmstat report.

```
vmstat 5
kthr          memory              page                faults           cpu
-------  -------------  -------------------------  -------------  -----------
 r  b       avm   fre   re  pi  po  fr  sr  cy    in   sy   cs   us sy id wa
 1  0     20172   399    0   0   0   0   0   0   138   92   42    1  4 95  0
 1  0     20187   378    0   0   0   0   0   0   134   69   32   32  3 65  0
 2  0     20194   371    0   0   0   0   0   0   137   29   26   99  0  0  0
 2  0     20200   365    0   0   0   0   0   0   134   38   28   99  1  0  0
 1  0     20172   399    0   0   0   0   0   0   132   43   29   17  2 81  0
```

Figure 3.1 Sample vmstat report

Before we go further, let me tell you the meanings of the more interesting columns of the vmstat report. Not all of the vmstat report is useful in analyzing system performance; I will discuss only the columns that convey useful information about AIX system behavior. If you are curious about parts of the report that I omit, you can consult the AIX Info-Explorer for more details.

The first group of two columns represents statistics about thread (process in the case of AIX 3.2) queues.

r   Number of threads waiting in the run queue averaged over the sample interval. On an idle system, this will almost always be zero, which denotes that there is nothing to run. The higher the number, the more CPU work there is to do—that is, CPU time is a bottleneck.

b   Average number of threads waiting on the wait queue. This statistic is an inexact indicator of how many threads are waiting on disk I/O.

The next group of two columns represents statistics about virtual- and real-memory usage.

avm   Active virtual memory in units of 4K pages. This value is the total number of pages allocated in page space. High values simply mean that the system has a high amount of virtual memory currently allocated; it is not an indicator of poor performance.

fre   Size of the list of free RAM pages. The AIX system will try to maintain a minimum-size free list so that pages will always be available when needed. The page stealer is responsible for keeping the free list at this minimum. See Chapter 2 for a description of the page stealer and how to tune the stealing algorithm. Please note that a small free list is not necessarily an indication that there is a real-memory shortage.

The next group of six columns are statistics concerning VMM page stealing. Note that the sy column in this group is different from the sy column in the CPU group.

pi   Average page-in rate from page space in units of pages per second. A nonzero value over an extended time (I consider one minute an extended time) means that real memory is constrained to some degree. To be more precise, five pages per second would have me worried, while 50 pages per second would have me pounding the desk in frustration. Also note that this statistic does not include paging in from a filesystem due to file I/O. We will see that statistic later in the filemon utility.

po   Average page-out rate to page space. Everything that applies to pi also applies to po.

fr   Page steal rate. The importance of page stealing is mentioned in Chapter 1 where I describe memory overcommitment.

The next group of three columns represents statistics about kinds of system interrupts.

cs   Average context switches per second. An idle system will typically exhibit about 20 to 60 per second. A system running two or more very compute-bound processes will typically show a rate of 100 because of the default AIX time slice is one hundredth second. Rates much greater than 100 mean that processes are voluntarily relinquishing the CPU by performing either a blocking I/O system call or a blocking IPC call. See Chapter 7 for more information about programming remedies for high cs rates.

The next four columns represent CPU utilization expressed in units of percent. These columns should total 100%, or very close to it. The percent is calculated by the clock-interrupt handler. One hundred times per second the clock interrupts and asks the question: What mode is the system in at this instant? There are four counters for each of these modes, and one counter is incremented at each clock interrupt. Vmstat computes each average by subtracting the last counter snapshot from the current snapshot and dividing that average by how many clock ticks occurred during the sample interval.

us   User-mode CPU average. What is a good value for user CPU time depends on whether you are trying to maximize throughput or response time. Ideally to maximize throughput, this value should be 100%; to maximize response time, this value would ideally be 0%.

sy   System-mode CPU average. Ideally system CPU time should be zero, but it never is. I would say that a value greater than 50% is usually cause for concern and further investigation.

id   Idle-time average. The ideal values are opposite those for user time.

wa   Disk I/O wait average. This is a special idle time when the system is idle, but there is at least one disk I/O pending on the system. Ideally this value should be zero. A nonzero value indicates there is some opportunity to improve system throughput by either tuning disk configurations so they complete faster, or somehow adding more non-I/O work load to the system.

Now, let's run a compute-bound program (see Figure 3.2) to see how vmstat reacts. I have a simple program that calculates prime numbers using the Sieve of Erosthenes algorithm. How it does this is not important, but you can view the source code in the Appendix. Perhaps we can guess what the sieve program is doing to cause the observed behavior.

```
./sieve   -d 20000
  kthr        memory              page                    faults          cpu
------- ----------- ----------------------- ----------- -----------
  r  b     avm    fre   re  pi  po  fr   sr   cy    in    sy   cs   us sy id wa
  1  0   20172   399    0   0   0   0    0    0   129    41   26    2  3 95  0
  1  0   20187   378    0   0   0   0    0    0   133  5050   30   28 41 31  0
  2  0   20187   378    0   0   0   0    0    0   133  7613   27   42 58  0  0
  2  0   20187   378    0   0   0   0    0    0   139  7571   28   45 55  0  0
```

Figure 3.2 Vmstat report showing CPU load

Notice that the values in both sy columns are significantly greater after the first invocation of sieve. This means that sieve is probably executing a large number of system calls that consequently contribute to the increased system-time utilization. If you consult the sieve source code, you will indeed see that this is the case. Later you will learn how to tell which system calls are being executed.

3.2   Iostat: Disk I/O Utilization

The next reading glass type of tool to use is the iostat command. Iostat is capable of reporting CPU statistics, terminal I/O statistics, and disk I/O statistics. Since vmstat also shows the same CPU statistics in a more readable format, I will ignore this portion of the iostat capability. Because I believe that terminal I/O is seldom a bottleneck concern, I will ignore this feature and instead refer you to the AIX InfoExplorer documentation to learn how to interpret this feature. I'll cover disk I/O reports for iostat next.

Let's run sieve as we did in the previous example and examine the iostat report.

```
sieve -d 20000
```

The iostat command to run is

```
iostat -d 5
```

Iostat takes the same arguments as vmstat to control sample interval and total sample size.

The report shows multiple lines per sample, which makes it extremely difficult to read. In Figure 3.3 each line represents statistics for one disk device. CD-ROM devices are considered disk devices. Remember to ignore the very first sample from an iostat report for the same reasons mentioned for vmstat.

```
Disks:        % tm_act      Kbps       tps    Kb_read    Kb_wrtn
hdisk0          0.4         0.6        0.1     283779    1254104
hdisk2          0.0         0.0        0.0      31300      55772
hdisk1          0.2         0.2        0.0      40457     419410
hdisk3          0.0         0.0        0.0       6323      21696
hdisk4          0.7         0.4        0.3     403333     683832
hdisk5          0.0         0.1        0.0       7135     334836
cd0             0.0         0.0        0.0       9732          0
hdisk0          0.0         0.0        0.0          0          0
hdisk2          0.0         0.0        0.0          0          0
hdisk1          4.2        25.5        1.6          0        128
hdisk3          0.0         0.0        0.0          0          0
hdisk4          0.0         0.0        0.0          0          0
hdisk5          0.0         0.0        0.0          0          0
cd0             0.0         0.0        0.0          0          0
hdisk0          0.0         0.0        0.0          0          0
hdisk2          0.0         0.0        0.0          0          0
hdisk1          3.4        22.4        1.4          0        112
hdisk3          0.0         0.0        0.0          0          0
hdisk4          0.0         0.0        0.0          0          0
hdisk5          0.0         0.0        0.0          0          0
cd0             0.0         0.0        0.0          0          0
```

Figure 3.3 Sample iostat report

Following is an explanation of the iostat columns:

Disks	Disk label
% tm_act	Disk utilization expressed in percent. This is calculated by the clock interrupt handler by incrementing a disk-busy counter, if the disk has at least one I/O event pending.
Kbps	Average total kilobytes transferred per second. Since today's hard disk drives can sustain about 1–5 megabytes per second, any value approaching one-half of a disk's theoretical maximum bandwidth would be considered a large number. To say this another way, a number exceeding 2000 would be cause for you to investigate the disk's true I/O throughput limitations and perhaps take some remedial action. You will learn what remedial actions to take later.
tps	Average number of I/O requests completed per second. Since the cost of a disk transaction varies with how much the disk must seek to complete the translation, it is difficult to identify a value of concern. Therefore I will guess that a range of concern is 10–100.
Kb_read	Total number of characters read during the sample interval.
Kb_wrtn	Total number of characters written during the sample interval. The total number is not important, but the transfer rate is. Kb_read and Kb_wrtn are most useful when expressed as a ratio to one another.

3.3   `Sar`: **System Activity Report**

The `sar` tool is also a reading glass tool. The `sar` command is derived from System V UNIX, but the AIX implementation of sar is of limited usefulness because the AIX implementation is not as complete as other UNIX implementations. However, I will tell you how to run it and which options are the most useful. To find details about the sections I omit, consult the AIX InfoExplorer.

The `sar` command runs the `sadc` command under the covers to capture the same kernel counters that vmstat reads. Sadc puts this binary information in a file, and `sar` formats the data. I prefer to run `sadc` directly because this eliminates the formatting that `sar` does concurrently with data capture. Figure 3.4 shows a simple script that uses `sadc` to capture data first and then uses `sar` to format the binary data in interesting reports. I will discuss only the `sar` options that I find useful. You can refer to AIX InfoExplorer if you are curious about the options that I have left out. Note that the options I recommend specifically omit the `-b` option, which reports the disk buffer cache ratios. These ratios are quite useful on other UNIX systems but not on AIX. AIX uses virtual memory as a disk cache for JFS-type files. The traditional buffer cache, which `sar -b` reports, is used for raw block devices. However, no application should use raw block devices, because they are the poorest performing type of disk I/O. There will be more on raw disk devices in Chapter 7.

```
/usr/lib/sa/sadc 5 10 > sadc.out
echo System calls >>sar.out.1
sar -f sadc.out   -c >>sar.out.1
echo Run queue >>sar.out.2
sar -f sadc.out   -q >>sar.out.2
echo CPU statistics >>sar.out.3
sar -f sadc.out   -u >>sar.out.3
echo Process switches >>sar.out.4
sar -f sadc.out   -w >>sar.out.4
```

Figure 3.4   Sample `sar` script

Don't be tempted to use the `-A` flag in order to save typing. The `A` option specifies `sar` format for all the possible options. Not only do you get a report with data that is not useful, but you get an extremely unreadable report as well. If you run `sar` several times in succession, as I have done, you get a report that has each section isolated with its own summary.

Figures 3.5, 3.6, 3.7, and 3.8 show the `sar` output that the script produced on my system. The first section, Figure 3.5, shows a system call summary in which the rates per second of total system calls, `read` and `write` system calls, `fork` and `exec` system calls, and total characters are displayed for each sample. It is difficult to gauge which values constitute large numbers; rather, I suggest you use `sar` as a way to tell when statistics have changed from the norm. Experience will tell you what normal values are for your own application, but norms aside, the sample report still tells a story about the application load being run. The write calls outnumber the read calls by a factor of 1000:1. Curiously enough the ratio of characters written to characters read is 1:1000.

```
System calls
AIX tampa 1 4 000102881000      04/24/95


17:19:47    scall/s    sread/s    swrit/s    fork/s    exec/s    rchar/s    wchar/s
17:19:52     7235         5        7211      0.00      0.00     266356     40047
17:19:57     7242         6        7220      0.00      0.00     266896     40134
17:20:02     7082        12        7041      0.00      0.00     267893     39179
17:20:07     7232         6        7196      0.00      0.00     266896     40319
17:20:12     7204         5        7176      0.00      0.00     266886     41443
17:20:17     5624        10        4966      0.59      0.59     271114     28827
17:20:22     6998         5        6915      0.40      0.00     266347     40047
17:20:27     7090         5        7049      0.00      0.00     256718     40819
17:20:33     7232         6        7204      0.00      0.00     266896     41729

Average      6994         7        6887      0.11      0.07     266181     39179
```

Figure 3.5   Sar report of system call usage

The second section, Figure 3.6, shows the run queue and swap queue average depth. The run queue depth is an indication of the degree of backlog that the system is facing due to the system being CPU-bound. One process in the run queue is ideal, meaning there is only one job to run. More than one means that other jobs could run only if there were more CPU power available to run them. The greater the run queue depth, the worse the response time of the individual processes that are waiting. The remedies include getting a faster CPU, using more CPUs (like buying a multiprocessor system), or somehow eliminating some of the process burden. The swap queue is more properly called a page-wait queue. Any processes that are waiting for a page fault to complete on disk I/O wait here. A high number of processes is an indicator of too little real memory. The paging columns of the vmstat report are a more accurate indicator of real memory shortage.

```
Run queue

AIX tampa 1 4 000102881000      04/24/95

17:19:47    runq-sz    %runocc    swpq-sz    %swpocc
17:19:52      2.0        100        0.0         0
17:19:57      3.0        100        0.0         0
17:20:02      3.0        100        0.0         0
17:20:07      3.0        100        0.0         0
17:20:12      2.0        100        0.0         0
17:20:17      2.8        100        0.0         0
17:20:22      2.0        100        1.0        20
17:20:27      2.0        100        0.0         0
17:20:33      2.0         83        0.0         0

Average       2.4        101        1.0         2
```

Figure 3.6   Sar report of run queue

```
CPU statistics

AIX tampa 1 4 000102881000      04/24/95

17:19:47       %usr      %sys      %wio      %idle
17:19:52        41        59         0         0
17:19:57        46        54         0         0
17:20:02        41        59         0         0
17:20:07        44        56         0         0
17:20:12        41        59         0         0
17:20:17        34        66         0         0
17:20:22        32        68         0         0
17:20:27        38        62         0         0
17:20:33        34        66         0         0

Average         39        61         0         0
```

Figure 3.7   Sar report of CPU usage

The third section, Figure 3.7, shows average CPU utilization. The most useful features of this sar report of CPU usage compared to the vmstat CPU report is that each sample has a leading time stamp, and there is an overall average at the end of the samples. Even with these handy features, I still prefer vmstat to sar because of the noticeable CPU overhead of sar.

The fourth and last section, Figure 3.8, shows the process switch rate per second. This should be identical to the cs column of the vmstat report.

```
Process switches

AIX tampa 1 4 000102881000      04/24/95

17:19:47              cswch/s
17:19:52                27
17:19:57                23
17:20:02                28
17:20:07                29
17:20:12                28
17:20:17                71
17:20:22                42
17:20:27                32
17:20:33                27

Average                 34
```

Figure 3.8   Sar report of process switch activity

3.4   Ps: **Process Status**

The ps command is one of the useful tools to help you to determine which processes are running and how much CPU time each has accumulated. Ps is also a reading glass tool and has about a dozen or so flags. Let's look at the most useful ones for our purposes.

Figure 3.9 shows a form of the ps report that specifies a *full* report listing.

```
ps -ef
        UID       PID     PPID    C    STIME      TTY      TIME    CMD
    chukran   22796    20488    0    Jun 09     lft0   254:04    /usr/lpp/X11/bin/X
    chukran   23056    21254    0    Jun 09     lft0     3:51    fvwm
    chukran   23318    23056    0    Jun 09     lft0     0:40    xbiff
    chukran   23586    23056    0    Jun 09     lft0     0:17    xclock
    chukran   23848    23056    0    Jun 09     lft0    10:48    xautolock
    chukran   24388    25150    0    Jun 09     pts/0    0:01    ksh
    chukran   24624        1    0    Jun 09     lft0     0:01    xcalc
```

Figure 3.9   Ps full report

The STIME column indicates the starting time for each process, TIME indicates accumulated CPU time for each process, and C is the CPU priority factor. In Chapter 2 priority scheduling is explained in further detail. In this example, we see that the X process has accumulated several hours of CPU time. This is normal since the system has been up for several weeks.

Figure 3.10 shows a *long* report form of ps. The most important fields in this report, different from those in the previous invocation, are located in the middle columns. The PRI column is the priority of process thread. If you keep in mind that small-valued priorities are good, then you would notice that the ps command itself had a priority that was not as good as the rest of the processes that are showing. This is because ps has recently been running, while all the other processes at priority 60 have not been running.

```
ps -el
     F  S  UID     PID     PPID   C PRI   NI   ADDR     SZ    WCHAN     TTY      TIME    CMD
200001  A  210   22796    20488   0  60   20   66cc   9104             lft0   254:04    X
200001  A  210   23056    21254   0  60   20    700    244             lft0     3:51    fvwm
200001  A  210   23318    23056   0  79   39   3f07    228             lft0     0:40    xbiff
200001  A  210   23586    23056   0  79   39   c718    216             lft0     0:17    xclock
200001  A  210   23848    23056   0  60   20    720    232   a4ad098   lft0    10:48    xautolock
240001  A  210   24388    25150   0  60   20   2764    156   5a13844   pts/0    0:01    ksh
200001  A  210   24624        1   0  60   20   ef3d    332             lft0     0:01    xcalc
```

Figure 3.10   Ps long report

Figure 3.11 shows a verbose format for ps. The most interesting columns are %CPU and %MEM. The %CPU value is an estimate of how much of the CPU resource the process has used since it started. For example, the X server (/usr/lpp/X11/bin/X) has accumulated 251 CPU minutes of time over its entire lifetime, but this represents only an estimate of 0.8% CPU burden.

```
ps wwvg
  PID    TTY STAT   TIME    PGIN  SIZE   RSS   LIM  TSIZ   TRS  %CPU  %MEM  COMMAND
22796   1ft0 A    251:08   4871  6784  6656  32768  1298   588   0.8   6.0  /usr/lpp/X11/bin/X
23056   1ft0 A      3:43     87   240   472  32768   117   140   0.0   0.0  fvwm
23318   1ft0 A      0:40    247   228   148  32768     6     8   0.0   0.0  xbiff
23586   1ft0 A      0:16    100   216   152  32768    36    12   0.0   0.0  xclock
23848   1ft0 A     10:44     50   232   192  32768     9     8   0.0   0.0  xautolock
24388   pts/0 A     0:01    135   156   384  32768   191   220   0.0   0.0  ksh
24624   1ft0 A      0:01    213   332   212  32768    78    12   0.0   0.0  xcalc
```

Figure 3.11   Ps report with CPU and memory usage

Note that this form uses options that don't begin with a "-" character. This convention was started with BSD UNIX. The AIX version of ps supports both System V UNIX and BSD UNIX syntax in the same command.

3.5   AIX Monitor

Now that we have covered the most basic performance monitoring tools that most UNIX systems offer, it is worth noting a monitoring tool that was not written by IBM. This monitor program is a reading glass tool that was written by Jusi Maki and donated to the public trust as free software. The program is similar to the top program found on many other UNIX systems. The source is available from many public Internet sites. Consult the Appendix for a location of where to find the monitor program. Once you find it, or it finds you, you must compile and link it. Directions for doing so are packaged with the source code. Figure 3.12 shows a sample report of monitor.

Monitor is a collection of the best statistics of sar, vmstat, iostat, and ps, all showing on one screen report. The top portion of the report labeled CPU shows CPU utilization both in a list and as a bar graph. This example shows that the system is totally CPU-bound because there is no wait-time percentage. Below the CPU usage section are averages of the run queue length, averaged for the last sample interval—the previous minute, the previous five minutes, and the previous fifteen minutes. These four averages show you whether the run queue load is increasing or decreasing at this moment; in this case the load is increasing. This is because I started the sieve program just before starting monitor. Next in the report is a summary of real and virtual memory usage. The Real column is obvious, but the Virtual column refers to how much page space is in use and free. The rows labeled files and total show how real memory is split between persistent and working segments. Files refers to percentage of real memory devoted to persistent segments, while total refers to the number of files working segments. In Chapter 4 we learn how to adjust these ratios to suit different situations. The Paging column shows paging in and out of page space, just as vmstat does; paging in and out of filesystems is also shown. The Process events column shows the same statistics as sar -c and sar -w. IO section shows disk statistics expressed as an aggregate; IO shows statistics for the hard disks, as in iostat. Clnt Serv NFS/s shows some of the statistics that the nfsstat command would display, and the Netw section is raw throughput of the network interfaces.

```
monitor -all -top 5

AIX System monitor v2.1.1, 26jun96: chukran        Wed Oct 30 12:50:40 1996
Uptime:  26 days, 20:05   Users:   1 of  10 active 0 remote 1754:04 sleep time
CPU: Sys  1.2% Wait  0.0% User 98.8% Idle  0.0%   Refresh: 10.00 s
0%            25%            50%            75%            100%
>>>>>>>>>>>>>>>>>>>>>>>>>>>>>>>>>>>>>>>>>>>>>>>>>>>>>>>>>>>>>>>>>>>>>>>>>>>>>>>>>

Runnable (Swap-in) processes  1.00 (1.00)  load average:  0.90,  0.39,  0.18

Memory     Real     Virtual   Paging (4kB)     Process events      File/TTY-IO
free        3 MB     46 MB       1.0 pgfaults      29 pswitch       9 iget
files      28 MB                 0.0 pgin          64 syscall       4 namei
total     128 MB    128 MB       0.0 pgout          2 read          6 dirblk
IO (kB/s) read  write busy%      0.0 pgsin          0 write       638 readch
hdisk0     0.0    0.0    0       0.0 pgsout         0 fork         33 writech
cd0        0.0    0.0    0                          0 exec          0 ttyrawch
                               Clnt  Serv NFS/s     0 rcvint        0 ttycanch
                                0.0    0.0 call     0 xmtint       33 ttyoutch
                                0.0    0.0 retr     0 mdmint
                                0.0    0.0 getattr
                                0.0    0.0 lookup   Netw  read  write kB/s
                                0.0    0.0 read     lo0   0.0    0.0
                                0.0    0.0 write    tr0   0.0    0.1
   PID USER      PRI NICE  SIZE   RES  STAT  TIME  CPU%        COMMAND
 30294 chukran   111   0  1588K 1640K Frun  2:04  98.4/97.6  sieve
 31314 chukran    60   0   422K  512K Frun  0:02   1.0/ 1.2  monitor
 31094 chukran    61   0    10M 9800K Fslp 32:32   0.2/ 0.3  X
 35756 chukran    60   0   795K  940K Fslp  0:11   0.2/ 0.0  aixterm
 17298 chukran    60   0   208K  260K Fslp  3:23   0.0/ 0.0  xautolock
```

Figure 3.12 Monitor sample screen showing all options on

The bottommost section of monitor is the list of the busiest processes sorted according to which uses the most CPU time in the interval. This list length is specified by the -top argument. Each row identifies process priority, size of data segment in units of pages, number of pages occupying RAM, total CPU minutes, and percentage of CPU time used during the last interval.

The beauty of monitor is that you can see everything important at one glance. Since the program is updating many variables on the screen, I suggest you not specify a sample rate less than the default of 10 seconds. If you specify a top option greater than 15, I suggest a sample interval of 20 seconds. In our example, monitor was using 1% of the available CPU, which is quite reasonable. If this percentage ever exceeds 5%, I recommend increasing the sample interval or eliminating top-process sampling.

Monitor is capable of showing details on a CPU basis. This is most useful for shared multiprocessor (SMP) AIX systems. Figure 3.13 shows monitor running on a two-processor system. The SMP option was added to the command invocation. The CPU section looks different from the non-SMP section because of the addition of statistics per processor as well as average statistics.

```
Load averages:   0.78,   0.21,   0.08               detroit    Tue Oct 29 17:12:29 1996
Cpu states: 19.3% user 11.0% system   0.0% wait 69.7% idle
Logged on:    2 users    2 active 2 remote 00:19 sleep time
Real memory:    83.9M procs    12.1M files  160.0M free  256.0M total
Virtual memory:               52.2M used  267.8M free  320.0M total
CPU   USER  KERN   WAIT   IDLE%   PSW   SYSCALL   WRITE   READ   WRITEkb   READkb
#0       4     6      0      91   682      5002    3776      2    36.65     0.00
#1      35    16      0      49   552      5439    4213      1    46.97     0.39
SUM     19    11      0      70  1234     10441    7988      3    83.62     0.39
    PID USER      PRI  NICE   SIZE    RES  STAT    TIME  CPU%        COMMAND
    516 root      127    21    16K    20K   run   11649  45.3/99.6  Kernel (wait)
  17770 chukran    63     0    15M    15M  Frun    0:16  29.7/56.8  vtest
    774 root      127    21    16K    20K   run   11647  24.2/99.6  Kernel (wait)
   5958 chukran    60     0   374K   460K  Frun    0:03   0.5/ 1.0  monitor
  11786 root       60     0  1970K  2324K   slp    0:39   0.0/ 0.0  dtwm
```

Figure 3.13   Monitor sample screen showing two CPUs active

A major drawback of monitor is that it does not show you any statistics history, as vmstat or sar does. Monitor output can not be captured to a file because the standard output has screen control sequences imbedded, therefore, the data captured to the file looks nothing like what you see on the screen. However, you can specify the -log option to dump unformatted statistics to a separate file.

3.6   Tprof: **Trace Profiler**

Tprof is the first AIX performance tool in our discussion that I classify as a magnifying glass tool. You should use tprof when vmstat or sar indicates that CPU utilization is high. It will answer the question: Which process is using the most CPU time? Sometimes, the process culprit is obvious, but quite often it is not. Haven't you at least once in your lifetime exclaimed, "Oh, gosh darn! The system is a trifle slow. What could the matter be?" Or perhaps your language was not so polite, but the mystery was still there. Trying to use ps to discover which processes are consuming the most CPU time is tedious and not always successful. Tprof is a more precise way to determine CPU bottleneck culprits.

Tprof is an example of a sampled profiler and is similar to prof and gprof, which I discuss in Chapter 5. Tprof uses the system event trace tool, which I also discuss in Chapter 5, to do the hard work of sampling, and the tprof program massages these samples into something understandable by ordinary mortals. Tprof instructs the trace program to sample the CPU program counter value 100 times per second. Other events such as fork and exec system calls and process switches are also remembered so that tprof can tell which process is running at any given sample. Thus for each sample, which is called a "tick" in tprof parlance, tprof records the process name and whether the program counter is in the kernel address space, the user address space, or shared library address space. Tprof creates an ASCII report of the statistics. What you see in the tprof report are sorted totals of process names and how many ticks are spent in the three address spaces. You can optionally see details like ticks for each subroutine in the main program and shared libraries. I will discuss profiling at the subroutine level in Chapter 5.

Following is an example of the simplest way to get a `tprof` profile of a specific program that you invoke on the command line:

```
tprof -x sieve 20000
```

This example is profiling sieve, and when the command is complete, several intermediate files will be in the current directory in addition to the report file named __prof.all. Figure 3.14 shows the report that was created. The `Total` column shows ticks for each

```
cat __prof.all
```

Process	PID	TID	Total	Kernel	User	Shared	Other
=======	===	===	=====	======	====	======	=====
sieve	17680	19225	2071	5	2066	0	0
sh	17680	19225	18	7	4	7	0
pcimapsvr.ip	7128	3553	12	11	1	0	0
wait	516	517	10	10	0	0	0
gil	1032	1291	9	9	0	0	0
gil	1032	1549	9	9	0	0	0
syncd	1902	2679	8	8	0	0	0
gil	1032	1807	5	5	0	0	0
dtfile	12820	6685	5	5	0	0	0
tprof	24078	5399	3	1	2	0	0
tprof	22268	19717	3	3	0	0	0
gil	1032	2065	2	2	0	0	0
sh	12818	6683	2	2	0	0	0
dtfile	21574	20047	2	2	0	0	0
dtwm	22596	23117	2	2	0	0	0
expr	12818	6683	2	2	0	0	0
netm	774	775	1	1	0	0	0
dtscreen	4592	7161	1	0	1	0	0
dtfile	22362	16995	1	1	0	0	0
pciconsvr.ip	18908	18917	1	1	0	0	0
rlogind	23918	21879	1	1	0	0	0
=======	===	===	=====	======	====	======	=====
Total			2168	87	2074	7	0

Process	FREQ	Total	Kernel	User	Shared	Other
=======	===	=====	======	====	======	=====
sieve	1	2071	5	2066	0	0
gil	4	25	25	0	0	0
sh	2	20	9	4	7	0
pcimapsvr.ip	1	12	11	1	0	0
wait	1	10	10	0	0	0
syncd	1	8	8	0	0	0
dtfile	3	8	8	0	0	0
tprof	2	6	4	2	0	0
dtwm	1	2	2	0	0	0
expr	1	2	2	0	0	0
netm	1	1	1	0	0	0
dtscreen	1	1	0	1	0	0
pciconsvr.ip	1	1	1	0	0	0
rlogind	1	1	1	0	0	0
=======	===	=====	======	====	======	=====
Total	21	2168	87	2074	7	0

Figure 3.14 Tprof report

process and thread. The columns `Kernel`, `User`, and `Shared` should add up to the value in `Total`. The column `Other` is always zero, so ignore it. We see that sieve takes 2071 out of 2168 ticks. We also see that only 5 ticks of 2071 were spent in the kernel. This is no surprise because `sieve` is a compute-bound program that computes prime numbers. Unfortunately if you want to see percentages, you will have to invest in a calculator because the `tprof` report does not calculate them for you.

The first part of the report is a list of every process that happened to run while `tprof` was running. More precisely, the list shows processes that were interrupted by the clock that ticks 100 times per second. The second part of the report is a somewhat redundant listing that totals each process that has the same name.

You are probably thinking that `tprof` is useless for programs that are not controlled by the command line, those programs such as with a GUI interface or programs that run in the background. Since the duration of the sampling session is determined by the duration of the program run via the `-x` argument of `tprof`, we can fake out `tprof` as

```
tprof -x sleep 60
```

Since `tprof` is executing a command that takes minimal CPU time, all the other processes running during the next 60 seconds will be measured. If you were not certain of exactly how long to specify for sleep, you could control the duration manually as

```
tprof -x cat
```

The `tprof` trace will run until you type control-D to terminate the cat command. I suggest that you make sure to avoid making the trace duration too short. This is because `tprof` uses a sampling technique that has inherent error built in. I suggest a minimum of 60 seconds of sampling time. The longer sampling time means more samples that will tend to have random errors cancel each other out.

3.7   `Filemon`: File I/O Activity

When `vmstat` indicates high CPU usage, you call `tprof` to investigate. But whom do you call when `iostat` says disk I/O is a bottleneck? You call `filemon`, a sibling of `tprof`. `Filemon` is another magnifying glass tool that uses trace to sample a limited number of interesting kernel disk I/O events.

`Filemon` is run somewhat differently than `tprof`. While `tprof` demands to run a synchronous command to define the capture duration, `filemon` does not take a command argument to execute. `Filemon` puts itself into the background and captures trace data. It is up to you to stop `filemon` with the `trcstop` command. Following is an example of how you would use the sleep command to capture `filemon` data:

```
filemon -O all -o filemon.out ; sleep 120; trcstop
```

You should use -O with every `filemon` invocation; otherwise the `filemon` report will not have the logical file statistics. Figures 3.15, 3.16, 3.17, 3.18, and 3.19 show the five parts of a sample `filemon` report.

```
Fri Apr 28 14:28:15 1995
System: AIX tampa Node: 4 Machine: 000102881000

120.134 secs in measured interval
Cpu utilization:  99.1%

Most Active Files
------------------------------------------------------------------------
  #MBs  #opns   #rds   #wrs  file                 volume:inode
------------------------------------------------------------------------
  12.9      1   3301      0  install_file         /dev/lv03:16408
   7.4      1   1889      0  compra.cdrs          /dev/lv03:26629
   6.0      1   1546      0  interior-53.cdrs     /dev/lv03:26625
   Most Active Segments
------------------------------------------------------------------------
  #MBs  #rpgs  #wpgs  segid  segtype              volume:inode
------------------------------------------------------------------------
  45.3  11589      0  d95b   persistent           /dev/lv03:4136
  12.9   3300      0  8b70   persistent           /dev/lv03:16408
   7.4   1888      0  53ea   persistent           /dev/lv03:26629

Most Active Logical Volumes
------------------------------------------------------------------------
  util   #rblk  #wblk   KB/s  volume               description
------------------------------------------------------------------------
  0.32  270464    264  530.6  /dev/lv03            /usr/cdrs6.1 Compressed:
  0.20  119416    952  235.9  <major=40,minor=9>   ???
  0.02     832    304    2.2  /dev/hd2             /usr Compressed:

Most Active Physical Volumes
------------------------------------------------------------------------
  util   #rblk  #wblk   KB/s  volume               description
------------------------------------------------------------------------
  0.31  264384    680  519.5  /dev/hdisk3          857   MB SCSI
  0.20  125656   1712  249.6  /dev/hdisk4          857   MB SCSI
  0.03    1152   1128    4.5  /dev/hdisk0          670   MB SCSI
  0.01     232    537    1.5  /dev/hdisk1          355   MB SCSI
  0.00     232     48    0.5  /dev/hdisk2          355   MB SCSI
```

Figure 3.15 Filemon report, part 1

```
--------------------------------------------------------------------------------
Detailed File Stats
--------------------------------------------------------------------------------

FILE: /usr/cdrs6.1/ibm-velocity/install_file  volume: /dev/lv03 (/usr/cdrs6.1)
inode: 16408
opens:                       1
total bytes xfrd:    13520896
reads:                    3301   (0 errs)
  read sizes (bytes):    avg  4096.0 min    4096 max       4096 sdev    0.0
  read times (msec):     avg  1.497 min  0.074 max   142.094 sdev  6.786

FILE: /usr/cdrs6.1/models/models/compra.cdrs  volume: /dev/lv03 (/usr/cdrs6.1)
inode: 26629
opens:                       1
total bytes xfrd:     7737344
reads:                    1889   (0 errs)
  read sizes (bytes):    avg  4096.0 min    4096 max       4096 sdev    0.0
  read times (msec):     avg  1.070 min  0.090 max    66.916 sdev  4.359

FILE: /usr/cdrs6.1/models/models/interior-53.cdrs  volume: /dev/lv03 (/usr/cdrs6.1)
inode: 26625
opens:                       1
total bytes xfrd:     6332416
reads:                    1546   (0 errs)
  read sizes (bytes):    avg  4096.0 min    4096 max       4096 sdev    0.0
  read times (msec):     avg  0.748 min  0.096 max    46.004 sdev  2.709
```

Figure 3.16 Filemon report, part 2

```
--------------------------------------------------------------------------------
Detailed VM Segment Stats    (4096 byte pages)
--------------------------------------------------------------------------------

SEGMENT: d95b  segtype:    persistent  volume: /dev/lv03  inode: 4136
segment flags:             pers
reads:                     11589 (0 errs)
  read times (msec):       avg  14.627 min     5.551 max  135.552 sdev   6.049
  read sequences:          1
  read seq. lengths:       avg 11589.0 min     11589 max    11589 sdev    0.0

SEGMENT: 8b70  segtype:    persistent  volume: /dev/lv03  inode: 16408
segment flags:             pers
reads:                     3300   (0 errs)
  read times (msec):       avg  15.919 min     5.431 max   86.344 sdev   9.299
  read sequences:          1
  read seq. lengths:       avg  3300.0 min     3300 max     3300 sdev    0.0

SEGMENT: 53ea  segtype:    persistent  volume: /dev/lv03  inode: 26629
segment flags:             pers
reads:                     1888   (0 errs)
  read times (msec):       avg  19.901 min     5.461 max  122.227 sdev  18.152
  read sequences:          1
  read seq. lengths:       avg  1888.0 min     1888 max     1888 sdev    0.0
```

Figure 3.17 Filemon report, part 3

```
------------------------------------------------------------------------
Detailed Logical Volume Stats    (512 byte blocks)
------------------------------------------------------------------------

VOLUME: /dev/lv03  description: /usr/cdrs6.1 Compressed:
reads:                    8905    (0 errs)
   read sizes (blks):     avg   30.4   min        8 max        64 sdev     17.1
   read times (msec):     avg 14.367 min    4.996 max   134.558 sdev    8.096
   read sequences:        281
   read seq. lengths:     avg  962.5 min        8 max     15240 sdev   2261.9
writes:                   31      (0 errs)
   write sizes (blks):    avg    8.5 min        8 max        16 sdev      2.0
   write times (msec):    avg 69.798 min   14.015 max   201.021 sdev   49.700
   write sequences:       31
   write seq. lengths:    avg    8.5 min        8 max        16 sdev      2.0
seeks:                    312     (3.5%)
   seek dist (blks):      init    1216,
                          avg 22095.5 min        8 max    375552 sdev 47149.3
time to next req(msec): avg  28.551 min    0.017 max   683.345 sdev  36.263
throughput:   530.6 KB/sec
utilization:        0.32

VOLUME: <major=40,minor=9>  description: ???
reads:                    5760    (0 errs)
   read sizes (blks):     avg   20.7 min        8 max        64 sdev     16.1
   read times (msec):     avg 12.336 min    4.931 max   207.125 sdev    8.822
   read sequences:        647
   read seq. lengths:     avg  184.6 min        8 max      2920 sdev    398.8
writes:                   92  (0 errs)
   write sizes (blks):    avg   10.3 min        8 max        40 sdev      6.4
   write times (msec):    avg 182.442 min  20.112 max   440.163 sdev  06.923
   write sequences:       92
   write seq. lengths:    avg   10.3 min        8 max        40 sdev      6.4
seeks:                    739     (12.6%)
   seek dist (blks):      init   32848,
                          avg 19630.4 min        8 max    129912 sdev 28413.9
time to next req(msec): avg  31.754 min    0.017 max 24515.854 sdev 322.238
throughput:   235.9 KB/sec
utilization:        0.20
```

Figure 3.18   Filemon report, part 4

The report, as shown in all five figures, is divided into a summary section and a detailed statistics section. The summary section shows sorted lists of most active files, virtual memory segments, logical volumes, and physical volumes. The I/O activity is sorted by amount of data transferred in both read and write directions. The Most Active Files section shows the amount of data transferred in megabytes, the number of opens, the number of reads and writes, the file name, and the device/inode pair. The Most Active Segments section shows the amount of data transferred, the number of pages read and written, the segment ID, and the device/inode pair. The Most Active Logical volumes and Most Active Physical Volumes sections show utilization, read and write transfer rate, and device name.

```
----------------------------------------------------------------------------
Detailed Physical Volume Stats   (512 byte blocks)
----------------------------------------------------------------------------

VOLUME: /dev/hdisk3   description: 857   MB SCSI
reads:                     7859        (0 errs)
  read sizes (blks):       avg         33.6 min        8 max        128 sdev        18.1
  read times (msec):       avg        9.776 min    4.685 max     61.853 sdev       4.115
  read sequences:          352
  read seq. lengths:       avg        751.1 min        8 max      13000 sdev      1665.8
writes:                    81          (0 errs)
  write sizes (blks):      avg          8.4 min        8 max         16 sdev         1.7
  write times (msec):      avg       24.567 min   12.433 max     40.812 sdev       6.301
  write sequences:         81
  write seq. lengths:      avg          8.4 min        8 max         16 sdev         1.7
seeks:                     433         (5.5%)
  seek dist (blks):        init     374208,
                           avg     244523.7 min        8 max    1004344 sdev    356286.9
  seek dist (cyls):        init        325,
                           avg        212.8 min        0 max        874 sdev       310.1
time to next req(msec): avg       31.704 min    0.151 max   1665.578 sdev      42.912
throughput:      519.5 KB/sec
utilization:          0.31

VOLUME: /dev/hdisk4   description: 857   MB SCSI
reads:                     5506        (0 errs)
  read sizes (blks):       avg         22.8 min        8 max         64 sdev        18.0
  read times (msec):       avg        8.903 min    4.635 max     37.860 sdev       4.047
  read sequences:          678
  read seq. lengths:       avg        185.3 min        8 max       4208 sdev       424.9
writes:                    127         (0 errs)
  write sizes (blks):      avg         13.5 min        8 max        104 sdev        15.8
  write times (msec):      avg       21.160 min    8.207 max     45.797 sdev       5.926
  write sequences:         112
  write seq. lengths:      avg         15.3 min        8 max        104 sdev        16.9
seeks:                     790         (14.0%)
  seek dist (blks):        init          0,
                           avg      44522.8 min        8 max    1171208 sdev     82632.3
  seek dist (cyls):        init          0,
                           avg         38.7 min        0 max       1019 sdev        71.9
time to next req(msec): avg       44.650 min    0.266 max  60295.341 sdev     863.433
throughput:      249.6 KB/sec
utilization:          0.20
```

Figure 3.19   Filemon report, part 5

The detailed statistics part of the filemon report presents an expanded amount of data for each row in the summary section and includes statistics such as read and write buffer sizes; minimum, maximum, and average transfer times; and number of seek sequences. These details can sometimes be useful but are usually not crucial to understanding a disk I/O bottleneck.

It is worth examining the file and segment summary sections in detail while we are trying to understand the report. In Figure 3.16, inode 26,629 shows up in both the file and segment sections with a transfer of 7.4 megabytes. In this case this means that all logical reads caused a corresponding physical I/O to occur. You might conclude that the effective cache hit ratio is zero, but that would be a very pessimistic definition. Recall that read-ahead happens whenever a program reads a file sequentially. If read-ahead is working properly, the program will always execute reads from the virtual memory cache, thus eliminating waiting. It is often the case that the transfer total for a file is much higher than the corresponding segment. If this happens, a program is rereading portions of the same file. In conclusion, calculating a ratio of logical reads to physical reads, as found in the filemon report, gives an inaccurate approximation to cache hit ratio. The accurate cache hit ratio cannot be determined with filemon. Later in this chapter I discuss how to adjust read-ahead to optimize this ratio.

The purpose of the report is to identify which storage entities are getting the most usage so that you can attempt to place them evenly on your physical volumes to accomplish optimum I/O overlap. Once you have performed this placement, a secondary purpose is to identify the optimum placement of these entities on the same disk to minimize seek distance. You achieve this by attempting to place the busiest entity, usually a filesystem, in the center of the physical volume in order to get the best average seek times. In Chapter 4, I discuss the mechanics of managing these storage entities for best placement.

3.8   Svmon: **Virtual Memory Report**

When vmstat shows a high rate of paging, you can often remedy the situation if you know which programs are consuming the most virtual and real storage. Once you discover which is the most humongous program, you can suggest, politely, of course, to the user executing this program that he would be much more considerate if he ran it at night. Or, if you wrote this program, you could take steps to make more efficient use of virtual memory.

Svmon is a magnifying glass tool that tells you precisely how much storage each process is using at any one time. Svmon takes a snapshot of the kernel virtual memory structures and formats them so you can make sense of them. The first svmon report we'll examine is the global memory report shown in Figure 3.20.

```
svmon -G
         memory                    in use                pin                 pg space
------------------------   ------------------   ----------------   ------------------
  size  inuse   free   pin   work   pers  clnt   work  pers  clnt    size   inuse
 32768  32620    148  4495  15942  15716   962   4495     0     0   32768   27566
```

Figure 3.20   Svmon global report

The first column titled memory shows real memory usage in units of 4K pages. Size is the total memory in the system, which is 128MB in this example. This total size is split between used and unused memory, denoted by inuse and free, respectively. Of the memory in use, there are 4495 pages pinned that cannot be paged out. The memory in use is categorized into the three segment types—working, persistent, and NFS client. The pinned memory is also categorized into those same segment types. The amount of storage allocated to page space is shown in the last two columns. Size is the total page space available, and inuse is the amount used. You must perform your own arithmetic to determine how much is free, or you can use the lsps -a command to see these same statistics.

The most interesting svmon report is the type that examines individual process usage of memory. Figure 3.21 shows part one of a svmon process report, including an index of each process and a summary of how much real memory, pinned memory (the amount of pinned memory for a process is rarely useful since it tends to be very constant), and page space usage (virtual memory) there is. The g flag specifies that usage is to be sorted by page space use. Figure 3.22 shows the topmost virtual memory user, X (the X server, process 13,612). This process has addressability to 16 segments. The Segid column identifies the segment so that you can see which segments may be shared by multiple processes. The type column identifies the kind of segment. Inuse is the portion of the global real-memory usage value used by this process; pgspace is the amount of page space. Address Range is applicable only for working segments. This field is an attempt to show the high-water mark of the address range for that segment.

```
svmon -Pag
       Pid             Command           Inuse           Pin          Pgspace
     13612                   X            8304          3547            11333
     29428             info_gr            6539          3541             6425
      2454                fkpr            4684          3543             6295
     20238               cdsadv           6360          3546             6248
```

Figure 3.21 Svmon process report index

```
Pid:   13612
Command:  X

Segid  Type      Description       Inuse   Pin   Pgspace          Address Range
 a294  pers   /dev/hd2:143397          0     0         0     0..0
 b296  pers   /dev/hd2:32870           0     0         0     0..0
 aa95  pers   /dev/hd2:32871           5     0         0     0..7
 6bcd  pers   /dev/hd3:25              0     0         0     0..-1
 2004  work   kernel extension        29    29         0     0..24590
  cc0  work   lib data                10     0        23     0..1468
 500a  work   shared library text   1495     0      1759     0..65535
 8191  work   sreg[9]                 32     0        32     0..32783
 8d10  work   sreg[8]                 29     0        29     0..32783
 3427  work   sreg[7]                 28     0        29     0..32783
 a515  work   sreg[6]                 14     0        17     0..32771
 ca99  work   sreg[5]                268     2      2301     0..65535
 9a93  pers   /dev/hd2:143396          0     0         0     0..0
 83d1  work   private               1797     5      3155     0..4075 : 65309..65535
 9292  pers   code,/dev/hd2:18595    217     0         0     0..443
    0  work   kernel                4380  3511      3988     0..32671 : 39532..65535
```

Figure 3.22 Svmon process report detail

Recall that since working segment pages are allocated on demand when the page is first referenced, page numbers may skip a value. Also recall that a process private segment has two portions—a data portion and a stack portion. To illustrate skips in page numbers, look at segment ID 83d1 in Figure 3.22. The low range is 0–4075, which means that there are at most 4076 pages comprising the data section of the segment. The high range is 65,309–65,535, which means there are at most 227 pages of stack and unblock. The total of these ranges equals 4303, but the page space column shows only 3155 pages allocated for the entire segment, proving that there are indeed skips in the sequences of pages. If you are curious about exactly where these skips are, you could run svmon -D to get a detailed segment report. I leave that exercise to you. This detail is rarely useful; however, knowing the relative sizes of data and stack could be useful. For example, a very large stack allocation could indicate a program bug involving uncontrolled function recursion.

Note some other interesting things about the X process. The largest virtual segment is the kernel segment (segid 0). This segment is shared with all the other processes in the system. You can identify whether a segment is shared if its segid shows up in another processes segment list. The other shared segments are cc0, 500a, and 2004. Try running svmon on your system and prove to yourself that these are shared segments. (The segids will be different on your system.) The open files are segments a294, b296, aa95, 6bcd, and 9292. All of these list a filesystem device and an inode number. The segments labeled sreg[5-9] are allocated as shared memory.

Be aware that sometimes you need to take steps to ensure that svmon gets a correct reading of the memory statistics. Svmon must perform many read operations to kernel memory to create a single report. If the system is very busy so that svmon does not get enough CPU time, the reads may be spaced too far apart. If this happens, virtual memory activity between reads could make the data that svmon collects inconsistent. To help ensure that this does not happen, you need to improve the scheduling priority of the svmon process. I will cover this topic in general in Chapter 4. But for now, the easiest way to boost priority is to run svmon with nice as the following shows:

```
nice --19 svmon -Pag >svmon.out
```

3.9   Rmss: Reduced Memory Simulator

When your system has too little memory, virtual memory paging is the most dire result. When your system has too much memory, the only dire result is that your wallet becomes too light too fast. Wouldn't it be nice if you could discover that magic point when your system has just enough memory, but not so much that it is wasted? You could remove memory modules and run your work load, but that can be laborious and is sometimes physically impossible. There is a way, however, to remove virtual memory modules so that the system behaves as if it had less RAM.

The rmss tool simulates reducing the amount of RAM by hiding real memory frames so that the system cannot use them for assigning virtual memory pages to them. Rmss is classified as a magnifying glass tool.

Using `rmss` is as easy as specifying how much real memory you want to simulate specified in units of megabytes. Here is how to reduce the RAM size to 35.5MB:

```
rmss -c 35.5
Simulated memory size changed to 35.50 Mb.
```

The memory frames are hidden in such a way that `svmon` can detect them, as shown here:

```
svmon -G
          memory                    in use              pin              pg space
------------------      ---------------      --------------      ----------------
 size  inuse  free     pin  work  pers    clnt work pers    clnt  size  inuse
10240   8881  1359    1664  5508  3060     313 1664    0       0 32768  11341
*
* Rmss has made 1138 free frames unusable.
*
```

The purpose of using `rmss` is to find the point at which reducing memory further causes degraded performance because of excess paging. You would take a work-load measurement at each memory setting, plot the results, and use those results to guess the optimum RAM size for that work load.

If you forget what the `rmss` setting is, just interrogate it as shown here:

```
rmss -p
  Simulated memory size is 64.00 Mb.
```

When you are done and want to set the simulated memory size to the real size, reset it as:

```
rmss -r
  Simulated memory size changed to 64.00 Mb.
```

3.10   PDT: Performance Diagnostic Tool

All the tools I have discussed so far are intended to be executed when you suspect or know you have a performance problem. But how are you alerted to the notion that something is wrong? Usually someone else tells you something is wrong. One of your system users may complain that response time is poor and you should fix it pronto! Quite often system administrators will write their own shell scripts in order to provide early warning of potential performance trouble. Well, you can burn your shell script programmer's manual; AIX has provided a program to do just that. PDT made its debut in AIX 4.1. It is kind of a vital signs monitor that you run on your system to alert you to performance trends that may someday require action.

Running PDT actually involves running a configuration program that sets up a permanent entry in the crontab file. Figure 3.23 shows an example of how to start `pdt_config`. The menu operation is simplistic. Select enable reporting and enter a recipient e-mail address; then enable collection. Once you have completed `pdt_config`, `cron` will be set up to run a data collection program at 9:00 A.M. every weekday. This `cron` job runs under the `adm` user ID, so you would have to switch to this user ID to change the time the statistics collection runs. At 10:00 A.M. the report program runs and mails you the results of the report. Figure 3.24 shows a sample report.

```
/usr/sbin/perf/diag_tool/pdt_config

_____PDT customization menu_____

1) show current  PDT report recipient and severity level
2) modify/enable PDT reporting
3) disable       PDT reporting
4) modify/enable PDT collection
5) disable       PDT collection
6) de-install    PDT
7) exit pdt_config
Please enter a number:
```

Figure 3.23   Pdt_config customization screen

```
Performance Diagnostic Facility 1.0

 Report printed: Fri Aug 18 10:00:02 1996

 Host name: chukran.austin.ibm.com
 Range of analysis includes measurements
 from: Hour 9 on Wednesday, July 19th, 1996
 to: Hour 9 on Friday, August 18th, 1996

 Notice: To disable/modify/enable collection or reporting
         execute the pdt_config script as root

---------------------- Alerts ---------------------

 I/O BALANCE
  -  Phys. vol. hdisk0 is significantly busier than others
        volume cd0, mean util. = 0.00 %
        volume hdisk0, mean util. = 1.62 %
        [based on 23 measurements, each consisting of 20 2-second samples]

 PROCESSES
  -  First appearance of 3316 (X) on top-3 memory list
        (memory % = 5.00)
  -  First appearance of 16492 (dtwm) on top-3 memory list
        (memory % = 4.00)
  -  First appearance of 2586 (dtsession) on top-3 memory list
        (memory % = 4.00)

 FILE SYSTEMS
  -  File system hd4 (/) is nearly full at 93 %
  -  File system hd2 (/usr) is nearly full at 98 %

 PROCESSES
  -  maxuproc (currently 80) may be too low for user chukran
        [based on 23 measurements, each consisting of 10 2-second samples]
```

```
-------------------- Upward Trends ---------------

   FILES
    -  File (or directory) /usr/adm/wtmp SIZE is increasing
       now, 44 KB and increasing an avg. of 728 bytes/day
    -  File (or directory) /tmp/ SIZE is increasing
       now, 11780 KB and increasing an avg. of 193369 bytes/day

   FILE SYSTEMS
    -  File system hd3 (/tmp) is growing
       now, 76.00 % full, and growing an avg. of 1.17 %/day
       At this rate, hd3 will be full in about 29 days

-------------------- System Health ---------------

   WORKLOAD TRACKING
    -  Workload nusers indicator is increasing;
       now 3.00, and growing an avg. of 0.23/day

   SYSTEM HEALTH
    -  Current process state breakdown:
       80.00 [ 99.9 %] : active
       0.10 [ 0.1 %] : zombie
       80.10 = TOTAL
       [based on 1 measurement consisting of 10 2-second samples]

-------------------- Summary -----------------------
    This is a severity level 3 report
    No further details available at severity levels > 3
```

Figure 3.24 PDT report

Note that the information in this report is not very specific. In order to isolate the warnings well enough to take some action would require configuring cron to take more statistics samples at various times in the day. Once you isolate the time of day of the problem, you would need to run additional scripts to gather more specific information. Such scripts would entail running one or more of the tools we have already discussed.

PDT is handy for telling you there might be a problem on your system and alerting you to that suspicion, but it is not helpful beyond this. Therefore I won't be using PDT to help solve any problems in any examples in this book.

3.11 Performance Toolbox

So far, all the statistics monitoring tools I have discussed have produced reports of ASCII text. These reports are valuable, but they leave much to be desired when you are trying to visualize trends or trying to correlate multiple data along a time line. For example, if the system has several brief spikes of I/O activity, it would be nice to determine whether this activity was caused by paging. And it would be nice to tell what time this happened so you could determine if an annoyed system user called you at this same time to complain of poor response. Iostat will give you some of this information, but it won't tell you the time the problem occurred. Filemon will tell you which disks are involved, but it won't pinpoint the time either. It would be nice to know how often these spikes occur to determine if they are a significant source of system performance degradation.

Fortunately for us, AIX has a product that looks at all the stuff `monitor` does, but it goes one step better. The AIX Performance Toolbox displays all this data and more in a graphical form as an X Window client. This data is mostly systemwide data, so Performance Toolbox is mostly a reading glass tool that you would use to gather your initial data. Many UNIX systems have the xload graphical monitor that displays CPU usage as a strip chart plotted against time. I like to call the Performance Toolbox an xload on steroids. You can display all manner of statistics in several choices of graphs. Not only can you display strip-chart graphs, but you can also choose speedometer-style dials, pie charts, and idiot-light indicators. You can get all these choices and change the configuration of the data that is displayed and how it is displayed right on the graph in real time.

The Toolbox is designed in a flexible client-server manner. The client is the program that you start on your AIX workstation to monitor system statistics. These system statistics are collected by a server daemon running in the background. The server can run on your local system as well as on remote systems. These systems can be AIX, HPUX, or Solaris. The idea behind all this is that you can have a single AIX workstation monitoring many other workstations on your network.

Enough commercials already! The Toolbox is started with a single invocation of the `xmperf` command. The first window to be displayed is the main configuration window shown in Figure 3.25. This window has a scrollable log area that shows you status of the client start-up. After this window appears, a default monitoring console appears as shown in Figure 3.26. This console is one of several consoles that have been configured for you.

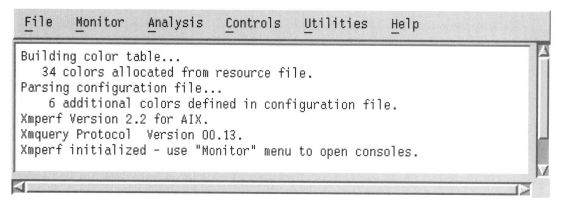

Figure 3.25 `Xmperf` main window

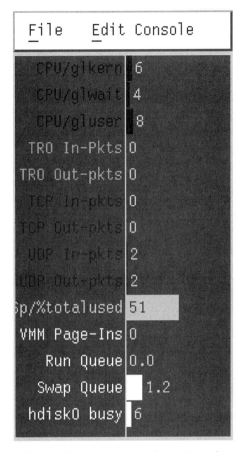

Figure 3.26 Xmperf sample miniconsole

Let's take a quick tour of the Performance Toolbox to get a feeling of what you can do. First from the configuration window, select the Local CPU Sample that is provided for you. This is shown in Figure 3.27. I'll show you some basic examples of how to configure this monitor console.

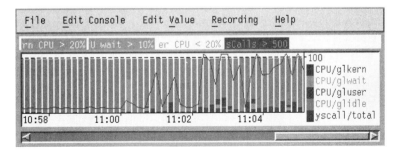

Figure 3.27 Xmperf local CPU sample console

Each console is a collection of rectangular panes called instruments. Each instrument can show several values at once by using color coding to distinguish the values. Click on the bottom pane of the `Local CPU Sample`. This instrument will now have a dotted border around it to show it has been selected. From the `Edit Console` menu, select `Modify Instrument`, followed by Interval, as shown in Figure 3.28. We are going to slow down the sample interval from a feverish one second to a more leisurely ten seconds. You will see a dialog with a slider bar that you can move to increase the number of samples that are saved. Change this value to ten or to some value you like, and then press Proceed. Observe that the movement is ten times slower.

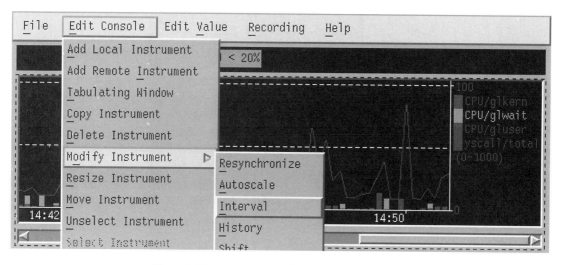

Figure 3.28   `Xmperf` example customization menu

Now let's change some of the colors of the values in the instrument. Select the `Edit value` menu, and select `Change Value`. In the next dialog, select the `glkern` value, which is the same as the system-time statistic in `vmstat`. You are presented with a `Changing Properties` of a Value dialog, in which you select the color button. You now get a color palette with which to select another color, like red. Before hitting `Proceed`, look at the console and note that the color change has taken effect immediately. In this way you can easily punch a few color blocks to see how the colors meld. Before leaving the Properties dialog, key a more useful label into the `Your label` box. How about something like: `CPU system %`. Hit the `Proceed` button, and all the changes you made will take effect.

Next let's change a value to a different value in the same instrument. Select `Edit Value` and `Delete`; then select the `glidle` value to delete. Since the sum of system, user, wait, and idle always totals 100%, showing idle explicitly is redundant and clutters the graph. Let's add a value in its place. Select Edit Value and Add Value. You will get a mind-numbing list of system statistics from which to choose. Select Proc, and then select pswitch, which is the same as the cs context switch statistic in vmstat. Pick some pleasing values for pswitch, and proceed. Note that you might have to stretch the console window in order to see all five values in the instrument. Before leaving this exercise, save the configuration changes with the Save Changes selection under the File menu.

You probably questioned what all the statistics in the selection panels mean. The Appendix explains these lists so you can choose which ones are useful. From this information you can build your own consoles to view the statistics meaningful to you.

Not only can you configure the Toolbox from menus, but you can also edit the xmperf.conf ASCII configuration file. Figure 3.29 shows the section of this file that identifies the new instrument we added. With your favorite text editor search for Local CPU Sample, and examine the pswitch value that we added. Editing the configuration file is useful if you need to change one item in many instruments. For example, if you wanted to change the sample interval to 60 seconds, it would require changing each instrument one by one. You can change these same instruments with one global change command; however, adding instruments or values to instruments is most easily done through the graphical menus.

```
monitor.Local CPU Sample.2.background:   black
monitor.Local CPU Sample.2.foreground:   white
monitor.Local CPU Sample.2.style:        bar
monitor.Local CPU Sample.2.stacked:      true
monitor.Local CPU Sample.2.input.1:      Proc/pswitch
monitor.Local CPU Sample.2.color.1:      ForestGreen
monitor.Local CPU Sample.2.range.1:      0-5000
monitor.Local CPU Sample.2.label.1:      Context Switches
monitor.Local CPU Sample.2.input.2:      CPU/glkern
monitor.Local CPU Sample.2.color.2:      sienna
monitor.Local CPU Sample.2.range.2:      0-100
monitor.Local CPU Sample.2.thresh.2:     90
```

Figure 3.29   Xmperf.cf configuration file

Now that I have shown you the basic operations, you should explore for yourself. You should particularly try the Recording menu in a console and the playback option in the File menu of the configuration window. Also try displaying values from remote hosts. Refer to *Performance Toolbox for AIX—Guide and Reference* for more complete information on how to use the Performance Toolbox.

3.12 Summary

The following are the most important points of this chapter:

1. Vmstat is the first monitoring tool to use in order to gain initial information about the operation of the AIX system. Vmstat will concisely convey CPU usage and memory usage in a single line per sample format.

2. Iostat is the monitoring tool to use to determine the degree to which disk I/O impacts the system. Together iostat and vmstat comprise the minimum set of tools with which to gather preliminary performance data.

3. Tprof is the monitoring tool to use when vmstat indicates that the system is significantly CPU-bound.

4. Filemon is used when iostat indicates that the system is significantly disk I/O bound.

5. Svmon is used when vmstat indicates a large amount of virtual-memory usage or a large degree of virtual-memory paging.

6. Performance Toolbox is used when you want a graphical view of the system-performance statistics.

7. The AIX monitor is a good value for the price (it's free) because it collects all the global system-performance statistics in one concise screen.

4

Remedies

This chapter discusses the "how" of tuning system configurations; it will appeal primarily to system administrators. Please assume that all command sequences mentioned are to be run as the root user. Quite often the only authority necessary to view statistics or configurations is membership in the system group. It is even possible to change some system configurations with SMIT while being merely a system group member. Every once in a while, though, system group membership is not sufficient for inexplicable reasons. So when something doesn't work the way I show it, make sure you are running as the root user.

Recall in Chapter 2 I said that AIX is not one of those UNIX kernels where tuning means setting kernel allocations in a file and then rebuilding the kernel to pick up these new allocations. AIX has a very dynamic kernel. You will find that all of your tuning efforts mentioned in this chapter can be accomplished in real time. By that I mean you can change values on the fly without a reboot.

Most of the changes to configurations and settings that you will perform will persist across a system reboot. These settings are stored somewhere on disk, and they are recalled every time the system is booted. Some notable exceptions to this rule are settings controlled with vmtune, schedtune, nice, and renice. These commands write directly into kernel virtual memory but not onto disk. When you use these commands, remember to embed their invocation in a script that is always called at boot time. One way to do this is to create an `inittab` entry that calls the script; another way is to edit one of the system `/etc/rc` scripts that are always invoked at boot time.

4.1   CPU-Bound Remedies

When `vmstat` indicates that the total of system and user CPU usage is approaching 100%, the system is said to be CPU-bound. Even if the average CPU usage over a moderately long interval is noticeably less than 100%, there could be smaller subintervals during which the total is 100%. The higher the percentage of CPU usage, the higher the probability that there are completely CPU-bound periods. It is useful to determine if and where these periods exist because this knowledge can help you to understand the relative importance of various bottlenecks that you may find. An application can experience different bottlenecks at different times.

4.1.1   Faster CPU

In theory a faster CPU can help to speed up your system, but the speedup may not be worth the cost of the new hardware. Estimating how much a faster processor could speed up your applications is a complex task on paper. Let's take the simplest case of a system with a 66 MHz CPU that is performing less than adequately at 90% CPU usage. Let's say you were considering a new system identical in every way to your current system except that the CPU is 100 MHz. Your estimate of performance improvement would be a simple ratio of CPU usage and CPU speed improvement. In this case the CPU speedup would be 50%, and the estimated improvement would be $50\% \times 90\% = 45\%$.

That was easy. You could estimate the improvement of any system upgrade. You should be so lucky! Things are not as easy as they seem if you have to take into account system hardware enhancements beyond faster CPUs. Hardware enhancements, such as larger memory caches, faster and wider memory buses, and more parallel instruction units internal to the CPU chip, can all boost CPU performance without boosting the clock speed. A method that is commonly used to estimate the performance-boost potential of hardware platforms is to use a standard industry benchmark as a relative figure of merit. One of the most common benchmarks used for these comparisons is the Standard Performance Evaluation Corporation (SPEC) suite of tests. SPEC tests the speed of the hardware by using several real-world programs that completely exhibit user CPU-bound behavior. These programs use very few system calls and, therefore, test the CPU and cache parts of a computer system. At this writing the most commonly used SPEC benchmarks are the SPECint95, which tests integer CPU performance, and SPECfp95, which tests floating-point performance. This assumption is the basis for using SPEC benchmark results to estimate system performance. If System B has a SPECint95 rating that is X% more than that of system A, then my application should likewise experience a performance boost of approximately X% when measured on the same systems. The more closely your application behaves like the SPEC suite, the truer the above assumption will hold. To learn more about the SPEC benchmark suites, visit the SPEC World Wide Web site at http://www.specbench.org/.

4.1.2   More CPUs

If the system you are analyzing happens to be a symmetric multiprocessor (SMP) that runs AIX, you potentially have the ability to add a CPU card that would increase the number of CPUs to the system, thus increasing CPU power.

Estimating the performance boost of additional CPUs is similar to the case of comparing systems with different bus or cache configurations. The problem is that adding CPUs does not scale linearly. A 4-CPU system will not necessarily run twice as fast as a 2-CPU system, even if the work load is 100% CPU-bound. This is because the operating system and the application overhead that handles mutual exclusion locking that is necessary for correct operation on an SMP system isn't necessary on a uniprocessor system.

Now that I have mentioned getting more CPUs, it is worth mentioning how to determine if all the CPUs you already have are really working. It is possible that one or more CPUs may have become disabled due to hardware failure or system administrator configuration error. To examine the state of the CPU complex try

```
cpu_state -l
        Name        Cpu       Status          Location
        proc0       0         enabled         00-0P-00-00
        proc1       1         enabled         00-0P-00-01
        proc2       2         enabled         00-0Q-00-00
        proc3       -         disabled        00-0Q-00-01
```

If you see any of the CPUs disabled, something is wrong. First try enabling the disabled unit with

```
cpu_state -e proc3
```

and then reboot. If the problem is simply that someone disabled a processor (with the -d flag), then the cpu_state listing would now show all enabled. If you still have disabled processors, you have a hardware failure, and you should consult your hardware maintenance person.

4.1.3   Scheduling Tasks at Other Times

If your system is CPU-bound, one remedy might be to do some of the work at another time. For example, if a user is building a rather large program with the make utility, the compiler compiling source code will be CPU-bound. You could easily schedule this kind of task to be run at another time using cron or equivalent alternatives. This sort of remedy is accomplished by system administrator edict that is rarely followed and even more rarely welcomed. Your user's reaction is likely to be, "If I wanted to run my jobs batched at night, I would have bought a mainframe running OS/360." However, some environments, like system compilation or noninteractive analysis runs, are suited to "running batch." See the AIX documentation on cron, crontab, and batch queue submission for more information on how to reschedule noninteractive work.

4.1.4   Finding Runaway Processes

One cause of a chronically sluggish system might be a runaway process that somehow, probably due to a bug in the program, gets into a CPU-bound infinite loop. You have several commands to use to check for runaway processes.

The easiest approach is to use `ps`. See Section 3.4 on how to use `ps` with the vg options. You will have to search manually for the highest percentage CPU user and determine if this CPU usage is excessive or even appropriate.

Another approach is to use `monitor` with the -top option. See Section 3.5 for more information about `monitor`.

`Ps` and `monitor` are quick, but they don't tell the whole story. For example, neither will catch short-lived processes that are run repetitively. To see every process that runs for some period of time, run

```
tprof -x sleep 60
```

for a short while for a fixed duration. If there is a runaway process, it will show up at the top of the list of processes in the `tprof` report. `Tprof` will also show if lots of small processes are running for short durations.

Once the process has been identified, you may take immediate action to kill it and hope the piggish behavior doesn't happen again. Or you may contact the user running the application to deal with the problem.

4.1.5   Tuning Scheduler Algorithm

If you can't manage to off-load work from your CPU-busy system, you could try to affect how much CPU resource a particular process or thread is allowed to have by altering the thread priority. This sort of remedy is indeed another statement of policy that does not go over well with independent users on a multiuser AIX system. Not only is this tactic unpopular, it is often difficult to implement. The various priority alterations require that either the user voluntarily demote his own processes or the root user demote single processes or groups of processes. A user is rarely going to want to have his own programs run more slowly, and it is difficult for an administrator to decide which users or processes to demote. For a system in which an application consists of several cooperating threads, altering one or more thread priorities might improve system performance. For example, a thread, the job of which is to read a socket for incoming requests, might be considered more important than its sibling processes and could benefit by a priority boost. Since you best understand your application's interdependencies, only you can determine if this priority alteration is necessary.

4.1.5.1   Nice and Renice

In Chapter 2 you learned about the computation of the thread priority. Recall that one of the sums is the `nice` value, N, which can have the range of 0 to 40. The default value is 20. Even with the CPU penalty, C, with a value of zero, the best that P can be during the life of a thread is heavily influenced by N. Making N small would tend to favor the probability of the thread using a CPU; making N large will do the opposite.

The `nice` and `renice` commands can accomplish this task but not without drawbacks. The basic premise is, that as a nonsuperuser, you are privileged only to increase `nice` of your program processes, thus making them less favored. You are being nice to your fellow users when you do this, since their programs will consequently be relatively more favored. If you have root privilege, you may decrease or increase the `nice` value of any thread or process on the system.

One example command-line use of nice would be

```
nice -10 make
```

The option is interpreted as a signed integer that is added to the thread's current `nice` value. The `nice` program accomplishes its task by first incrementing its own `nice` value; it then forks and execs the remaining arguments as a command string. This method relies on the fact that children processes inherit the `nice` value of their parent.

If you were root, you could do

```
nice --20 svmon -Pag
```

This looks tricky, but it is how you improve your nice value. Strip off the first "-" which is simply an option prefix, leaving the integer -20. Adding -20 is another way of setting the `nice` value to zero. I chose to use `nice` with `svmon` because it is often necessary to boost the priority of `svmon` on a busy system to get a good sample.

`Nice` is useful when you can plan ahead and specify a `nice` value before you run the program. But what if you didn't plan ahead, and you need to adjust `nice`? Renice accepts a process ID in addition to a `nice` value. It has the same privilege restrictions as `nice`. Nonsuperusers can increment only their own processes; superusers can change any process. If you knew the process of a user you wanted to demote, you would do the following:

```
renice -n 10 -p 21396
```

This would affect just that one process and all threads in that process. If you wanted to affect everything that a particular user was doing, you could do

```
renice -n 10 -u bigjohn
```

This would effectively demote every process that bigjohn has running at the moment, including any shells. Since the `nice` value is inherited across fork, `renice` will affect any future programs that might be run.

Playing with the `nice` value will have an effect only if two conditions apply. First, there must be more than one thread in the run queue. The r column of vmstat will tell you if that is the case. Second, there must be some logical advantage to making some threads more important than other threads. One very good advantage is the case of many cooperating threads in a complex program that somehow creates computing bottlenecks among themselves. One quite common scenario is a client-server application program consisting of many processes. One of these processes is responsible for reading messages from a network socket. In heavy-load situations, it is possible to lose UDP datagrams if the network reader thread does not get enough processing time to save the datagrams before they are lost. In this case improving the priority of this thread with `nice` might be in order. Shortly I will discuss an alternative method that would work better in this situation.

You should also be aware that creating a background job in the `ksh` shell causes the nice value to be incremented by 4. The `csh` shell does not change nice for backgrounded processes. Knowing this will allow you to compute your nice values accordingly.

In order to experiment, I created two competing processes that are completely CPU-bound. I started them simultaneously with the following commands:

```
spin& spin&
```

Figure 4.1 shows these processes accumulating equal CPU time after a few minutes. Note that the nice values of spin are 24, which is 4 more than the default 20. The nice value was changed by the `ksh` shell (the shell I was running in this case) because it considers background jobs implicitly to be less important than foreground jobs. Different shells will adjust the nice value by differing amounts.

```
ps -fl -uchukran
  F   S    UID     PID  PPID   C  PRI  NI  ADDR   SZ   WCHAN     STIME    TTY   TIME  CMD
240001 A  chukran  5706 7496   0   60  20  42f0  160             12:56:29 pts/1  0:01 -ksh
240001 A  chukran  6200 5942   0   60  20  49b2  156  5a10a44    12:54:29 pts/0  0:00 -ksh
200001 A  chukran  6554 5706  47   87  24  1ee7   32             13:39:54 pts/1  1:16 spin
200001 A  chukran  7064 5706  47   87  24  372d   32             13:39:54 pts/1  1:16 spin
```

Figure 4.1   Ps listing before applying `renice`

I now use the `renice` command to degrade one of the `spin` processes,

```
renice -n 20 -p 7064;sleep 60
```

In Figure 4.2 process 6554 has gained about 10 CPU seconds over process 7064, which is not much of a difference. But that is about all the control you have if you are a nonroot user.

```
ps -fl -uchukran
  F   S    UID    PID  PPID  C PRI NI ADDR   SZ   WCHAN    STIME    TTY   TIME CMD
240001 A  chukran 5706 7496  1  60 20 42f0  160            12:56:29 pts/1  0:01 -ksh
240001 A  chukran 6200 5942  0  60 20 49b2  156  5a10a44   12:54:29 pts/0  0:00 -ksh
200001 A  chukran 6554 5706 85 106 24 1ee7   32            13:39:54 pts/1  1:51 spin
200001 A  chukran 7064 5706 53 106 40 372d   32            13:39:54 pts/1  1:41 spin
200001 A  chukran 8614 5706 38  79 20 7d9f  152            13:43:30 pts/1  0:00 ps -fl -uchukran
```

Figure 4.2   Ps listing after applying `renice`

4.1.5.2   Tuning the Scheduler with `Schedtune`

You saw that adjusting the `nice` value does not give much control over competing threads. Chapter 1 explained how thread priorities change with time. Now you can learn how to adjust parameters of the thread priority calculation.

AIX provides a command, `/usr/samples/kernel/schedtune`, to manipulate these parameters. Notice that schedtune is not in a familiar directory that is likely to be in your PATH search string. This is because the designers of AIX initially chose to classify this command as a "sample" program, which I instead call a "patch" program. It is a command to patch values into the kernel; it does not have a SMIT interface and was not mentioned in InfoExplorer until AIX Version 4.1. It was intended for expert use only, and tuning the parameters was not well understood. Consequently `schedtune` was shipped on AIX as a sample program with its source code file. A binary executable is provided for your use.

The `schedtune` command allows you to specify values for R and D in the priority calculation by specifying the r and d flags respectively. The -r flag represents the value R, while the -d flag represents the value D.

The most likely reason you might want to change R and D is to ensure that background threads don't ever compete with foreground threads. The most useful bit of information to know is that making R smaller restricts the range of possible priority values, making it possible to have totally separate ranges for foreground and background categories of threads. Figure 4.3 shows a conceptual example of two threads running on a system with a default R=16. Thread 1 has a default nice=20, while thread 2 represents a background thread with nice=40. Notice that it is possible for these threads to compete with one another because the resultant priority ranges overlap. Setting R=5 reduces the swing in CPU penalty and consequently reduces the swing in resultant priority. Now threads 1 and 2 do not compete because their priority ranges do not overlap.

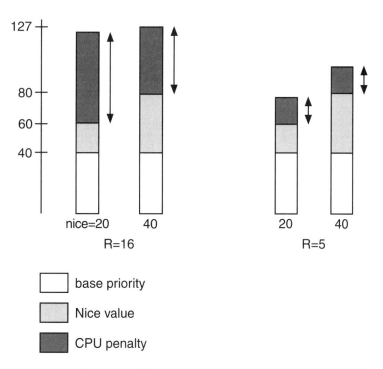

Figure 4.3   Effects of R scheduling parameter

Other settings of R and D may be useful for your particular environment. I suggest you experiment with schedtune if you think that competing threads are restricting your system's optimum behavior.

4.1.5.3 Setpri

A more forceful method of adjusting a process priority, as in the client-server example, is to fix the priority instead of allowing the priority to float. You will have to have root privilege to do this. There is no AIX command to do this, but you can create your own. Figure 4.4 shows an example C program that implements such a command.

```
#include <sys/types.h>
usage(char *name)
{
        printf(" usage: %s process_id priority \ n", name);
}
main(int argc,char **argv)
{
    pid_t pid, pri;
    if ( ( argc !=  3  ) || ! strcmp(argv[1] , "-?" ) )
        { usage(argv[0]); exit(1); }
    pid = atol(argv[1]);
    pri = atol(argv[2]);

    if (-1 == setpri( pid, pri)) /* <== important stuff is here */
    {
        perror("setpri failure ");
        usage(argv[0]);
        exit(1);
    }
    else exit(0);
}
```

Figure 4.4 Setpri priority program

Using setpri to fix the priority wouldn't work for the spin example since spin does not sleep. If you used setpri to set the priority of one of the spin processes to something less than 60, then the other floating process would starve, and the "golden" spin process would hog the CPU. This is not useful, but it is useful to set fixed priorities for competing processes that eventually do relinquish the CPU voluntarily.

If you have a situation where a process is unimportant, setpri can come in handy. If you want this process to run only when there is nothing else to do, use setpri to fix this priority to 126, which is one better than the wait kernel thread.

The same advice about determining the advantage of making certain processes more important applies for setpri. But a warning is in order. With setpri you have the power to set the priority to anything you want. Take care to not interfere with AIX kernel threads by setting the priority of your processes too good. Locking out the kernel netw network process will not be a pretty sight if you are doing any networking. I suggest examining all the kernel process priorities on your system, making sure you pick values larger than those given.

Figure 4.5 shows a listing of the values on my system. Note that the fixed priority processes are noted with a "--" nice value. Since the nice value is not used to calculate fixed priorities, this notation is a handy, compact way to identify fixed priority processes. You will see this only when viewing the "ps -el" command. Other commands that show nice values may not use this notation.

```
ps -elk
       F S UID   PID PPID   C PRI NI ADDR    SZ      WCHAN    TTY   TIME    CMD
     303 A   0     0   0 120  16 -- 2008     4                 -   8:26    swapper
  200003 A   0     1   0   0  60 20 1405   176                 -  25:01    init
     303 A   0   516   0 120 127 -- 2409     0                 - 17247:01  kproc
     303 A   0   774   0   0  36 -- 1806     8                 -   1:26    kproc
     303 A   0  1032   0   4  37 -- 300c    40           *     -  89:27    kproc
   40201 A   0  1878   0   0  60 20 2c2b     8                 -   0:00    kproc
```

Figure 4.5   Ps listing showing nice process values

4.1.5.4   Time Slice

Chapter 2 explained that the running process had its priority changed every 1/100th second. This happens regularly when the clock interrupt occurs. But a process could wake up a few microseconds before a scheduled clock tick and consequently have to give up the CPU without getting to use a full time slice. It is possible to lengthen the time interval in which a priority scan is done by changing the time-slice interval. The priority scan is done every time slice + 1 ticks. Figure 4.6 shows the default situation; that is, a priority scan is done every clock tick. The lower part of the figure shows the time slice lengthened to a value of 1, meaning that a priority scan is done every two clock ticks.

Increasing the time-slice setting could enable threads to get more processing done with less chance of involuntary preemption; however, this would potentially cause interactive

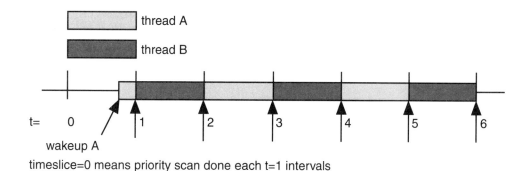

Figure 4.6   Illustration of time slice quanta (*continued on next page*)

wakeup A

timeslice=1 means priority scan done each t=2 intervals

Figure 4.6   Illustration of time slice quanta (*cont.*)

programs to respond more sluggishly. The only situation in which increasing time slice might help is multiple CPU-bound threads competing for CPU time and interactive performance is not a concern. However, the likelihood of larger time slices being helpful is rather low. Because threads can get such an enormous amount of processing done in 10 ms, it is rare to want to run multiple CPU-bound threads. Usually the threads will voluntarily relinquish their time slice by doing some sort of I/O.

If vmstat shows that the system is approaching 100% user percentage and the run queue is greater than one most of the time, then increasing time slice may be something to try. Otherwise, it may waste time to worry about this. Figure 4.7 shows an example of changing the time slice to 3.

```
/usr/samples/kernel/schedtune -t 3
        THRASH                SUSP        FORK               SCHED
  -h     -p     -m      -w     -e      -f       -d        -r        -t
  SYS   PROC  MULTI   WAIT  GRACE   TICKS   SCHED_D  SCHED_R  TIME SLICE
   6      4      2      1      2      10       16        8         3
```

Figure 4.7   Use of schedtune to change time slice

4.2   Memory-Bound Remedies

Memory-boundedness is noted by nonzero values for pi and po in the vmstat reports; this means that some virtual memory is forced out to disk. Memory-boundedness becomes a performance issue because it really means that the system ends up waiting for relatively slow disks instead of relatively fast RAM. Memory-bound remedies will attempt to reduce virtual memory paging.

4.2.1   Adding More Real Memory

There are two things in life that you just can't have too much of. One is money; the other is real memory. If you have a lot of the former, then enough of the latter is no problem.

There really is no good way to estimate how much things will improve after adding RAM. A cost-effective experiment is to borrow more RAM than you will possibly need and install it in your system to observe worst-case load. Then remove memory one piece at a time to observe the results on the system.

Removing RAM by yanking out SIMMs or RAM boards is tedious at best and requires some hardware repair skills and special equipment. A quicker and better way to measure the effects of reduced RAM is to use an AIX tool that simulates reduced system memory. The rmss tool can simulate removing memory by hiding RAM pages from the VMM. The free pages are specially marked with a flag so they can be found again later. While the pages are marked, they cannot be used by the VMM. You hide these pages by specifying a desired simulated memory size in fractions of a megabyte. Figure 4.8 shows an example of setting the memory size to 35.2MB. This assumes that the system has more than 35.2MB of RAM. Notice that global svmon statistics show 1210 frames (another term for pages) that are hidden. The command rmss -r resets the simulated memory to the real-memory value and unhides all the hidden pages.

```
rmss -c 35.2
Simulated memory size changed to 35.19921875 Mb.
svmon -G
        memory                in use              pin            pg space
   size inuse  free   pin   work  pers   clnt  work  pers   clnt   size  inuse
  10240  5532  4708   924   2610  2922      0   924     0      0  21504   2133
*
* Rmss has made 1210 free frames unusable.
*
```

Figure 4.8 Use of rmss to simulate reduced memory

4.2.2 Tuning File Memory Allocation

In Chapter 2 you learned how the page stealer decides which pages to replace in order to keep the free RAM list at a minimum value. The two parameters that are used are minperm and maxperm. Situations involving very heavy periods of filesystem I/O tend to cause paging to and from paging space. Lowering maxperm can reduce this paging by causing the VMM to devote less memory to file pages and more memory to nonfile pages. There are many ways to determine if you have this situation. As you have already seen, you could run filemon and observe that significant I/O was occurring to both a JFS logical volume and page-space logical volumes. Note that vmstat will not help you much, because vmstat reports only paging activity from page space. (Actually, vmstat -s will produce statistics about filesystem paging, but you have to work to calculate these figures. See the AIX manual page for vmstat.) Figure 4.9 shows an example of a snapshot of AIX monitor that illustrates this case. Note that both filesystem statistics, pgin and pgout, and page space, pgsin and pgsout, have high I/O activity. This is a tip-off that file pages are fighting with nonfile pages for memory.

The program that was being examined is a rather common type of program. It reads in a large file into its data area, 32MB in this case, manipulates the file in memory, and then writes the file out to disk. The program starts out by being file I/O intensive. The second phase is a combination of compute intensive and data-segment reference intensive.

```
AIX monitor v1.12: philly                       Fri Oct 13 16:35:47 1995
Sys 10.8% Wait 34.3% User 54.9% Idle  0.0%      Refresh: 31.08 s
0%            25%                50%             75%                 100%
======WWWWWWWWWWWWWWWWWWWWWWWWW>>>>>>>>>>>>>>>>>>>>>>>>>>>>>>>>>>>>>>>>>
Runnable processes  1.51 load average:  1.69,  1.32,  1.33

Memory      Real      Virtual    Paging (4kB)     Process events      File/TTY-IO
free        0.3 MB    44.7 MB      74.6 pgfaults    158 pswitch          0 iget
procs      36.3 MB    39.3 MB      71.1 pgin          6 syscall          0 namei
files       3.4 MB                  2.1 pgout         3 read             0 dirblk
total      40.0 MB    84.0 MB      68.9 pgsin         0 write         8079 readch
                                    1.6 pgsout        0 fork            35 writech
                                                      0 exec             0 ttyrawch
DiskIO       Total Summary                            0 rcvint           0 ttycanch
read        284.5 kByte/s                             0 xmtint          17 ttyoutch
write         8.4 kByte/s
transfers    71.6 tps                               Netw    read      write
active        4/6 disks                             lo0     0.0      0.0 kB/s
                                                      0     0.0      0.0 kB/s
TOPdisk     read      write  busy
hdisk0       282    8 kB/s   42%
hdisk4         1    0 kB/s    0%
hdisk5         1    0 kB/s    0%
hdisk3         0    0 kB/s    0%
hdisk2         0    0 kB/s    0%
```

Figure 4.9 Monitor showing large paging values

The third phase is again file I/O intensive. In other words, the program becomes file-page intensive then working-page intensive and then file-page intensive again. The total amount of virtual memory required would be 32MB of file pages plus 32MB of working pages, which is allocated as buffer space. But, alas, my system has only 40MB of RAM, so some heavy paging is expected. The ideal solution would be to add more RAM so that I have at least 64MB.

There is a cheaper solution, however. AIX provides a command, /usr/samples/ kernel/vmtune, that allows you to specify the maxperm and minperm. Vmtune is similar to schedtune in that it is a patch program and does not have a SMIT interface. Figure 4.10 shows setting maxperm to 50 and minperm to 10, which is expressed in units of percent of RAM. Be careful how you interpret the vmtune output. The values under the -p and -P columns are page counts and are not to be supplied as parameters. The new values are reflected at the bottom of the report near the line maxperm=.

I experimented with two different settings of minperm and maxperm. Figure 4.11 summarizes the values I chose and the resultant improvement in completion time of the program. The top row represents the starting value before I changed anything. Picking good values will require experimentation. I can't recommend any rules of thumb other than decreasing minperm and maxperm as the starting point.

```
/usr/samples/kernel/vmtune -p 10 -P 50
vmtune:   new values:
   -p         -P         -r          -R          -f        -F         -N          -W
minperm   maxperm   minpgahead   maxpgahead   minfree   maxfree   pd_npages   maxrandwrt
  1024      5120         2            64          72        80       524288         0

   -M         -w         -k          -c          -b        -B          -u
maxpin    npswarn    npskill    numclust    numfsbufs   hd_pbuf_cnt  lvm_bufcnt
  8192      672        168          1           93          128           9

number of valid memory pages = 10240      maxperm=50.0% of real memory
maximum pinable=80.0% of real memory     minperm=10.0% of real memory
number of file memory pages = 1683       numperm=16.4% of real memory
```

Figure 4.10   Using vmtune to change paging parameters

Time (s)	minperm %	maxperm %
159	19	75
120	10	50
103	**10**	**30**

Figure 4.11   Results of adjusting paging parameters

4.2.3   Tuning Memory Overcommitment Algorithm

In Chapter 2 you learned how the VMM controls overcommitment of memory by suspending processes. Now it's time for you to learn how to tune the five parameters for the suspension algorithm. As a reminder, the following are the default values:

Thrashing threshold: $H = 1/h = 1/6$

Process paging threshold: $P = 1/p = 1/4$

Minimum time in suspension queue: $w = 1$

Minimum number on run queue: $m = 2$

Exemption time: $e = 2$

Figure 4.12 shows an example of using schedtune to report the current settings of the suspension algorithm.

```
/usr/samples/kernel/schedtune

        THRASH                  SUSP        FORK                    SCHED
  -h      -p     -m       -w       -e        -f       -d        -r          -t
  SYS    PROC   MULTI    WAIT    GRACE     TICKS   SCHED_D   SCHED_R    TIME SLICE
   6      4      2        1        2        10       16        8           1
```

Figure 4.12 Using `schedtune` to show current setting for memory control

If you didn't quite understand all of these parameters, don't worry about it. There is really only one parameter that you need to learn to use—the thrashing threshold. Setting h=0 has the effect of setting the threshold to infinity, effectively disabling suspension. If your system has 128 megabytes or more of RAM, then just skip this whole section because memory overcommitment (also called *thrashing*) control is disabled by the AIX kernel. The value of h is effectively set to zero.

If your system has less than 128MB, you can disable thrashing as shown here:

```
/usr/sample/kernel/schedtune -h 0
```

In fact, I recommend you do this as a preventive measure, regardless whether thrashing is occurring. If you are really curious, you can determine whether thrashing is happening by calculating the thrashing ratio. Recall that the thrashing ratio is

```
T=page-outs/page reclaims
```

From the `vmstat` report, page-outs is the `po` column, and page reclaims is the `fr` column. To state this as a Boolean expression,

```
Thrashing occurs if po/fr > 1/h
```

If we eliminate the fractions by multiplying by fr*h,

```
Thrashing occurs if po*h > fr
```

Setting h to zero ensures the inequality is always false, and that is the extent to which you should try to tune it. Memory thrashing control was never designed to be a general useful mechanism; it was designed to be a safety valve mechanism for customers who insisted on putting too much computing into too little RAM. Just as you wouldn't want to play with the safety valve on your home hot-water heater while it is blowing steam, you shouldn't mess with memory thrashing control while your memory is blowing steam. Get more RAM instead. If you get enough RAM so that you have more than 128MB, thrashing control will never again be a worry.

4.2.4   Page Space Configuration

AIX paging volumes, or *page spaces* as they are also called, are implemented as raw logical volumes. Later you will learn general tuning tips for any logical volume, but you should be aware of advice specific to paging volumes.

If your system pages to any measurable extent, you should consider optimizing placement of the paging volumes. If you need more paging space than the default installation gives you, consider creating additional space on a new paging volume, and place the new volume on a different physical volume than the default paging volume, hd6. Page volumes on multiple disks will improve the concurrency opportunity for the system as a whole. Figure 4.13 shows an example of a SMIT screen in which you would add additional paging volumes.

```
Fastpath:smit mkps
                              Add Another Paging Space

Type or select values in entry fields.
Press Enter AFTER making all desired changes.

                                                       [Entry Fields]
   Volume group name                                   vg2
   SIZE of paging space (in logical partitions)        [40]            #
   PHYSICAL VOLUME name                                                 +
   Start using this paging space NOW?                  yes             +
   Use this paging space each time the system is       yes             +
     RESTARTED?
```

Figure 4.13   SMIT screen to add more page space

If you don't have an additional disk with space to accommodate another paging volume, then increasing the size of an existing default volume is likely to be better than creating a new one. Increasing the size of an existing volume will try to allocate new partitions close to the existing partitions. Creating a new page space will assign it to a default position of center band.

4.2.5   Isolating Memory Leaks

A memory leak is a program bug that can have system performance side effects. A memory leak occurs when a program inadvertently does not release all the memory that it allocates from the operating system. Programs often have many cycles of dynamically obtaining memory from the process heap, manipulating that memory, and then freeing the memory back to the process heap. Sometimes the programmer forgets to free the memory, even though the program is done using it. The program will consequently allocate more storage than it frees, and the process data segment, which holds the heap, will grow without bound.

Since a memory leak is a program logic bug, complete isolation of a memory leak goes beyond performance tuning into that twilight zone of debugging. I will give you a simple procedure to determine if you have a memory leak and, if so, which program contains it. Once you have done the procedure, you can get the guilty party (hopefully that guilty party is not you) to find and fix the leak by examining program logic.

A program leak will manifest itself with two seemingly different symptoms. One symptom is one or more programs dying unexpectedly due to lack of paging space. The other symptom is performance degrading due to paging activity. Both of these symptoms are related because their root cause is an unanticipated amount of virtual memory usage that increases over a long period of time.

Don't think that these two symptoms always mean a memory leak on the system. It may be that the system simply did not have enough page space or RAM to accommodate a completely correct program. The key difference is that a correct program will eventually reach a steady-state memory usage in a few minutes. A leaky program's virtual memory will grow over time and will never reach a steady state.

Proving whether you are dealing with a memory leak requires that you take virtual-memory measurements repetitively over a long period of time. If you suspect a memory leak, reboot your system, and start vmstat with a somewhat long sample interval with the output going to a file. A shell script similar to that in Figure 4.14 might be something you could run over a period of hours after booting. If you pick the vmstat technique, you would monitor the avm column for unbounded growth. If you are using the svmon command, examine the page space column.

```
#Comment out one of the CMD variables
# The CMD runs for a duration of 1 hour and takes 60 samples at 1 minute
# intervals
CMD="vmstat 60 60"
#CMD="svmon -G -i 60 60"
#CMD="svmon -Pag -i 600 6"
while true
do
date
$CMD
done
```

Figure 4.14   Sample script to monitor memory leaks

Once you are certain that you have a memory leak in progress, you may have to go a step further by identifying the process. Using the same script, substitute a new CMD variable. This time, you are looking for the guilty process whose virtual-memory size grows without bound. It is very likely that the data segment of the process will be the one that is growing.

4.3   Disk-Bound Remedies

If your system is disk I/O bound, your options to improve performance involve buying new hardware or improving utilization of the hardware you have. Buying new hardware would consist of buying more RAM, which I have already discussed, and buying new disks. Describing how to buy these disks is outside the scope of this book, so I will concentrate on improving utilization of the hardware you do have.

4.3.1   Importance of Data Placement on a Disk

If you find your system is I/O bound, the I/O wait percentage will be high. A value of concern is when I/O wait exceeds 20%. This figure means that you could get 20% more work done if only you did not have to wait for the disk to complete its tasks. The figure of 20% is somewhat arbitrary; however, ridding the system of the last few percentage points of I/O wait is a difficult task. If you see 5% average I/O wait, be satisfied that you are doing that well.

The wait time can be reduced three ways. The first way is to reduce the average seek time for disk data transfers. In general, data access patterns of computer systems tend mostly to be random in nature. Some types of applications have predominately sequential access, but we will talk about that next. When you don't know if your access patterns are random, assume they are. For random access, seek latency dominates. If the data you want to access is on closely clustered cylinders on the disk, then the head seek time will be less than if the data is widely spread across the disk. For random accesses, reducing seek latency means placing the most heavily accessed data closest to the center of arm travel.

The second way to reduce wait time is to reduce disk rotational latency. If the access patterns are sequential, then rotational latency dominates seek latency, and you want to minimize rotational latency. One way is to make the disks spin faster, but disks don't come with a speed adjustment knob as record turntables once did. Just buy faster spinning disks for more money. However, there is a sneakier way to minimize rotational latency effectively. Some disk drivers pack more sectors on the outer edges than on the inner edges. This means that the drive is capable of reading more bytes per second at the outer edges than on the inner edges. For sequential accesses, reducing latency means placing the most heavily accessed data closest to the outer edge, but only for disks that have a greater sector density at the outer edge. If the disk has a constant sector density, then center placement is optimal. To determine which type of disk you have requires examining the detailed technical specifications for the disk drive. There is no way to determine the sector density using AIX commands. The rest of the examples illustrating choice of data placement on the disk show random access patterns and assume the optimum placement is in the center.

The third way to reduce wait time is to do some work that doesn't require waiting on a busy disk. However, there is a more practical way to accomplish this. When you are ready to check out in the grocery store, you search for the shortest line. This is what happens naturally as a result of human nature. On a computer system, you may have to intervene in order to ensure that the disks are equally busy so that one disk doesn't work harder than another. When the checkout lines are the same length, but are very long, the store manager will open another register. Some people will rush to that new line, and eventually the length of the lines will rebalance and become shorter. Using this analogy, add another disk, manually move data to the new disk, and try to ensure that the disks are equally balanced.

Your job will be to determine which data is accessed the most on the disks you have by using filemon. Filemon will tell you which files, filesystems, raw logical volumes, and disks are being utilized to what degree. It also identifies the degree of randomness of the data-access patterns. You then use AIX commands to determine where this data is physically located. Finally, move the data to better spots on the disks. The reapportionment of your data is based on three major remedies:

1. Make the disk utilization uniform across all the disks you already have.
2. Cluster the most heavily used data close in the optimal spot on the disk.
3. Add disks, and balance resulting utilizations.

Let's look at the specifics of how to accomplish these remedies.

4.3.2   Examples of Data Placement

I have created some nonoptimal disk I/O scenarios in order to illustrate these concepts. After applying standard remedies to these scenarios, we will observe the amount of improvement. I use a program that performs I/O on a file or logical volume. It does uniformly random seeks on files with multiple processes and can also weight the I/O to bias either reading or writing. For all the subsequent examples, I use a 75% read to 25% write ratio. This program does no computation and exaggerates the I/O characteristics of typical multiuser client/server transaction processing applications.

4.3.2.1   One Disk with Data on Edges

The first example (see Figure 4.15) examines a single disk where only two logical volumes are being accessed, and they happen to be on opposite ends of the disk. Running my test program on just these two logical volumes produces the output report shown in Figure

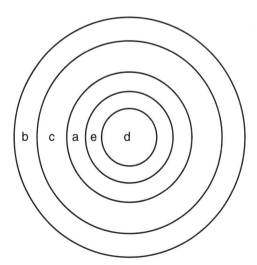

Figure 4.15   Example disk arrangement

4.16. The corresponding filemon report is shown in Figure 4.17, and the corresponding vmstat report is shown in Figure 4.18.

185.633 Kbytes/s

Figure 4.16   Result of experiment 1

```
Most Active Logical Volumes
------------------------------------------------------------------------
   util  #rblk  #wblk   KB/s  volume              description
------------------------------------------------------------------------
   0.97  18064   5936   92.6  /dev/b              N/A
   0.97  17536   6464   92.6  /dev/d              N/A
   0.01      0    160    0.6  /dev/hd4            /
   0.00      0    192    0.7  /dev/hd2            /usr
   0.00      0    109    0.4  /dev/hd1            /home Frag_Sz.= 512
   0.00      0    112    0.4  /dev/hd8            jfslog

Most Active Physical Volumes
------------------------------------------------------------------------
   util  #rblk  #wblk   KB/s  volume              description
------------------------------------------------------------------------
   0.99  35600  12400  185.2  /dev/hdisk1         400   MB SCSI
   0.01      0    573    2.2  /dev/hdisk0         400   MB SCSI


------------------------------------------------------------------------
Detailed Physical Volume Stats   (512 byte blocks)
------------------------------------------------------------------------

VOLUME: /dev/hdisk1  description: 400   MB SCSI
reads:                     4450      (0 errs)
  read sizes (blks):       avg      8.0 min       8 max       8 sdev      0.0
  read times (msec):       avg  21.080 min   5.007 max  40.691 sdev    7.231
  read sequences:          4450
  read seq. lengths:       avg      8.0 min       8 max       8 sdev      0.0
writes:                    1550      (0 errs)
  write sizes (blks):      avg      8.0 min       8 max       8 sdev      0.0
  write times (msec):      avg  22.513 min   9.306 max  41.826 sdev    7.064
  write sequences:         1550
  write seq. lengths:      avg      8.0 min       8 max       8 sdev      0.0
seeks:                     6000      (100.0%)
  seek dist (blks):        init 115264,
                           avg 175440.4 min       8 max  756768 sdev 259254.7
  seek dist (cyls):        init     175,
                           avg    267.4 min       0 max    1153 sdev    395.2
time to next req(msec):    avg  21.570 min   0.235 max 219.607 sdev    8.489
throughput:    185.2 KB/sec
utilization:   0.99
```

Figure 4.17   Filemon report for experiment 1

```
kthr       memory              page                    faults         cpu
-----  -----------  ------------------------  ------------  -----------
 r  b   avm   fre  re  pi  po  fr   sr  cy   in   sy   cs us sy id wa
 1  0  2343  3831   0   0   0   0    0   0  159  112  115  2 10  0 88
 1  0  2346  3828   0   0   0   0    0   0  163  118  121  2  9  0 90
 1  0  2351  3823   0   0   0   0    0   0  161  116  117  2 12  0 86
 1  0  2355  3819   0   0   0   0    0   0  160  109  115  2 11  0 87
 1  0  2360  3814   0   0   0   0    0   0  165  125  125  2 12  0 86
```

Figure 4.18   Vmstat report for experiment 1

There are several things to note in these reports. The vmstat report shows that there is a great amount of I/O wait (in the wa column), and the filemon report shows, under Most Active Physical Volumes, that the utilization for hdisk1 is 99%. These two indicators are consistent with one another and show that the system is definitely I/O bound. The Most Active Logical Volumes part of the filemon report shows that b and d are the LVs that are getting all the I/O. Recall that Figure 4.15 shows these LVs at opposite ends of hdisk1, which is nonoptimal. The Detailed Physical Volume Stats of Figure 4.17 shows seek statistics. The seek percentage is 100%; that is, every physical read and write is preceded by a physical seek. This program would be classified as performing completely random I/O.

The solution is to move the b and d logical volumes to the center of hdisk1. Rather than actually moving those logical volumes, I have just modified the program to perform I/O to two logical volumes near the center of hdisk1, namely to a and e. I'll save the mechanics of moving logical volumes for later in the chapter. You can read it, perhaps, some evening when you have a case of insomnia.

```
206.166 KB/sec
```

Figure 4.19   Result of experiment 2

Figure 4.19 shows the results of the output of the test program with a more optimal modification. Figure 4.20 shows the corresponding filemon report.

```
Most Active Logical Volumes
------------------------------------------------------------------------
 util  #rblk  #wblk   KB/s  volume            description
------------------------------------------------------------------------
 0.95  17568   6432   99.7  /dev/e            N/A
 0.95  18144   5856   99.7  /dev/a            N/A
 0.00      8    152    0.7  /dev/hd4          /
 0.00      8    114    0.5  /dev/hd1          /home Frag_Sz.= 512
 0.00      8    176    0.8  /dev/hd2          /usr
 0.00      8    168    0.7  /dev/hd8          jfslog

Most Active Physical Volumes
------------------------------------------------------------------------
 util  #rblk  #wblk   KB/s  volume            description
------------------------------------------------------------------------
 0.96  35728  12288  199.5  /dev/hdisk1       400  MB SCSI
 0.01     32    610    2.7  /dev/hdisk0       400  MB SCSI
```

```
-----------------------------------------------------------------------
Detailed Physical Volume Stats    (512 byte blocks)
-----------------------------------------------------------------------

VOLUME: /dev/hdisk1   description: 400  MB SCSI
reads:                    4466   (0 errs)
  read sizes (blks):      avg     8.0 min        8 max        8 sdev    0.0
  read times (msec):      avg  18.883 min    4.998 max   33.468 sdev    4.994
  read sequences:         4466
  read seq. lengths:      avg     8.0 min        8 max        8 sdev    0.0
writes:                   1536   (0 errs)
  write sizes (blks):     avg     8.0 min        8 max        8 sdev    0.0
  write times (msec):     avg  20.541 min    9.811 max   33.661 sdev    5.007
  write sequences:        1536
  write seq. lengths:     avg     8.0 min        8 max        8 sdev    0.0
seeks:                    6002   (100.0%)
  seek dist (blks):       init   4360,
                          avg 60670.6 min        8 max   614392 sdev 75176.8
  seek dist (cyls):       init      6,
                          avg    92.5 min        0 max      936 sdev  114.6
time to next req(msec): avg  20.025 min    0.423 max 2945.975 sdev 39.529
throughput:   199.5 KB/sec
utilization: 0.96
```

Figure 4.20   Filemon report for experiment 2

This new program report shows a change in throughput from 185 to 206 kilobytes per second, a 10% improvement. This is a result of reducing the seek distance between the two logical volumes. Note that the seek percentage is still 100% because the test program has not been changed. What has changed is the average elapsed time for each of these seeks.

The filemon report agrees that the throughput has increased. Also note in the Detailed Physical Volume Stats section that the average seek distance has decreased 65% from 175,440 to 60,670 blocks. These statistics show that throughput is inversely, but nonlinearly, proportional to seek distance.

4.3.2.2   Two Disks with One Disk Dominating

In the previous example, you saw the effects of moving data on the same disk to accomplish clustering most used data around the center band. In this section I demonstrate the effects of balancing utilization. The example I use has the test program accessing three logical volumes clustered about the center of hdisk1 and one logical volume clustered about the center of hdisk2. Figure 4.21 and Figure 4.22 show the test output and filemon reports, respectively.

```
281.515 KB/s
```

Figure 4.21   Result of experiment 3

```
Most Active Logical Volumes
-------------------------------------------------------------------
  util  #rblk  #wblk   KB/s  volume                description
-------------------------------------------------------------------
  0.95   7512   2392   69.4  /dev/c                N/A
  0.95   7672   2288   69.8  /dev/a                N/A
  0.95   7816   2224   70.4  /dev/e                N/A
  0.35   7352   2744   70.8  /dev/j                N/A
  0.01      0     96    0.7  /dev/hd4              /
  0.00      0    112    0.8  /dev/hd2              /usr
  0.00      0     43    0.3  /dev/hd1              /home Frag_Sz.= 512
  0.00      0     40    0.3  /dev/hd8              jfslog

Most Active Physical Volumes
-------------------------------------------------------------------
  util  #rblk  #wblk   KB/s  volume                description
-------------------------------------------------------------------
  0.99  23000   6904  209.6  /dev/hdisk1           400  MB SCSI
  0.35   7352   2744   70.8  /dev/hdisk2           400  MB SCSI
  0.01      0    291    2.0  /dev/hdisk0           400  MB SCSI


-------------------------------------------------------------------
Detailed Physical Volume Stats    (512 byte blocks)
-------------------------------------------------------------------

VOLUME: /dev/hdisk1  description: 400   MB SCSI
reads:                    2875    (0 errs)
  read sizes (blks):      avg      8.0 min       8 max        8 sdev     0.0
  read times (msec):      avg  18.479 min   6.750 max  36.353 sdev   5.134
  read sequences:         2875
  read seq. lengths:      avg      8.0 min       8 max        8 sdev     0.0
writes:                    863    (0 errs)
  write sizes (blks):     avg      8.0 min       8 max        8 sdev     0.0
  write times (msec):     avg  20.292 min   9.904 max  36.878 sdev   5.207
  write sequences:        863
  write seq. lengths:     avg      8.0 min       8 max        8 sdev     0.0
seeks:                    3738    (100.0%)
  seek dist (blks):       init 163592,
                          avg 55038.6 min      24 max  450160 sdev 98367.9
  seek dist (cyls):       init    249,
                          avg    83.9 min       0 max     686 sdev   150.0
time to next req(msec):   avg  19.050 min   0.223 max 207.631 sdev  12.500
throughput:     209.6 KB/sec
utilization:    0.99

VOLUME: /dev/hdisk2  description: 400   MB SCSI
reads:                     919    (0 errs)
  read sizes (blks):      avg      8.0 min       8 max        8 sdev     0.0
  read times (msec):      avg  19.243 min   8.048 max  31.176 sdev   4.427
  read sequences:         919
  read seq. lengths:      avg      8.0 min       8 max        8 sdev     0.0
writes:                    343    (0 errs)
  write sizes (blks):     avg      8.0 min       8 max        8 sdev     0.0
  write times (msec):     avg  20.614 min  10.380 max  33.146 sdev   4.437
  write sequences:        343
  write seq. lengths:     avg      8.0 min       8 max        8 sdev     0.0
seeks:                    1262    (100.0%)
  seek dist (blks):       init 374616,
                          avg 47800.1 min      88 max  139352 sdev 33323.8
  seek dist (cyls):       init    571,
                          avg    72.9 min       0 max     212 sdev    50.8
time to next req(msec):   avg  56.350 min   0.856 max 523.385 sdev  61.881
throughput:      70.8 KB/sec
utilization:     0.35
```

Figure 4.22   Filemon report for experiment 3

The `Most Active Physical Volumes` part of the filemon report shows that `hdisk1` is fully utilized, while `hdisk2` is only 35% utilized. Note that all four logical volumes are getting about the same throughput of 70K per second, so it should be easy to balance the throughput by moving one volume from `hdisk1` to `hdisk2`. I simulate this movement by substituting logical volume i, which is on `hdisk2`, for volume e, which is on `hdisk1`. Figure 4.23 and Figure 4.24 show the test output and the `filemon` output, respectively, of the optimal scenario.

390.727 KB/S

Figure 4.23 Result for experiment 4

The composite throughput of both disks improves from 281K to 390K per second, for an increase of 38%. The lesson learned here is that when you encounter both conditions of unbalanced hard disk utilization and dominating I/O occurring on uncentered portions of the disk, fix the former first, for two reasons. Measuring the effect of the former will let you estimate an upper bound of the effect of the latter, which is sure to be less.

```
Most Active Logical Volumes
-------------------------------------------------------------------------
  util  #rblk  #wblk   KB/s  volume              description
-------------------------------------------------------------------------
  0.92   7656   2440   98.1  /dev/a              N/A
  0.91   7624   2336   96.8  /dev/c              N/A
  0.90   7352   2688   97.5  /dev/j              N/A
  0.88   7616   2288   96.2  /dev/i              N/A
  0.01      0     96    0.9  /dev/hd4            /
  0.01      0    112    1.1  /dev/hd2            /usr
  0.00      0     43    0.4  /dev/hd1            /home Frag_Sz.= 512
  0.00      0     40    0.4  /dev/hd8            jfslog

Most Active Physical Volumes
-------------------------------------------------------------------------
  util  #rblk  #wblk   KB/s  volume              description
-------------------------------------------------------------------------
  0.97  14968   4976  193.8  /dev/hdisk2         400  MB SCSI
  0.97  15280   4776  194.9  /dev/hdisk1         400  MB SCSI
  0.01      0    291    2.8  /dev/hdisk0         400  MB SCSI


-------------------------------------------------------------------------
Detailed Physical Volume Stats    (512 byte blocks)
-------------------------------------------------------------------------

VOLUME: /dev/hdisk2  description: 400  MB SCSI
reads:                        1871    (0 errs)
  read sizes (blks):          avg     8.0 min      8 max        8 sdev     0.0
  read times (msec):          avg  19.566 min  7.593 max  33.227 sdev     4.990
  read sequences:             1871
  read seq. lengths:          avg     8.0 min      8 max        8 sdev     0.0
writes:                        622    (0 errs)
  write sizes (blks):         avg     8.0 min      8 max        8 sdev     0.0
  write times (msec):         avg  21.666 min  9.697 max  33.532 sdev     5.183
  write sequences:             622
  write seq. lengths:         avg     8.0 min      8 max        8 sdev     0.0
```

Figure 4.24 `Filemon` report for experiment 4 (*continued on next page*)

```
seeks:                          2493      (100.0%)
   seek dist (blks):            init 586032,
                                avg 70978.7 min      24 max   287264 sdev 73136.0
   seek dist (cyls):            init    893,
                                avg   108.2 min       0 max      437 sdev   111.5
time to next req(msec):         avg  20.590 min   0.226 max 209.440 sdev  16.685
throughput:     193.8 KB/sec
utilization:    0.97

VOLUME: /dev/hdisk1  description: 400  MB SCSI
reads:                          1910      (0 errs)
   read sizes (blks):           avg      8.0 min       8 max        8 sdev    0.0
   read times (msec):           avg  19.439 min   7.158 max   33.384 sdev    5.213
   read sequences:              1910
   read seq. lengths:           avg      8.0 min       8 max        8 sdev    0.0
writes:                         597       (0 errs)
   write sizes (blks):          avg      8.0 min       8 max        8 sdev    0.0
   write times (msec):          avg  21.449 min  10.420 max   33.865 sdev    4.892
   write sequences:             597
   write seq. lengths:          avg      8.0 min       8 max        8 sdev    0.0
seeks:                          2507      (100.0%)
   seek dist (blks):            init 428032,
                                avg 71702.8 min      24 max   296928 sdev 77343.3
   seek dist (cyls):            init    652,
                                avg   109.3 min       0 max      452 sdev   117.9
time to next req(msec):         avg  20.486 min   0.228 max 228.066 sdev  16.642
throughput:     194.9 KB/sec
utilization:    0.97
```

Figure 4.24   Filemon report for experiment 4 (*cont.*)

4.3.3   Determining Your Disk Configuration

The disk configurations for the previous examples were determined in advance in order to make the examples obvious. But what if you had a system for which you wanted to determine the data layouts? You didn't put the data on the system—you just wanted to determine the configuration in your discovery process. Let's look at some AIX commands that give you enough data to draw pictures. Figure 4.25 shows an example of the lspv command used to find out how the various logical volumes are laid out on the physical disks.

```
lspv -l hdisk1
hdisk1:
LV NAME              LPs    PPs    DISTRIBUTION            MOUNT POINT
b                    19     19     19..00..00..00..00      N/A
c                    19     19     00..19..00..00..00      N/A
a                    19     19     00..00..18..01..00      N/A
e                    18     18     00..00..00..18..00      N/A
d                    19     19     00..00..00..00..19      N/A
```

```
lspv -l hdisk2
hdisk2:
LV NAME                    LPs     PPs     DISTRIBUTION            MOUNT POINT
l                          19      19      19..00..00..00..00      N/A
k                          19      19      00..19..00..00..00      N/A
j                          18      18      00..00..18..00..00      N/A
i                          19      19      00..00..00..19..00      N/A
h                          19      19      00..00..00..00..19      N/A
lspv -l hdisk3
hdisk3:
LV NAME                    LPs     PPs     DISTRIBUTION            MOUNT POINT
s                          19      19      19..00..00..00..00      N/A
r                          19      19      00..19..00..00..00      N/A
q                          18      18      00..00..18..00..00      N/A
p                          19      19      00..00..00..19..00      N/A
o                          19      19      00..00..00..00..19      N/A
```

Figure 4.25 Showing data arrangement with `lspv -l`

A similar invocation of `lspv`, shown in Figure 4.26, shows the same information in a different form. This form is the most useful in that it gives both the band names and the exact range of the physical partitions used.


```
lspv -p hdisk1
hdisk1:
PP RANGE   STATE   REGION          LV NAME         TYPE      MOUNT POINT
  1-19     used    outer edge      b               jfs       N/A
 20-38     used    outer middle    c               jfs       N/A
 39-56     used    center          a               jfs       N/A
 57-57     used    inner middle    a               jfs       N/A
 58-75     used    inner middle    e               jfs       N/A
 76-94     used    inner edge      d               jfs       N/A
lspv -p hdisk2
hdisk2:
PP RANGE   STATE   REGION          LV NAME         TYPE      MOUNT POINT
  1-19     used    outer edge      l               jfs       N/A
 20-38     used    outer middle    k               jfs       N/A
 39-56     used    center          j               jfs       N/A
 57-75     used    inner middle    i               jfs       N/A
 76-94     used    inner edge      h               jfs       N/A
lspv -p hdisk3
hdisk3:
PP RANGE   STATE   REGION          LV NAME         TYPE      MOUNT POINT
  1-19     used    outer edge      s               jfs       N/A
 20-38     used    outer middle    r               jfs       N/A
 39-56     used    center          q               jfs       N/A
 57-75     used    inner middle    p               jfs       N/A
 76-94     used    inner edge      o               jfs       N/A
```

Figure 4.26 Showing data arrangement with `lspv -p`

4.3.4   Specifying Where Your Data Goes

Now that you know how the logical volumes are laid out, you need to know how I got them in their places. The easiest way to get a logical volume in its proper place on the physical volume is to know the I/O utilization of each logical volume beforehand and to place the logical volumes on initial creation. Starting with a blank canvas (an empty hard disk), you can paint your scene with the most flexibility.

Oh, so you claim you are not an artist, and you couldn't paint the short side of a barn? Well, even Picasso had to start someplace. We will "paint by number" to start. Using the disk band names is a sort of painting by number. It is easy and you get a moderately nice picture, but this method does not give you full control. First let's see how `hdisk1` was laid out. I picked the size of each logical volume to be 20% of the total size of the disk. That way each logical partition occupies exactly one full band. See Figure 4.27 for an example of the SMIT screen in which you would create a logical volume.

```
Fastpath: smit mklv
                          Add a Logical Volume

Type or select values in entry fields.
Press Enter AFTER making all desired changes.

[TOP]                                              [Entry Fields]
  Logical volume NAME                              [x]
* VOLUME GROUP name                                vg5
* Number of LOGICAL PARTITIONS                     [18]           #
  PHYSICAL VOLUME names                            []             +
  Logical volume TYPE                              []
  POSITION on physical volume                      center         +
  RANGE of physical volumes                        minimum        +
  MAXIMUM NUMBER of PHYSICAL VOLUMES               []             #
    to use for allocation
  Number of COPIES of each logical                 1              +
    partition
  Mirror Write Consistency?                        yes            +
  Allocate each logical partition copy             yes            +
[MORE...11]
```

Figure 4.27   SMIT screen to add logical volume

The fields that were changed are logical volume name, number of logical partitions, and position on physical volume. The position field can be specified to be one of the five disk position bands. You would repeat this creation scenario for the other logical volumes on the disk that you wish to create.

The paint-by-number method of specifying location by band doesn't always give you enough control. When conflicts occur, AIX, rather than you, will decide how to resolve them. A more precise method is to create a volume map of exactly where each logical partition should go. Figure 4.28 shows an example of a logical volume allocation map.

```
hdisk5:82-87
```

Figure 4.28 Example of a physical partition map

The map specifies precisely which physical partitions of which disk will comprise the logical volume. Figure 4.29 shows use of the `lslv` command for the logical volume "a" and the resultant output. The map in Figure 4.28 is used in the same `Add a Logical Volume` SMIT dialog, as shown in Figure 4.30. The `ALLOCATION MAP` field specifies the file I stored in `/tmp/newlv.map`. If you ever forget the syntax of an allocation map, you can create a template by inquiring about an existing logical volume.

```
lslv -m a
a:N/A
LP    PP1  PV1              PP2  PV2              PP3  PV3
0001  0039 hdisk1
0002  0040 hdisk1
0003  0041 hdisk1
0004  0042 hdisk1
0005  0043 hdisk1
```

Figure 4.29 `Lslv` showing partition map

```
Fastpath: smit mklv

                        Add a Logical Volume

Type or select values in entry fields.
Press Enter AFTER making all desired changes.

[MORE...10]                                    [Entry Fields]
    partition
  Mirror Write Consistency?                    yes             +
  Allocate each logical partition copy         yes             +
    on a SEPARATE physical volume?
  RELOCATE the logical volume during           yes             +
    reorganization?
  Logical volume LABEL                         []
  MAXIMUM NUMBER of LOGICAL PARTITIONS         [128]
  Enable BAD BLOCK relocation?                 yes             +
  SCHEDULING POLICY for writing logical        parallel        +
    partition copies
  Enable WRITE VERIFY?                         no              +
  File containing ALLOCATION MAP               [/tmp/newlv.map]
  Stripe Size?                                 [Not Striped] +
[BOTTOM]
```

Figure 4.30 SMIT screen showing use of allocation map

These ways of creating logical volumes are fine if you have the foresight to plan the precise locations. But what if you did not have the foresight to plan, and it is your task to fix the current situation? You could certainly use the brute-force technique of dumping all the data to tape, removing everything, creating new logical volumes in new and better places, and restoring the data from tape. You may be able to make some shortcuts, depending on how much free space you may have on your disk drives and how little data you actually want to move.

Figure 4.31 shows a disk that I configured rather unoptimally just by using SMIT to place the logical volumes. Note that `lv03` is split with half on the outer edge and half on the inner edge. If a scenario found `lv03` with the most I/O traffic, it would clearly be better to move it. Since there is no place to move `lv03`, let's consider what we could do if we had an empty disk drive to add to the system. I'll now introduce the concept of a volume group with more than one physical volume.

```
hdisk5:
PP RANGE   STATE   REGION          LV NAME     TYPE      MOUNT POINT
   1-19    used    outer edge      lv03        jfs       /w
  20-20    used    outer middle    loglv00     jfslog    N/A
  21-38    used    outer middle    lv00        jfs       /x
  39-43    used    center          lv00        jfs       /x
  44-56    used    center          lv01        jfs       /y
  57-66    used    inner middle    lv01        jfs       /y
  67-75    used    inner middle    lv02        jfs       /z
  76-89    used    inner edge      lv02        jfs       /z
  90-93    used    inner edge      lv03        jfs       /w
  94-94    free    inner edge
```

Figure 4.31   Example of poorly configured disk

Volume group `vg5` contains only `hdisk5`. Add the new disk to this same volume group by extending the volume group. Figure 4.32 shows how to do this in SMIT.

```
Fastpath: smit extendvg
                    Add a Physical Volume to a Volume Group

Type or select values in entry fields.
Press Enter AFTER making all desired changes.

                                                   [Entry Fields]
  * VOLUME GROUP name                              [vg5]           +
  * PHYSICAL VOLUME names                          [hdisk4]        +
```

Figure 4.32   SMIT screen to extend a volume group

Once this is done, change the position of lv03 to the center position, as shown in Figure 4.33.

```
Fastpath: smit chlv1
                              Change a Logical Volume

Type or select values in entry fields.
Press Enter AFTER making all desired changes.

[TOP]                                                      [Entry Fields]
  Logical volume NAME                                      lv03
  Logical volume TYPE                                      [jfs]
  POSITION on physical volume                              center        +
  RANGE of physical volumes                                minimum       +
  MAXIMUM NUMBER of PHYSICAL VOLUMES                       [32]          #
     to use for allocation
  Allocate each logical partition copy                     yes           +
     on a SEPARATE physical volume?
  RELOCATE the logical volume during                       yes           +
     reorganization?
  Logical volume LABEL                                     [/w]
  MAXIMUM NUMBER of LOGICAL PARTITIONS                     [128]
  SCHEDULING POLICY for writing logical                    parallel      +
[MORE...5]
```

Figure 4.33   SMIT screen to change logical volume

The next step is to reorganize the volume group with the reorgvg command. There is a SMIT dialog to do this, but it doesn't supply reorgvg with the crucial logical volume name. The command form is simply as follows:

```
reorgvg lv03
```

The system will try to place lv03 in the center of any disk in the vg5 volume group. The only choice is to copy lv03 to the center of hdisk4. Figure 4.34 shows the results of the reorganization after a few minutes.

```
lspv -p hdisk4
hdisk4:
PP RANGE    STATE    REGION          LV ID      TYPE      MOUNT POINT
   1-19     free     outer edge
  20-38     free     outer middle
  39-56     used     center          lv03       jfs       /w
  57-61     used     inner middle    lv03       jfs       /w
  62-75     free     inner middle
  76-94     free     inner edge
```

Figure 4.34   Example report after using reorgvg (*continued on next page*)

```
lspv -p hdisk5
hdisk5:
PP RANGE    STATE    REGION              LV ID       TYPE       MOUNT POINT
   1-19     free     outer edge
  20-20     used     outer middle        loglv00     jfslog     N/A
  21-38     used     outer middle        lv00        jfs        /x
  39-43     used     center              lv00        jfs        /x
  44-56     used     center              lv01        jfs        /y
  57-66     used     inner middle        lv01        jfs        /y
  67-75     used     inner middle        lv02        jfs        /z
  76-89     used     inner edge          lv02        jfs        /z
  90-94     free     inner edge
```

Figure 4.34   Example report after using `reorgvg` (*cont.*)

4.3.5   JFS Considerations

Thus far all the disk illustrations comparing disk positioning have involved raw logical volumes. Filesystems are implemented in a logical volume, so logical volume considerations apply. But filesystems have their own set of problems to worry about.

4.3.5.1   Filesystem Placement

Even when these logical volumes contain a filesystem, all the concepts of positioning still apply. However, you should be aware that positioning a filesystem is not as straightforward as you might want it to be. Figure 4.35 shows the SMIT dialog to create a filesystem. This dialog first creates the logical volume and then the filesystem and places them wherever it wants. You have no control concerning placement. Note that there is no field that specifies disk position.

```
Fastpath: smit crjfsstd
                             Add a Journaled File System

Type or select values in entry fields.
Press Enter AFTER making all desired changes.

                                                        [Entry Fields]
    Volume group name                                   vg5
  * SIZE of file system (in 512-byte blocks)            []                #
  * MOUNT POINT                                          []
    Mount AUTOMATICALLY at system restart?              no                +
    PERMISSIONS                                         read/write        +
    Mount OPTIONS                                       []                +
    Start Disk Accounting?                              no                +
    Fragment Size (bytes)                               4096              +
    Number of bytes per inode                           4096              +
    Compression algorithm                               no                +
```

Figure 4.35   SMIT screen to add filesystem

In order to place filesystems where you want them, you have to create a filesystem in a two-step process. The first step is creating a logical volume, just as I have demonstrated in previous examples. The next step involves creating the filesystem on a previously created logical volume. Figure 4.36 shows the SMIT dialog that performs this step.

```
Fastpath: smit crjfslvstd
        Add a Journaled File System on a Previously Defined Logical Volume

Type or select values in entry fields.
Press Enter AFTER making all desired changes.

                                                        [Entry Fields]
* LOGICAL VOLUME name                                   z                  +
* MOUNT POINT                                           [/z]
  Mount AUTOMATICALLY at system restart?                no                 +
  PERMISSIONS                                           read/write         +
  Mount OPTIONS                                         []                 +
  Start Disk Accounting?                                no                 +
  Fragment Size (bytes)                                 4096               +
  Number of bytes per inode                             4096               +
  Compression algorithm                                 no                 +
```

Figure 4.36   SMIT screen to add filesystem on existing logical volume

You now know how to create filesystems and place them where you want. You also know how to create multivolume volume groups. It is time to combine these skills and create filesystems that span multiple volumes. This is a very powerful concept that allows you to create large filesystems and not be limited by the size of your physical volumes. However, this concept doesn't help us to improve I/O performance; what does help is the notion that a filesystem can be spread across multiple volumes in a regular and controlled way. Figure 2.9 in Chapter 2 shows a multivolume volume group where the filesystems do not span disks. The logical volumes are allocated to use the minimum number of disks, namely one. This is the Range field shown in Figure 4.33 and is defaulted to minimum.

What if the range is specified to be maximum? The partitions for the logical volume would be allocated to use the maximum number of volumes. Figure 2.10 in Chapter 2 shows logical volumes spread across all three disks.

In order to compare how maximum range improves I/O throughput, I first created three filesystems specifying minimum default range on the center, inner edge, and outer edge bands. Figure 4.37 shows the resulting configuration. Each filesystem occupies its own disk and is arranged somewhat around the center band.

Next I created three filesystems by first creating three logical volumes placed on the center, inner edge, and outer edge bands. Figure 4.38 shows how I created the first logical volume. Figure 4.39 shows the results of the layout.

```
hdisk3:
LV NAME                     LPs    PPs    DISTRIBUTION            MOUNT POINT
lv01                        60     60     00..04..18..19..19      /test2
hdisk4:
LV NAME                     LPs    PPs    DISTRIBUTION            MOUNT POINT
lv02                        60     60     00..04..18..19..19      /test3
hdisk5:
LV NAME                     LPs    PPs    DISTRIBUTION            MOUNT POINT
loglv00                     1      1      00..01..00..00..00      N/A
lv00                        60     60     00..04..18..19..19      /test1
```

Figure 4.37   Example of filesystem arrangement


```
Fastpath: smit mklv

                            Add a Logical Volume

Type or select values in entry fields.
Press Enter AFTER making all desired changes.

[TOP]                                                    [Entry Fields]
  Logical volume NAME                                    []
  VOLUME GROUP name                                      vg5
  Number of LOGICAL PARTITIONS                           [60]              #
  PHYSICAL VOLUME names                                  []                +
  Logical volume TYPE                                    []
  POSITION on physical volume                            edge              +
  RANGE of physical volumes                              maximum           +
  MAXIMUM NUMBER of PHYSICAL VOLUMES                     []                #
    to use for allocation
  Number of COPIES of each logical                       1                 +
    partition
  Mirror Write Consistency?                              yes               +
  Allocate each logical partition copy                   yes               +
[MORE...11]
```

Figure 4.38   SMIT screen specifying maximum allocation


```
lspv -l hdisk3; lspv -l hdisk4 ; lspv -l hdisk5
hdisk3:
LV NAME                     LPs    PPs    DISTRIBUTION            MOUNT POINT
lv02                        20     20     19..01..00..00..00      /test3
lv00                        20     20     00..00..18..02..00      /test1
lv01                        20     20     00..00..00..01..19      /test2
hdisk4:
LV NAME                     LPs    PPs    DISTRIBUTION            MOUNT POINT
lv02                        20     20     19..01..00..00..00      /test3
lv00                        20     20     00..00..18..02..00      /test1
lv01                        20     20     00..00..00..01..19      /test2
```

```
hdisk5:
LV NAME                 LPs   PPs   DISTRIBUTION          MOUNT POINT
lv02                    20    20    19..01..00..00..00    /test3
loglv00                 1     1     00..01..00..00..00    N/A
lv00                    20    20    00..00..18..02..00    /test1
lv01                    20    20    00..00..00..01..19    /test2
```

Figure 4.39   Example filesystem arrangement

This configuration shows that the /test1 filesystem is spread across the center band of all three disks, the /test2 filesystem is on the inner edge band, and the /test3 filesystem is on the outer edge band. If we measure the speed of the random and sequential benchmarks, we see the results in Table 4.1.

4.3.5.2   Disk Striping

There is another variation of spreading logical volumes across physical disks. Interleaving sequential blocks of a few kilobytes across more than one disk is called striping. Each block is called a *stripe*. This configuration enables programs that read or write sequentially to boost I/O throughput dramatically.

I have taken the same three filesystems and put them on the same bands on the disks. The only difference from the preceding configuration is that the logical volumes were striped instead of set just to maximum range. Figure 4.40 shows the SMIT screen that created the logical volume.

Note that the different fields that you must specify to get striped logical volumes are PHYSICAL VOLUME names and Stripe Size. You must leave RANGE of physical volumes to be the default setting of minimum, even though striping is a special form of maximum range.

What makes the throughput of striping better than maximum range is VMM read-ahead, which I discuss in Chapter 2. It is rarely true that if some medicine is good, more medicine is better. But in the case of read-ahead, more read-ahead is better for sequential reading of files—at least to a point. The vmtune command can allow you to change the maximum read-ahead value. Figure 4.41 shows how to change the maximum read-ahead value to 64 pages from the default value of 8.

Random	Sequential
791.860 KB/S	1372.349 KB/S

Table 4.1   Throughput results for example filesystem arrangement

```
Fastpath: smit mklv
                            Add a Logical Volume

Type or select values in entry fields.
Press Enter AFTER making all desired changes.

[TOP]                                                    [Entry Fields]
    Logical volume NAME                                  [lv00]
*  VOLUME GROUP name                                     vg5
*  Number of LOGICAL PARTITIONS                          []                    #
    PHYSICAL VOLUME names                                [hdisk3
                                                          hdisk4
                                                          hdisk5]              +

    Logical volume TYPE                                  []
    POSITION on physical volume                          center                +
    RANGE of physical volumes                            minimum               +
    MAXIMUM NUMBER of PHYSICAL VOLUMES                   []                    #
      to use for allocation
    Number of COPIES of each logical                     1                     +
      partition
    Mirror Write Consistency?                            yes                   +
    Allocate each logical partition copy                 yes                   +
    Mirror Write Consistency?                            yes                   +
    Allocate each logical partition copy                 yes                   +
      on a SEPARATE physical volume?
    RELOCATE the logical volume during                   yes                   +
      reorganization?
    Logical volume LABEL                                 []
    MAXIMUM NUMBER of LOGICAL PARTITIONS                 [128]
    Enable BAD BLOCK relocation?                         yes                   +
    SCHEDULING POLICY for writing logical                parallel              +
      partition copies
    Enable WRITE VERIFY?                                 no                    +
    File containing ALLOCATION MAP                       []
    Stripe Size?                                         [32K]                 +
[BOTTOM]
```

Figure 4.40   SMIT screen to add striped logical volume

As you can see in Table 4.2, increasing the maximum read-ahead to 32 pages improved throughput by 33%. I initially discovered that 32 pages was optimum by repetitively doubling the default until the test stopped improving. However, there is a formula to calculate what the stripe and read-ahead settings should be. I chose 32K because that happened to be the fastest setting for the disks that I had, old and slow SCSI 1 disks. A good starting point would be 32K, but 64K or 128K would probably be better choices for your disks. Once you have picked the stripe size, set the read-ahead amount to read one stripe from each disk when read-ahead has reached the read-ahead maximum. For my configuration, three disks times 32K stripes equals 96K, and dividing by 4K per page yields 24 pages. Also keep in mind that changing read-ahead may be totally unnecessary if the I/O mix is predominantly random rather than sequential.

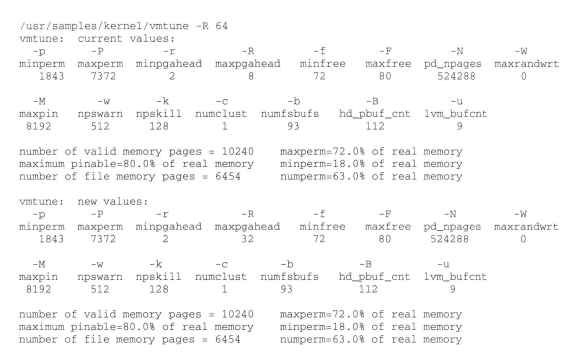

```
/usr/samples/kernel/vmtune -R 64
vmtune:   current values:
   -p         -P          -r          -R          -f          -F          -N          -W
minperm    maxperm   minpgahead  maxpgahead   minfree     maxfree   pd_npages  maxrandwrt
  1843       7372         2           8          72          80       524288        0

   -M         -w          -k          -c          -b          -B          -u
maxpin     npswarn    npskill    numclust   numfsbufs   hd_pbuf_cnt  lvm_bufcnt
  8192       512        128          1          93          112          9

number of valid memory pages = 10240      maxperm=72.0% of real memory
maximum pinable=80.0% of real memory      minperm=18.0% of real memory
number of file memory pages = 6454        numperm=63.0% of real memory

vmtune:   new values:
   -p         -P          -r          -R          -f          -F          -N          -W
minperm    maxperm   minpgahead  maxpgahead   minfree     maxfree   pd_npages  maxrandwrt
  1843       7372         2          32          72          80       524288        0

   -M         -w          -k          -c          -b          -B          -u
maxpin     npswarn    npskill    numclust   numfsbufs   hd_pbuf_cnt  lvm_bufcnt
  8192       512        128          1          93          112          9

number of valid memory pages = 10240      maxperm=72.0% of real memory
maximum pinable=80.0% of real memory      minperm=18.0% of real memory
number of file memory pages = 6454        numperm=63.0% of real memory
```

Figure 4.41   Using vmtune to change read-ahead value

	Random Kbytes/s	**Sequential Kbytes/s**
Minimum	588	1706
Maximum	792	1894
Striped	686	2330
Striped—32 read-ahead	NA	3111
Striped—32 read-ahead with 2 SCSI adapters	NA	4096

Table 4.2   Throughput results of striped filesystem

4.3.5.3   Disk Caching Effects

Filesystem cache tuning was discussed in Section 4.2.2. We showed that reducing the effective size of the filesystem cache can help performance. Vmtune was used to limit the size of the cache and also to control the degree of "dirty page write-through." The problem scenario is illustrated by a program I/O mix that is predominately random-write. We learned in Chapter 2 that write-behind is triggered only for sequential-write. This means that writes done in a random fashion will accumulate in the filesystem cache until either a sync system call occurs (caused by the syncd daemon) or page replacement forces dirty pages out to their filesystems. The latter happens when real memory is constrained (we have already discussed the remedies). The cause of the former is more insidious. The system disks will be quiet until the sync occurs, usually once every 60 seconds as a default. Then the affected disks will become 100% busy as the pages are written out in one batch. During this time, all other I/O is suspended on the affected disks. This has the effect of freezing the system once per minute for tens of seconds at a time, annoying users in interactive environments. The solution is to force these dirty pages to be written sooner. One of the obscure vmtune options is the maxrandwrit (maximum random write) value that controls how many dirty pages may be cached for a file before those pages are flushed to the filesystem. The command would be invoked as shown in Figure 4.42. Since you have seen this output in previous figures, I have edited the output to show only the changed parameters.

```
/usr/samples/kernel/vmtune -W 32
```

```
vmtune:   new values:
   -p        -P          -r          -R          -f          -F          -N          -W
minperm   maxperm   minpgahead  maxpgahead   minfree     maxfree    pd_npages   maxrandwrt
   6348      25395         2           8         120         128       524288        32

   -M        -w          -k          -c          -b          -B          -u
maxpin    npswarn     npskill     numclust    numfsbufs   hd_pbuf_cnt  lvm_bufcnt
  26215      1024        256          1           93           64           9
```

Figure 4.42   Using vmtune to change random write value

This command specifies that a threshold of 32 dirty pages will be maintained in filesystem cache per file. (I chose the parameter 32 arbitrarily.) Once that threshold is exceeded, the dirty pages for that file will be purged to the filesystem. The smallest value that could be specified is 1, which means that dirty pages would be written one page at a time, which is clearly inefficient. It is more efficient to batch the writes into a bigger bundle. But the larger the bundle of dirty pages, the more the remedy begins to revert to the initial problem. I chose 32 to match the maximum number of pages that could be read ahead in a sequential-read scenario, so the size is not totally arbitrary. I would suggest starting at 32 and trying larger values by doubling to see the effect. Remember, the expected effect will be lower average response time, not necessarily improved throughput.

The scenario we just remedied was caused by intense random write I/O. What if a program were writing sequentially instead of randomly? In this case, write-behind would engage without resorting to using vmtune. However, consider the issue of fairness. If a particular program (or user) consistently hogged the disks by writing files, it might be nice to "throttle back" that user. SMIT gives you a way to specify that processes whose write I/O backlog exceeds a certain amount will be suspended until that backlog is cleared out. Figure 4.43 shows the SMIT panel that sets these values. When a process performs more writes to a file than the high-water mark allows, the process is suspended. When the number of pending I/Os drops below the low-water mark, the process is awakened again. This write throttling will not improve throughput of a single process, nor will it help aggregate I/O throughput of the whole system. It only prevents disk starvation due to disk-hogging processes.

```
Fastpath: smit chgsys
               Change / Show Characteristics of Operating System

Type or select values in entry fields.
Press Enter AFTER making all desired changes.

                                                  [Entry Fields]
    Maximum number of PROCESSES allowed per user    [40]        +#
    Maximum number of pages in block I/O BUFFER CACHE [20]      +#
    Maximum Kbytes of real memory allowed for MBUFS [2048]      +#
    Automatically REBOOT system after a crash       false       +
    Continuously maintain DISK I/O history          true        +
    HIGH water mark for pending write I/Os per file  [17]       +#
    LOW water mark for pending write I/Os per file   [10]       +#
    Enable memory SCRUBBING                         false       +
    Amount of usable physical memory in Kbytes      40960
    State of system keylock at boot time            normal
    Enable full CORE dump                           false       +
```

Figure 4.43 SMIT screen to change file write pacing

4.3.6 SCSI Bus Speed Limitations

Every SCSI disk has a rating for maximum transfer rate stated in megabytes per second. This is a statement of the speed of the electrical interface for the most optimal data transfer. The best-case transfer is when there is no seek or track switching involved. The data we have seen so far confirms that sequential-read scenarios generate the highest disk throughput.

SCSI host adapters also have a rated transfer speed that is limited by the SCSI architecture itself. The burst transfer speed for the SCSI 1 adapter that I used was 4MB. Most modern SCSI-2 adapters are rated at 10MB. There is nothing you can do to change the speed of a single adapter, and typically you do not have to worry about it. But if you have a lot of busy disks all trying to transfer data at the same time, something might have to wait. There is a limit to the SCSI bus capacity. Unfortunately, there is no good, cheap way to measure to what degree this capacity is being exceeded and becoming a bottleneck. Estimates based on empirical measurements will be the best we can do.

The fastest sequential-read example I have discussed exhibited 3111K throughput. All three disks are connected to a single SCSI-1 adapter, which is rated at 4MB per second burst. A very comfortable margin under 5MB might be 3MB, but if I move one of the three disks to a second adapter, throughput increases by 30%. Thus if you have an aggregate actual transfer rate between 50% and 75% of the SCSI adapter burst rate, you may want to consider adding an additional adapter and moving one or more disks to this new adapter. If the measured throughput on one adapter exceeds 75%, you should definitely move one or more disks to another adapter and remeasure your resulting SCSI adapter load.

See Figure 4.44 for an example of the lsdev command that can be used to verify which disks are attached to which adapters. The figure shows that I have six disks attached to the SCSI adapter in slot 8. Figure 4.45 shows the same report after I moved hdisk5 to the second adapter in slot 3.

```
lsdev -C -c disk
hdisk0 Available 00-08-00-0,0 400 MB SCSI Disk Drive
hdisk1 Available 00-08-00-1,0 400 MB SCSI Disk Drive
hdisk2 Available 00-08-00-2,0 400 MB SCSI Disk Drive
hdisk3 Available 00-08-00-3,0 400 MB SCSI Disk Drive
hdisk4 Available 00-08-00-4,0 400 MB SCSI Disk Drive
hdisk5 Available 00-08-00-5,0 400 MB SCSI Disk Drive
```

Figure 4.44   First example using lsdev to list disk adapter positions

```
hdisk0     Available 00-08-00-0,0 400 MB SCSI Disk Drive
hdisk1     Available 00-08-00-1,0 400 MB SCSI Disk Drive
hdisk2     Available 00-08-00-2,0 400 MB SCSI Disk Drive
hdisk3     Available 00-08-00-3,0 400 MB SCSI Disk Drive
hdisk4     Available 00-08-00-4,0 400 MB SCSI Disk Drive
hdisk5     Available 00-03-00-5,0 400 MB SCSI Disk Drive
```

Figure 4.45   Second example using lsdev to list disk adapter positions

4.3.7   Miscellaneous Tuning Parameters

AIX has more tuning parameters that can be set by vmtune and SMIT. Since some of these parameters are not documented anywhere in the AIX documentation, I think it is worthwhile to mention them briefly, although my experience has not shown them to be effective in cases most system administrators are likely to encounter. You can read and then decide whether you want to try experimenting with them. When in doubt, however, leave these at their system defaults.

Vmtune has the following parameters that I have not yet mentioned:

minfree: -f :   This is the low-water mark for free frames. When free frames drop
                           below this number, the page stealer starts scanning pages to steal.

maxfree: -F :

This is the high-water mark for free frames. The page stealer stops stealing pages once free pages exceed this value.

maxpin: -M :

This is a maximum amount of memory that can be pinned by the kernel expressed in percentage of real memory. This should be a concern only to kernel extension and device driver developers.

npswarn: -w :

When free-page-space pages drop below this value, the AIX kernel will send a SIGDANGER signal to processes that indicates a low page-space condition. This value is in units of pages. The error report will indicate that this condition has occurred. If this happens chronically, it may mean you have a memory leak somewhere on your system.

npskill: -k :

When free-page-space pages drop below this value, the AIX kernel will select one or more processes to which to send the SIGKILL signal. The error report will indicate that this condition has occurred. Npskill should be less than npswarn.

numclust: -c :

This is the value that is used to detect sequential write-behind. When sequential writes are greater than this value, the AIX kernel will initiate write-behind. This value is in units of 16K (four pages). Increasing this value could improve write performance of very fast disk devices.

numfsbufs: -b :

This is the number of filesystem buffers that are reserved for JFS write operations. Increasing this value could improve write performance of very fast disk devices. If you change this value, you must unmount and remount the appropriate filesystems in order for the new value to take effect.

lvm_bufcnt: -u :

This is the number of LVM buffers allocated for raw I/O to logical volumes. Increasing this value could improve I/O performance of very fast disk devices.

pd_npages: -N :

This value controls how many pages of a file are deleted at once when a file is removed. Lowering this value could improve performance of programs that remove large files.

maxrandwrt: -W :

Heavy random write I/O initiated by a program often causes intense physical I/O to occur at the time of the regularly scheduled sync from the syncd daemon. This cyclic occurrence can often be annoying to interactive users. Specifying a value for maxrandwrt initiates flushing of dirty pages when that many pages accumulate for a particular file. If you leave the default setting at zero, dirty-page flushing will occur only when the pages are being written sequentially. This value is related to numclust.

4.4   Summary

The following are the most important points in this chapter:

1. Remedies that a system administrator can take to relieve CPU bottlenecks are very limited in effectiveness. Short of adding more CPU power, remedies are limited to changing process priorities with renice, setpri, and schedtune.

2. Remedies to relieve RAM bottlenecks are limited to tuning the amount of RAM devoted to file caching with vmtune.

3. Remedies to relieve disk I/O bottlenecks can be much more effective than remedies concerning CPU and memory bottlenecks. Disk I/O remedies are accomplished by careful data placement, making more efficient use of the existing disk hardware.

   a. Randomly accessed data should be placed nearest the center track of the disk to minimize average seek time.

   b. Sequentially accessed data should be placed nearest the outer edge of disks that have variable sector density.

   c. Concurrency of multiple disks should be exploited by employing striped filesystems for sequentially accessed data or by employing maximum allocated filesystems for randomly accessed data in a multiuser environment.

   d. Paging space is a special case of data placement where multiple paging spaces on different disks can exploit concurrent access.

5

Local Area
Network Tuning

This chapter discusses TCP/IP local area network (LAN) bottlenecks and remedies to relieve these bottlenecks.

The most popular AIX networking subsystems are based on TCP/IP and NFS protocol suites. These subsystems are implemented from code licensed from the University of California (BSD 4.2-4.4) and SunSoft (NFS version 2). Even though AIX follows open systems networking standards, the implementation may vary slightly from other UNIX systems. I will concentrate on these implementation differences and emphasize how these differences affect performance. The causes of the poor network performance can be classified into one of the following general categories:

1. Too many network requests are made by the application. The remedy is to avoid making some of these requests.

2. Network requests are lost somewhere in the network, and subsequent retransmissions are taking extra time. The remedy is either to repair the real cause of the data loss or to reduce the rate of transmission.

3. Insufficient system memory causes either packet loss or automatic throttling of transmission rate to compensate for insufficient memory. The remedy is to allocate more memory.

4. Incorrect system configuration, hardware fault, or incorrect network topology causes long time-outs to occur, and the system uses an alternate means to accomplish the transmission. The remedy is to fix the incorrect configuration.

5. A system in the network is CPU-bound, causing delayed response to requests or complete loss of these requests. The remedy is to reduce the network load or to add CPU power.

After reading this chapter, you should understand how to search for faults that fit in these categories and to execute the appropriate remedy.

5.1   Network Monitoring Tools

You should invoke network monitoring tools in order to get more statistics for isolation when you suspect you have a network bottleneck. When vmstat shows a significant amount of idle that perhaps doesn't quite make sense, the system may be network-bound. Recall that vmstat separates wait time into two different kinds: disk I/O wait (wa column) and nondisk wait (idle column). Nondisk wait would also include network I/O wait and terminal I/O wait. Therefore significant vmstat wait time may indicate waiting for network I/O to complete.

   You should run one or more of the following network monitoring tools to find out if the wait is attributable to network wait.

5.1.1   Netstat

The command that most mimics vmstat for the network domain is netstat. Figure 5.1 shows how to get a repetitive sampling of the network interface every five seconds, in the manner of vmstat sampling. In this case my only network interface was tr0, a token ring interface. If I had been using Ethernet, I would have specified en0. As in vmstat, the very first line is a dump of the counters since boot and should be ignored. The first five columns, which are the most useful, are statistics for the tr0 interface, while the last five columns are statistics for all the interfaces. The first two columns are input packet rate in packets per second and error rate in errors per second. The next two columns are output packet rate and error rate. Ignore the colls column, which is not used on AIX and will always be zero. On other UNIX systems, this statistic counts the number of Ethernet collisions. The packet counts indicate a rough measure of network throughput through that particular interface. Typical Ethernet or token ring interfaces will be able to sustain about 2000 to 3000 packets per second. This figure will depend on how large the packets are and how fast the CPU is.

```
netstat -I tr0 -i 5
      input    (tr0)     output                 input    (Total)     output
   packets  errs  packets  errs colls   packets  errs  packets  errs colls
  10578435     0   394244    29     0  11092863     0   908672    29     0
        24     0        1     0     0        24     0        1     0     0
        26     0        1     0     0        26     0        1     0     0
        20     0        1     0     0        20     0        1     0     0
        26     0        1     0     0        26     0        1     0     0
```

Figure 5.1 The netstat report interface statistics

Figure 5.2 shows network memory buffer statistics. The first paragraph of data shows how much memory is allocated to kernel network buffers, called mbufs. The total number of bytes allocated for mbufs is the first of two very important statistics. In this case there are 72K allocated out of a possible limit of 8MB. A little later, I'll show you how to change this limit. The second important statistic is "request for mbufs denied," which indicates at some point a shortage since boot. A nonzero value here would indicate you should increase the limit. Ignore the rest of the statistics, for they are important primarily to network device programmers.

```
netstat -m
33 mbufs in use:
16 mbuf cluster pages in use
72 Kbytes allocated to mbufs
0 requests for mbufs denied
0 calls to protocol drain routines
```

Figure 5.2   The netstat memory report

Figures 5.3 and 5.4 show network adapter statistics for token ring and Ethernet, respectively.

```
netstat -v
TOKEN-RING STATISTICS (tok0) :
Device Type: Token-Ring High-Performance Adapter (8fc8)
Hardware Address: 10:00:5a:a8:2a:4a
Elapsed Time: 3 days 3 hours 17 minutes 44 seconds

Transmit Statistics:                           Receive Statistics:
--------------------                           --------------------
Packets: 54406                                 Packets: 4471095
Bytes: 13993563                                Bytes: 492234008
Interrupts: 54374                              Interrupts: 4471024
Transmit Errors: 0                             Receive Errors: 0
Packets Dropped: 0                             Packets Dropped: 0
Max Packets on S/W Transmit Queue: 45          Bad Packets: 0
S/W Transmit Queue Overflow: 0
Current S/W+H/W Transmit Queue Length: 0

Broadcast Packets: 11                          Broadcast Packets: 4404536
Multicast Packets: 2                           Multicast Packets: 2
Timeout Errors: 0                              Receive Congestion Errors: 0
Current SW Transmit Queue Length: 0
Current HW Transmit Queue Length: 0
```

Figure 5.3   The netstat report for token ring (*continued on next page*)

```
General Statistics:
-------------------
No mbuf Errors: 0                          Lobe Wire Faults: 0
Abort Errors: 0                            AC Errors: 0
Burst Errors: 139                          Frame Copy Errors: 0
Frequency Errors: 0                        Hard Errors: 0
Internal Errors: 0                         Line Errors: 4
Lost Frame Errors: 0                       Only Station: 0
Token Errors: 0                            Remove Received: 0
Ring Recovered: 0                          Signal Loss Errors: 0
Soft Errors: 0                             Transmit Beacon Errors: 0
Driver Flags: Up Broadcast Running
        AlternateAddress ReceiveFunctionalAddr 16 Mbps


Token-Ring High-Performance Adapter (8fc8) Specific Statistics:
--------------------------------------------------------------
DMA Bus Errors: 0                          DMA Parity Errors: 0
ARI/FCI Errors: 0
```

Figure 5.3   The netstat report for token ring (*cont.*)

```
netstat -v
ETHERNET STATISTICS (ent0) :
Device Type: Integrated Ethernet Adapter
Hardware Address: 08:00:5a:47:02:41
Elapsed Time: 3 days 3 hours 17 minutes 45 seconds

Transmit Statistics:                       Receive Statistics:
-------------------                        -------------------
Packets: 1853                              Packets: 4008
Bytes: 145562                              Bytes: 1152257
Interrupts: 1853                           Interrupts: 4008
Transmit Errors: 0                         Receive Errors: 0
Packets Dropped: 0                         Packets Dropped: 0
Max Packets on S/W Transmit Queue: 0       Bad Packets: 0
S/W Transmit Queue Overflow: 0
Current S/W+H/W Transmit Queue Length: 0

Broadcast Packets: 5                       Broadcast Packets: 6
Multicast Packets: 2                       Multicast Packets: 202
No Carrier Sense: 0                        CRC Errors: 0
DMA Underrun: 0                            DMA Overrun: 0
Lost CTS Errors: 0                         Alignment Errors: 0
Max Collision Errors: 0                    No Resource Errors: 0
Late Collision Errors: 0                   Receive Collision Errors: 0
Deferred: 0                                Packet Too Short Errors: 0
SQE Test: 0                                Packet Too Long Errors: 0
Timeout Errors: 0                          Packets Discarded by Adapter: 0
Single Collision Count: 0                  Receiver Start Count: 1
Multiple Collision Count: 0
Current HW Transmit Queue Length: 8
```

```
General Statistics:
-------------------
No mbuf Errors: 0
Adapter Reset Count: 0
Driver Flags: Up Broadcast Running
        Simplex AlternateAddress

Integrated Ethernet Adapter Specific Statistics:
------------------------------------------------
Packets with Transmit collisions:
  1 collisions: 0          6 collisions: 0         11 collisions: 0
  2 collisions: 0          7 collisions: 0         12 collisions: 0
  3 collisions: 0          8 collisions: 0         13 collisions: 0
  4 collisions: 0          9 collisions: 0         14 collisions: 0
  5 collisions: 0         10 collisions: 0         15 collisions: 0
```

Figure 5.4   The netstat report for Ethernet

5.1.2   Netpmon

In Chapter 3 you saw how to use filemon and how useful that tool was for analyzing disk I/O. Netpmon is the tool to use to analyze network I/O. It uses trace as a means to collect statistics about events occurring in network code in the kernel. Figure 5.5 shows how I ran netpmon while trying a sample NFS work load; Figures 5.6, 5.7, and 5.8 show portions of the report, edited for brevity.

The CPU usage portion of the report shows the top processes using the CPU along with the network portion of CPU usage. Note that the cp and sum commands consumed the most CPU and were responsible for the files being copied across the network. However, the processes that were actually executing the most networking code in the kernel were the biod processes. These biods are surrogate processes that execute the NFS RPC calls. This is just a peculiarity of NFS. Had I been transferring the same file via ftp, the ftp process would show up as the top CPU user, both for network and nonnetwork code. The network device section shows the throughput of the device, in this case, token ring. The important fields are the packets and bytes per second and the utilization. This test example was able to use only 25% of the network capacity due to the inefficiency of the NFS protocol. Had I transferred the file via ftp, the utilization would have approached 80%. Statistics (by Destination Host) in Figure 5.7 show which hosts were comprising which portion of the total traffic.

NFS specific statistics, shown in Figure 5.7, indicate which files, server, and processes were causing the most traffic. The last important section in Figure 5.8 shows detailed statistics such as transfer times measured in milliseconds. Examining transfer times might uncover longer than usual times for a particular host, indicating a specific problem with that host or network.

```
netpmon -o netpmon.out
cp -r $HOME/test /remote.tmp
sum /remote.tmp/test/*
trcstop
```

Figure 5.5   Command line to run netpmon

```
Process CPU Usage Statistics:
-----------------------------
                                                     Network
Process (top 20)              PID  CPU Time   CPU %   CPU %
------------------------------------------------------------
sum                         29248   17.6944  20.125   0.004
cp                          20282    7.0257   7.991   0.005
netpmon                     29496    4.5608   5.187   0.000
biod                         8476    2.2765   2.589   2.589
biod                         9250    2.2540   2.564   2.564
biod                         5140    2.2277   2.534   2.534
biod                         8218    2.1812   2.481   2.481
biod                         8992    2.1783   2.477   2.477
biod                         8734    2.1425   2.437   2.437
kbio                         6544    2.1218   2.413   1.763
```

```
Network Device-Driver Statistics (by Device):
------------------------------------------------
                        ----------- Xmit -----------   -------- Recv ---------
Device                  Pkts/s  Bytes/s  Util  QLen   Pkts/s  Bytes/s  Demux
------------------------------------------------------------------------------
token ring 0            270.74   338710  26.4% 1.691   280.51   337129  0.0427
```

Figure 5.6   The netpmon report, part 1

```
==========================================================================
Network Device-Driver Transmit Statistics (by Destination Host):
------------------------------------------------------------
Host                    Pkts/s  Bytes/s
---------------------------------------
f94apps                 270.68   338703
ausgate                   0.05        4
splabgate                 0.02        3
==========================================================================
NFS Client Statistics for Server f94apps (by File):
---------------------------------------------------
                        ------ Read -----   ----- Write -----
File (top 20)           Calls/s  Bytes/s    Calls/s  Bytes/s
------------------------------------------------------------
gcc-2.7.0.tar             77.24   316362      77.23   316316
------------------------------------------------------------
Total (all files)         77.24   316362      77.23   316316

==========================================================================
```

```
NFS Client RPC Statistics (by Server):
---------------------------------------

Server                    Calls/s
---------------------------------------
f94apps                    77.61
-----------------------------------------------------------------------
Total (all servers)        77.61


=======================================================================

NFS Client Statistics (by Process):
------------------------------------
                                      ------ Read -----   ----- Write -----
Process (top 20)            PID     Calls/s   Bytes/s   Calls/s   Bytes/s
--------------------------------------------------------------------------
sum                       29248     77.24      316362     0.00         0
cp                        20282      0.00           0    77.23    316316
--------------------------------------------------------------------------
Total (all processes)                77.24     316362    77.23    316316
==========================================================================
```

Figure 5.7   The netpmon report, part 2

```
Detailed Network Device-Driver Statistics:
-------------------------------------------

DEVICE: token ring 0
recv packets:           24664
  recv sizes (bytes):   avg 1201.8   min 50      max 1514    sdev 519.5
  recv times (msec):    avg 0.089    min 0.051   max 0.178   sdev 0.013
  demux times (msec):   avg 0.152    min 0.034   max 0.556   sdev 0.136
xmit packets:           23805
  xmit sizes (bytes):   avg 1251.0   min 52      max 1514    sdev 471.2
  xmit times (msec):    avg 6.244    min 0.656   max 19.140  sdev 3.325


=======================================================================

Detailed Network Device-Driver Transmit Statistics (by Host):
-------------------------------------------------------------

HOST: f94apps
xmit packets:           23799
  xmit sizes (bytes):   avg 1251.3   min 170     max 1514    sdev 470.9
  xmit times (msec):    avg 6.246    min 0.684   max 19.140  sdev 3.324

HOST: ausgate
xmit packets:           4
  xmit sizes (bytes):   avg 97.8     min 74      max 117     sdev 15.5
  xmit times (msec):    avg 0.705    min 0.656   max 0.724   sdev 0.028
```

Figure 5.8   The netpmon report, part 3 (*continued on next page*)

```
HOST: splabgate
xmit packets:            2
  xmit sizes (bytes):    avg 111.0    min 52      max 170     sdev 59.0
  xmit times (msec):     avg 0.963    min 0.834   max 1.092   sdev 0.129


========================================================================

Detailed NFS Client Statistics for Server f94apps (by File):
------------------------------------------------------------

FILE: /f94tmp/rudy.junk/gcc-2.7.0.tar
reads:                   6791
  read sizes (bytes):    avg 4096.0   min 4096    max 4096    sdev 0.0
  read times (msec):     avg 1.305    min 0.134   max 87.560  sdev 3.041
writes:                  6790
  write sizes (bytes):   avg 4096.0   min 4096    max 4096    sdev 0.0
  write times (msec):    avg 1.344    min 0.555   max 141.777 sdev 3.637

SERVER: f94apps (All Files)
reads:                   6791
  read sizes (bytes):    avg 4096.0   min 4096    max 4096    sdev 0.0
  read times (msec):     avg 1.305    min 0.134   max 87.560  sdev 3.041
writes:                  6790
  write sizes (bytes):   avg 4096.0   min 4096    max 4096    sdev 0.0
  write times (msec):    avg 1.344    min 0.555   max 141.777 sdev 3.637
```

Figure 5.8   The `netpmon` report, part 3 (*cont.*)

5.1.3   `Tcpdump`

The tools discussed earlier let you see statistics that summarize the number of various network-type events in the AIX kernel. Usually this data is sufficient for most purposes in determining if a host network configuration is optimal. However, sometimes, you get one of these hard performance problems where statistics counters are not enough for you to determine the root problem. Sometimes you need to see the real data "coming across the wire." If you understand the guts of TCP/IP well enough, then `tcpdump` is the command for you. `Tcpdump` will let you see every packet that enters or leaves your system, if you wish to see it. Better yet, `tcpdump` will intelligently filter only the packets you want to see and throw out the rest, thus vastly cutting down the amount of manual scanning you have to do. Figure 5.9 shows an example of how to examine the network traffic for a Telnet connection between two hosts. `Tcpdump` gives extremely detailed information about the network traffic, but most of the time, you will not need to rely on this kind of detail to

```
19:22:45.580738560 philly.austin.ibm.com.telnet > tampa.austin.ibm.com.1038:   P 4:22(18)   ack 16 win 15972
19:22:45.583226624 tampa.austin.ibm.com.1038   > philly.austin.ibm.com.telnet: P 16:39(23)  ack 22 win 15972
19:22:45.630656768 philly.austin.ibm.com.telnet > tampa.austin.ibm.com.1038:   P 22:55(33)  ack 39 win 15972
19:22:45.633556992 tampa.austin.ibm.com.1038   > philly.austin.ibm.com.telnet: P 39:42(3)   ack 55 win 15972
```

Figure 5.9   The `tcpdump` report

solve network problems. If you do, I suggest reading the `tcpdump` command description in AIX InfoExplorer to determine how to use `tcpdump` and how to interpret the output. In addition, you might want to consult *Internetworking with TCP/IP,* Volume 1, by Dougles E. Comer and *TCP/IP Illustrated,* Volume 1, by W. Richard Stevens to learn more about TCP/IP internal architecture.

5.2   Network Tuning Remedies

Now that you have a basic understanding of the kinds of statistics you can gather, you can apply some of these skills to remedy configuring your network subsystem. Be warned that much of what you may have to remedy may be done "in the blind." That is, there are some bottleneck areas that just don't have any statistic counters to tell you they are bottlenecks.

5.2.1   Adapter

5.2.1.1   Transmit and Receive Queues

One of the most common configuration items that needs to be fixed is the network adapter transmit queue length. AIX uses a default value that is too small for moderately heavy traffic and the packets get lost before they ever get transmitted to the receiver. Rather than spend a lot of time determining if you have this condition, it is best just to set the value to the maximum allowable. Setting the value to the maximum is not wasteful since no significant memory is used.

There are two ways to change this value. The first way uses SMIT and allows you to make the change from a remote network connection. Figure 5.10 shows the SMIT panel to change this value for a token ring device. The transmit queue is set to the maximum of 160. Note that the field "Apply change to DATABASE only" is set to yes. This means that the value will not take effect until the next reboot. You must resort to rebooting because the network device cannot be changed while it is in available state, which it is if the network interface is up. Once you have exited SMIT, you can accomplish a reboot from the remote connection with the following command sequence:

```
nohup shutdown -Fr & exit
```

The second way to change this value avoids rebooting, but you have to make the changes from a locally attached terminal. This technique requires bringing the network interface down, changing the device setting, and then bringing the interface back up. The example in Figure 5.11 shows the change for a token ring device. This technique should be attempted from a network connection only if you have been spending too much time at your desk and need more exercise. The `ifconfig tr0 detach` command, which brings down the interface, will be your last from the remote terminal. You will definitely have to don your walking shoes and log in on a local terminal to do the rest of the sequence.

```
smit chtok
  Change / Show Characteristics of a Token Ring Adapter

Type or select values in entry fields.
Press Enter AFTER making all desired changes.

                                                      [Entry Fields]
  Token Ring Adapter                                  tok0
  Description                                         Token-Ring High-Perfor>
  Status                                              Available
  Location                                            00-07
  TRANSMIT queue size                                 [160]          +#
  RING speed                                          16             +
  Receive ATTENTION MAC frame                         no             +
  Receive BEACON MAC frame                            no             +
  Enable ALTERNATE TOKEN RING address                 no             +
  ALTERNATE TOKEN RING address                        [0x]           +
  Apply change to DATABASE only                       yes            +
```

Figure 5.10   Screen to change transmit queue

```
ifconfig tr0 detach              # bring down interface and close device
chdev -l tok0 -a xmt_que_size=160  # change queue size
ifconfig tr0 up                  # bring up interface
```

Figure 5.11   How to change transmit queue

If you are a true UNIX guru, you have probably figured out that I haven't told the whole truth. The commands in Figure 5.11 could be typed on the same command line separated by semicolons, or they could be put into a shell script. Either way, you could execute them from one command line and get away with executing them from a remote terminal. If you are confident enough to do this, please do. Just don't try to interrupt the commands before the last ifconfig is done.

5.2.2   TCP/IP Memory Options

AIX usually does a credible job of allocating virtual memory for various TCP/IP networking tasks. Heavy network load can use up more virtual memory; too little virtual memory for network use can cause a receiver to lose packets or a sender to send less than an optimum amount of data. In the case of packet loss, the sender will usually detect this and retransmit the data, thus reducing the effective transmission throughput. In the case of suboptimum transmission amounts, the sender will not take full advantage of the TCP sliding window acknowledgment with a consequent reduction in throughput. Consult Comer to learn more about TCP sliding window acknowledgment.

All TCP/IP options are set by the no command. Figure 5.12 shows all the options that can be set from no. In the sections ahead, I will discuss only those options that affect performance characteristics of TCP/IP. I suggest that you consult the *AIX 4.1 Performance Tuning Guide* or the InfoExplorer article on the no command to learn the meaning of the other options.

```
                        no -a
                                    thewall = 8192
                                    sb_max = 65536
                           net_malloc_police = 0
                                    rto_low = 1
                                   rto_high = 64
                                  rto_limit = 7
                                 rto_length = 13
                                arptab_bsiz = 7
                                  arptab_nb = 25
                                  tcp_ndebug = 100
                                     ifsize = 8
                             subnetsarelocal = 1
                                     maxttl = 255
                                   ipfragttl = 60
                             ipsendredirects = 1
                                ipforwarding = 0
                                    udp_ttl = 30
                                    tcp_ttl = 60
                                 arpt_killc = 20
                              tcp_sendspace = 16384
                              tcp_recvspace = 16384
                              udp_sendspace = 9216
                              udp_recvspace = 41600
                               rfc1122addrchk = 0
                              nonlocsrcroute = 0
                               tcp_keepintvl = 150
                               tcp_keepidle = 14400
                                  bcastping = 0
                                   udpcksum = 1
                                tcp_mssdflt = 512
                             icmpaddressmask = 0
                               tcp_keepinit = 150
                    ie5_old_multicast_mapping = 0
                                    rfc1323 = 0
                                  ipqmaxlen = 100
                         directed_broadcast = 1
```

Figure 5.12   Network options report

5.2.2.1   `Thewall`

The `thewall` setting is an upper limit to the amount of memory that can be allocated to mbufs. AIX chooses a default setting that is tailored to the amount of system RAM. The default setting is 1/8 the amount of RAM with an upper limit of 16MB. If there is evidence of memory shortages from the field "requests for mbufs denied," then you should increase `thewall` by setting it as

```
no -o thewall = 8192
```

You can also check for evidence of shortages in the recent past by checking the AIX error log with the errpt command. I suggest increasing `thewall` by a factor of 2 until the denied requests disappear.

You may choose to set `thewall` as high as you like, but there may be a subtle penalty to pay for being extravagant. The intention of `thewall` setting is a sanity check for aberrant network behavior. If there were no sanity check, an unusual network event like a bad broadcast storm could cause the network subsystem to allocate a disproportionate amount of RAM to junk network packets and possibly cause a system crash. My observation has been that the default setting has always been sufficient for systems with a single Ethernet or token ring device. If you have more than one of these devices active or if you have faster network devices, you may need to increase `thewall`.

5.2.2.2 TCP and UDP Send and Receive Buffers

Both UDP and TCP have default socket-data buffer limits that can either limit throughput or cause data loss. Whenever a socket is opened by a program, these default limits will be associated with the socket. The program can change these defaults via a `setsockopt` call, which is covered in Chapter 7.

UDP on AIX uses `udp_sendspace` and `udp_recvspace` to reserve the amount of send and receive buffer space for a UDP socket. Since UDP datagrams must be sent or received in one go, insufficient space to send or receive can prevent a UDP program from operating properly. If a host receives a datagram that exceeds the `udp_recvspace`, the datagram is silently discarded. If a program attempts to send a UDP datagram that is larger than the `udp_sendspace`, the system call fails. A UDP program can increase its own UDP-socket send space, but it cannot increase the space of the receiver process, which is often on another host.

TCP on AIX uses `tcp_sendspace` and `tcp_recvspace` to reserve space for a TCP domain socket. For TCP sockets, the buffer space size is not as critical as it is for UDP. Since TCP is a stream protocol, the data can be sent out in sufficiently small chunks to accommodate whatever buffer space is left. Therefore insufficient buffer space for TCP sockets will merely inhibit throughput but not inhibit proper operation. It is `tcp_recvspace` that controls the TCP advertised window, which cannot be larger than the socket-receive buffer space. The TCP window limits the amount of data pending to be acknowledged and effectively limits the throughput of the socket. To state this another way, with a sufficiently powerful CPU and sufficiently large TCP window, it is possible for a single socket to utilize 100% of the effective bandwidth of the transmission medium.

To make a rough guess for an upper bound on the optimum receive buffer size, use the following calculation:

```
s = rtt * bw
```

`s` is the size of the buffer, `rtt` is the average round-trip time of a packet, and `bw` is the maximum bandwidth. For example, let's use an ordinary Ethernet network that typically has a round-trip time, measured by `ping`, of 2 ms. Plugging in these numbers gives

```
s = .002s * ( 10,000,000 bytes per second/ 8 bits per byte)
  = 2500 bytes
```

Fortunately the default, `tcp_recvspace`, is 16,384 bytes, which is plenty large. But if the round-trip time got worse by a factor of 10, then the upper bound on receive space would be 25,000 bytes. All it would take is to put a gateway or two between the two endpoints; the round-trip packet time could then easily become 20 ms, and 16,384 bytes might not be adequate. This calculation establishes just a theoretical upper bound. It notes that, for the second example, the upper bound for receive buffer size is not larger than 25,000 bytes; the true optimum size could actually be smaller. This rough calculation lets you make some intelligent guesses for `tcp_recvspace`; the `tcp_sendspace` should be equal to the `tcp_recvspace`.

If you are not familiar with TCP sliding window acknowledgment and round-trip time calculations, it would be a good time to consult Stevens, *TCP/IP Illustrated*, Volume 1, on how TCP does this.

Figure 5.13 shows an example of how to set buffer spaces for TCP and UDP.

```
no -o tcp_sendspace  = 16384
no -o tcp_recvspace  = 16384
no -o udp_sendspace  =  9216
no -o udp_recvspace  = 41600
```

Figure 5.13   Setting TCP and UDP buffers

Since these values do not persist, you need to put the changes into some script that gets executed when the system is first booted. The best place is in /etc/rc.net, since AIX already has a handy spot there where these defaults are set. If you attempt to set any of these space values larger than 65,384 (16 bits in length), you will also need to change settings for `rfc1323` and `sb_max`.

5.2.2.3   Rfc1323

If the value of the `rfc1323` flag is nonzero, it allows the TCP window size to be a maximum of 32 bits instead of 16 bits. What this means to you, the TCP/IP tuner, is that you can set `tcp_sendspace` and `tcp_recvspace` to be greater than 65,384. This becomes important for faster media such as FDDI, but it is not needed for Ethernet and token ring media. An example of how to enable 32-bit window sizes is

```
no -o rfc1323 = 1
```

5.2.2.4   Sb_max

In order that programs don't hog kernel memory by sending a flood of data to another program, there is a limit to the amount of memory buffers a socket can take up on the send or receive side. The `sb_max` value, the buffer memory limit expressed in bytes, also limits `udp_sendspace`, `udp_recvspace`, `tcp_sendspace`, and `tcp_recvspace`. No matter how large you try to set the space values with `no`, the AIX kernel will silently limit these values to `sb_max`, because the actual value is interrogated only when a socket is opened by an application. At this time the socket will fail to open, and the application will experience an operational failure.

All these settings may seem like a bit of overkill, and they are. But they are a legacy of BSD that harkens back to the days of the mid-1980s when RAM sizes where relatively small. Udp_sendspace, udp_recvspace, tcp_sendspace, and tcp_recvspace are default limits that can be changed by any program, whether it has root authority. Sb_max, an upper limit to these other space limits, can be changed only by root via a command interface.

The greatest danger of sb_max being too small is that input UDP packets will be dropped. Since NFS runs on top of UDP, sb_max is an important setting for NFS servers. I will discuss NFS in a later section and will revisit sb_max there. An example of how to change sb_max is

```
no -o sb_max = 65536
```

5.2.2.5 Ipqmaxlen

Another limit is that you must be concerned about is the length of the IP input queue. The default is 100 packets long, which is sufficient for single-network device systems. You may have to increase this value for systems with multiple network devices. The penalty for insufficient queue length is silently dropped packets. Use the netstat command to interrogate the number of IP input queue overflows, shown as

```
netstat -s |fgrep ipintrq
  0 ipintrq overflows
```

And this is how the IP queue length is changed:

```
no -o ipqmaxlen = 100
```

5.2.2.6 Summary of Recommendations

I have described how to change many of the TCP/IP settings from a theoretical view-point, but what you really want is a list of values to use. Table 5.1 is a starting point for all the values I have just described. Once you have set them, analyze them to see if they are large enough for your situation.

5.2.3 Network Interface

5.2.3.1 MTU

The media transmission unit (MTU) size is an aspect of network configuration that must be considered for the entire network rather than just for a local host. The MTU is the size of frames at the media layer. Every host on the same network must agree on the same size; therefore it is not always possible to change the MTU to a more optimum value without changing the entire network.

Let's assume that you can change the MTU, and let's consider which networks benefit from changing the default MTU size. In general, larger MTU is better than smaller

Media type	Ethernet	Token Ring 16MB	FDDI	SP Switch
sb_max	default	default	256K	1280K
rfc1323	default	default	1	1
thewall	default	default	default	default
tcp_sendspace	default	default	128K	384K
tcp_recvspace	default	default	128K	384K
udp_sendspace	default	default	64K	64K
udp_recvspace	default	default	128K	640K

Table 5.1   TCP/IP setting for different media

because it lessens the likelihood of fragmentation of UDP datagrams. Whether UDP is being used can be understood by examining the output of `netstat -s` and examining the proportion of IP packets that were fragmented. Figure 5.14 shows an edited `netstat` report with the reassembled packet count a very negligible part of the total. Be aware that NFS RPCs are based solely on UDP datagrams.

Datagram fragmentation puts a CPU usage burden on intervening routers between source and destination. This burden may not be noticeable until one or more routers becomes saturated with packet traffic. The intervening routers will have to pass along more packets compared to the unfragmented case, and the destination host will have to perform IP packet reassembly.

```
netstat -s

ip:

        31 packets reassembled ok
   2838802 packets for this host
```

Figure 5.14   Abbreviated report of IP statistics

Table 5.2 shows a list of the most common LAN devices, their default MTU, their maximum MTU, and whether increasing MTU would help. Note that changing Ethernet or FDDI cannot help because the MTU should be set at its maximum.

Network device	Default MTU	Max MTU	Increase?
Ethernet	1500	1500	N
Token Ring 4MB	1492	3900	Y
Token Ring 16MB	1492	17,960	Y
FDDI	4352	4352	N
SP Switch	65,520	65,520	N

Table 5.2   Recommended MTU sizes

Figure 5.15 shows how to change the MTU for a token ring device. Other devices would be changed similarly.

```
SMIT ch nfs
        Network Interface Drivers

Type or select values in entry fields.
Press Enter AFTER making all desired changes.

                                                        [Entry Fields]
   Network Interface                                    tr0
   Maximum IP PACKET SIZE for THIS DEVICE               [1492]       +#
```

Figure 5.15   SMIT screen to change MTU size

5.2.3.2   Tcp_mssdflt

A TCP connection that has both endpoints on the same network will use the MTU value for the maximum segment size (MSS), which is a limit on how much data that TCP will attempt to send at one time. See Stevens, *TCP/IP Illustrated,* Volume 1, for more details on MSS.

The MSS value for a connection for which both endpoints are on different networks cannot be determined, because the receiver host MTU is not known. AIX TCP uses a value called the default MSS value, tcp_mssdflt, which has a default value of 512 bytes. If the endpoint network is guaranteed to have an MTU larger than 512, it may improve throughput by increasing tcp_mssdflt to this known value of MTU. An example of changing the MSS default is

```
no -o tcp_mssdflt = 4096
```

5.2.4   TCP/IP Setup Errors

5.2.4.1   Name Resolution

If network transactions seem inexplicably slow sometimes but all right at other times, it is usually a good idea to do a basic diagnosis on your system nameserver configuration to make sure it is responding to name requests. The system name resolution may be served through either a remote DNS server or a remote NIS server. Quite often in these circumstances, the nameserver will be down, and a time-out occurs. The name then ends up being resolved by an alternate means, which might be a secondary nameserver or the local hosts file.

The primary isolation technique to determine if your nameserver is down is to notice how the `ping` command behaves. Try to `ping` any host on the network and observe if `ping` reports an IP address immediately or if it just hangs. If `ping` hangs with no IP address reported, then your nameserver is snoozing or misconfigured. If `ping` immediately reports an IP address being pinged, then the nameserver is working all right. The IP address of a DNS server can be found in the `/etc/resolve.conf` file; the IP address of an NIS server can be found with the `ypwhich` command.

If you do find that the nameserver is the culprit of your slow response, it may be more expedient simply to bypass remote name service rather than try to debug the real problem. The quickest way to see if local name resolution would help your application performance is to set the `NSORDER` environment variable to specify that the local `/etc/hosts` file be tried first before trying remote name service. You would set the variable something like this:

```
export NSORDER="hosts=local,nis,bind"
```

This setting would force the name resolution search for any child processes to be worked through by local `/etc/hosts`, then by NIS, and finally by DNS. If this experiment proves fruitful, then you could set the order permanently for the entire system by putting the same values in the `/etc/netsvc.conf` file. The contents of this file would look like this:

```
cat /etc/netsvc.conf
hosts=local,nis,bind
```

5.2.5   NFS

NFS protocol maps the various filesystem operations into remote procedure calls (RPC) that are transmitted to the NFS server via UDP datagrams. Since UDP is not reliable delivery, NFS adds a layer of reliability by detecting RPCs that don't get answered and generating a time-out. If a time-out occurs, the client host assumes that the first request was lost and is retransmitted. Since RPC is based on UDP, there is no sort of pacing mechanism that ensures the server has room to receive the request. It is this time-out feature that can turn an NFS client from a kitten into a dragon.

The first order of business is to ensure that the UDP transport layer is performing properly by taking the tuning steps outlined in the previous sections. Once you have done that, you can begin to analyze NFS performance.

5.2.5.1 Nfsstat

The nfsstat command reports statistics on NFS requests. Figure 5.16 shows a client-side report of the requests that have occurred since the last time the statistics were cleared. The client rpc section shows how many RPCs have been sent and how many have made it to the server all right. Pay particular attention to ratio of retransmissions (retrans) to calls. If this is high, some remedial action is necessary. Also pay attention to the bad transmission ID (badxid) figure, the count of server replies that were redundant. A redundant reply means that a retransmission happened unnecessarily. The first request was eventually received by the server and answered, but the reply wasn't fast enough to prevent the time-out. The ratio of badxid to retrans approaching one implies that the server is just overloaded. When this ratio approaches zero, the network is losing the requests either before they arrive at the server or after the response is sent back.

```
nfsstat -c

Client rpc:
calls        badcalls    retrans      badxid       timeout      wait         newcred
88607        2           8            0            10           0            0

Client nfs:
calls        badcalls    nclget      nclsleep
88606        0           88606       0
null         getattr     setattr     root         lookup       readlink     read
0   0%       11158 12%   217   0%    0   0%       30977 34%    0   0%       12862 14%
wrcache      write       create      remove       rename       link         symlink
0   0%       21317 24%   4432   5%   4429   4%    0   0%       0   0%       0   0%
mkdir        rmdir       readdir     fsstat
222  0%      221   0%    2000   2%   771   0%
```

Figure 5.16 Nfsstat client report

Since time-outs have such a devastating effect on NFS performance, I would consider any ratio over 10% high enough to warrant concern. Figure 5.17 shows a server-side report of requests. Both client and server reports show a breakdown of the different kinds of RPCs. This data may be interesting but goes beyond the scope of this book. I would recommend *Managing NFS and NIS* by Hal Stern for more detailed information on the operation of NFS.

```
$ nfsstat -s

Server rpc:
calls        badcalls    nullrecv    badlen       xdrcall
106163       0           12          0            0
```

```
Server nfs:
calls         badcalls
106116        0
null          getattr      setattr      root         lookup       readlink     read
0   0%        11251 10%    217  0%      0    0%      31225 29%    68   0%      12901 12%
wrcache       write        create       remove       rename       link         symlink
0   0%        20797 19%    4430   4%    4429   4%    0    0%      0    0%      0    0%
mkdir         rmdir        readdir      fsstat
222  0%       221   0%     2000   1%    18355 17%
```

Figure 5.17 Nfsstat server report

5.2.5.2 Nfso

In an earlier section, I discussed udp_recvspace and the implications of this value being too small. For NFS servers the nfsds can lose packets because the receive buffer is too small. You could increase the value of udp_recvspace, and that would allocate a larger receive buffer for all the nfsd sockets. However, all other UDP sockets in the system would get larger default receive buffers. A more direct way to change only the receive buffer size of nfsd is to change the nfs_socketsize value with nfso. Remember to ensure that the sb_max is greater than the new value of nfs_socketsize. An example of changing nfs_socketsize would be

```
nfso -o nfs_socketsize=128000
```

5.2.5.3 Client NFS Daemons

NFS clients use surrogate processes, called biods, to speed up reading and writing of NFS files. The job of biods is to perform read-ahead and write-behind for client-type pages. For RPCs other than read and write, the application process does not use a surrogate process but rather performs the RPC itself. For sequential read, the process that initiated the read is the one that performs the read RPC. Rather than fetch only the amount of data that the program's read call specifies, fetch a larger buffer size. This size is controlled by the NFS rsize value. Once read-ahead goes into action, the biods are used to make the read-ahead happen in parallel with the execution of the requesting process. The read-ahead amounts will also be done in rsize chunks. If all the biods are busy, then read-ahead will not happen, and the read will be performed in a normal manner by the requesting process.

When an application process performs a write on an NFS file, the data is cached into virtual memory until a contiguous amount exceeding the NFS wsize has been written. Then a biod is dispatched to perform a write RPC for that entire wsize chunk. The process that initiated the writing is free to continue processing while the biod does its work, but the biod will not wake up until the NFS server has acknowledged that the data really is written to disk. This is an important point that makes NFS writing very expensive in terms of performance. The application process writes data asynchronously, the same as if the file were a local file. Both the biod and the NFS server write the data synchronously.

If all the `biods` are busy, the process must perform the RPC itself, and writing effectively becomes synchronous from the application perspective, too.

The default number of `biods` is set to 6, which supports an average client NFS load. Even with one application process writing to one NFS file, all the biods can be busy working on one file for one application process. The same can be true of sequential reading. If the client system has lots of application processes, the `biods` have a greater likelihood of being busy. When all the biods are busy, the application processes must perform all the reads and writes themselves, decreasing aggregate throughput for NFS I/O. Increasing the number of `biods` can increase throughput, if there are a lot of application processes performing NFS I/O concurrently. A loose rule of thumb is to allocate 2 to 4 `biods` per NFS file to be accessed concurrently. Once you have your system running with that number of `biods`, you can tune the number, usually by increasing biods and observing changes in throughput.

In a perfect world, you could add more `biods` than you really need without much penalty. Each biod process would take a dozen pages or so of data and stack space. Having extra `biods` would ensure you always have enough and would cost just a pittance in virtual memory—in a perfect world, that is. But your world, like mine, probably tends to be somewhat less than perfect; network routers can often be overloaded, and Ethernets can become saturated with collisions. When this happens, NFS RPCs can get lost, causing NFS retransmissions.

As I said earlier, lost packets should be dealt with by tuning sender and receiver to ensure that packet loss does not occur, but tuning the end points of a transmission doesn't help if the message gets lost in the middle. Our imperfect world often prevents us from tuning those things in the network that make up the middle. The next best thing is to live with the imperfect network by throttling back on the client side until packet loss disappears. The key indicator to look for is the following statistics from `nfsstat -c`:

high (>10%) ratio of retrans/calls

low ratio of badxid/retrans

Throttling back of client requests can be accomplished in two ways. The first and better way is to reduce the number of `biods`. Often it is expedient to shut off all the `biods` rather than try to experiment to find an optimum number. Shutting down all the `biods` can be done with a single command:

```
stopsrc -s biod
```

This command will terminate all `biods`, but there will be one kernel process left to act as a `biod` surrogate. In cases of significant retransmissions, I have known this quick, expedient method to improve NFS throughput as much as ten times for NFS-intensive commands.

This point is important to repeat. If the client and server could have been magically put on the same network, the biod-shutdown technique not only would have been unnecessary but would have degraded throughput. Don't use it unless `nfsstat` says that NFS RPCs are getting lost.

If the `biod` shutdown helped, then I suggest you find out exactly how many `biods` are optimum. Figure 5.18 shows how to adjust the number of `biods` to something other than none. This will set a total number of `biod` kernel processes that are free to service any of the NFS mounts on the client. It is also possible to control the number of concurrent `biod` requests on a mount basis.

```
SMIT ch nfs
                         Change Number of nfsd & biod Daemons


Type or select values in entry fields.
Press Enter AFTER making all desired changes.

                                                          [Entry Fields]
* NUMBER of nfsd (Server) daemons to run                  [20]          #
* NUMBER of biod (Client) daemons to run                  [10]          #
* CHANGE number now, system restart or both               both          +
```

Figure 5.18   SMIT screen to change number of NFS daemons

The second technique of throttling client requests is to reduce the `wsize` and `rsize` mount options. This will cause RPCs to occur more often but with smaller amounts of data being transmitted. This may improve performance by reducing the degree of burst network activity, which may, in turn, improve a packet loss situation. However, if the server is overloaded and responding slowly, this technique will only compound the problem. The server will have to receive more RPCs and perform more disk fetches for the same amount of transferred data. If `nfsstat` says that `badxid/retrans` is approaching 1, don't consider reducing `wsize` or `rsize`. Instead, reduce the number of `biods`, or take some remedial action, such as changing the number of `nfsds`, on the server. I will discuss this remedial action next.

5.2.5.4   Server NFS Daemons

Once the client RPC is received by the NFS server in the NFS socket, it is fielded by `nfsd` processes. On AIX, the default number is 8.

Tuning the number of `nfsds` on the server is about as straightforward as tuning the `biods` on the client. To increase performance, you increase `nfsds`, decrease `nfsds`, or leave them alone. Now that I have become purveyor of the obvious, let me explain all the bottlenecks you can run into.

If `nfsds` are a bottleneck, then adding more will probably increase NFS throughput. The easiest approach is to increase the number of `nfsds` by 25% and see if there is a corresponding increase in throughput. Another indicator that there are too few `nfsds` is when `netstat` reports any socket buffer overflows. If all the `nfsds` are busy while more NFS requests come in, the request will stay in the socket buffer. If even more requests come in and the socket buffer is full, the requests will be dropped. In the case of server NFS sockets repeatedly overflowing and causing client time-outs, increasing `nfsds` can cure this symptom. If socket buffer overflows are occurring, it is also a good idea to increase the depth of the receive buffer for `nfsd`, as discussed earlier.

There is one situation that overrules increasing the number of `nfsds`, even if socket buffer overflows are occurring. If the server system is CPU-bound, adding `nfsds` will not help; the server will become severely disk I/O bound long before it becomes CPU-bound. However, it is possible that a server could become CPU-bound if it had an under-powered CPU, a high read request load, a heavy non-NFS load, or some combination of these. In the case of the server being CPU-bound, the remedy is to decrease the number of `nfsds` and increase the `nfsds` socket buffer depth to compensate.

5.2.5.5   Mount Options

The mount command has several NFS-specific options that may affect performance. An example of changing all of these is

```
mount -o\
rsize=4096,wsize=4096,acregmin=60,acregmax=120,acdirmin=60,\
acregmax=120 philly:/work /mnt
```

`Rsize` is the minimum chunk size for which RPC reads are done; `wsize` is the buffering threshold for RPC writes. The AIX default for both of these is 8K. Oddly enough, this default is also the enforced maximum. It is possible to make these values smaller, but I don't recommend changing them. It is almost always better to reduce the number of `biods`. Making `wsize` or `rsize` smaller than 4K is definitely inadvisable. The AIX page size is 4K, and it can be grossly inefficient to perform I/O of any sort in less than a page size of 4K. I will discuss the reasons in depth in Chapter 7.

Control of flushing the NFS attribute cache is controlled by `acregmin`, `acregmax`, `acdirmin`, and `acdirmax`, which are specified in seconds. NFS attributes are the values contained in the inode of the physical file. For example, doing `ls -l` on a directory would execute a `getattr` for every file in that directory. The `getattr` RPC gets attributes for a file and caches them on the client for a period of time specified by `acregmin`. Likewise, attribute flushing for a directory is controlled by `acdirmin`. If a second `ls -l` were done on the same directory immediately, the attributes would be in the client attribute cache, and all those getattr RPCs would be avoided. If the minimum period expires and the client did not change any of the files that had cached attributes, the file and directory attributes are flushed in such a way that a subsequent `ls -l` would require getattr RPCs. The moral of the story is that increasing `acregmin` and `acregmax` could improve performance if the client were performing many `getattr` RPCs.

Determining if adjusting attribute cache flush time-outs can help is fairly straight-forward. If `nfsstat` shows a significant number of getattr calls on the client, then adjusting the cache time-out may be in order. Figure 5.16 showed that there was a moderate amount (11%) of `getattr` calls executed by the client. I would predict that 11% would not warrant changing the `acregmin` and `acdirmin` values, but perhaps 50% would be worth the trouble to try.

Determining which time-out values to try is less straightforward. The entire point of keeping an attribute cache is to avoid expensive `getattr` RPCs for the second and subsequent time, as file attributes are needed. However, if another client happens to be modifying the same file, the attributes on the first client will become stale. Longer time-out periods increase the likelihood that some client will have stale attributes; shorter time-outs will keep the attributes more current but will incur a greater performance penalty.

In the case of NFS filesystems that are consistently mounted read-only by all clients, you might be able to make a simplifying assumption that there is little or no chance of anyone modifying files in that filesystem. If that assumption can be made, then the time-out values for `acregmin` and `acdirmin` can be significantly increased without any danger of obtaining stale data. Figure 5.19 shows an example of setting these values to 60 seconds.

```
mount -o
"acregmin=60,acdirmin=60" chukran:/tools /mnt
```

Figure 5.19   The mount command to set NFS time-out values

In the case where an NFS filesystem is mounted read-write by a client, you might be able to make a simplifying assumption that this client is the only client that will be modifying files in this filesystem. In this case you can increase the values of acregmax and `acdirmax` so that caching of modified attributes will occur for a longer period before the modified attributes are flushed back to the server. However, file attribute modification typically happens because the file data is being modified. There is no way to prevent modified data pages from being written to the server immediately. Therefore write RPCs will tend to dominate `setattr` RPCs. Hal Stern's *Managing NFS and NIS* discusses attribute caching in more depth.

Figure 5.19 showed how mount options are set using a mount command. NFS mounts typically are not done manually, though. Figure 5.20 shows the SMIT way of

```
                 Add a File System for Mounting

   Type or select values in entry fields.
   Press Enter AFTER making all desired changes.

   [TOP]                                                    [Entry Fields]
   * PATHNAME of mount point                                [/mnt]           /
   * PATHNAME of remote directory                           [/work]
   * HOST where remote directory resides                    [philly]
     Mount type NAME                                        []
   * Use SECURE mount option?                               no               +
   * MOUNT now, add entry to /etc/filesystems or both?      filesystems      +
   * /etc/filesystems entry will mount the directory        yes              +
       on system RESTART.
   * MODE for this NFS file system                          read-only        +
   * ATTEMPT mount in background or foreground              background       +
```

Figure 5.20   SMIT screen to mount NFS filesystems (*continued on next page*)

```
    NUMBER of times to attempt mount                    []              #
    Buffer SIZE for read                                []              #
    Buffer SIZE for writes                              []              #
    NFS TIMEOUT. In tenths of a second                  []              #
    Internet port NUMBER for server                     []              #
  * Mount file system soft or hard                       hard           +
    Allow keyboard INTERRUPTS on hard mounts?            yes            +
    Minimum TIME, in seconds, for holding               [3]             #
      attribute cache after file modification
    Maximum TIME, in seconds, for holding               [60]            #
      attribute cache after file modification
    Minimum TIME, in seconds, for holding               [30]            #
      attribute cache after directory modification
    Maximum TIME, in seconds, for holding               [60]            #
      attribute cache after directory modification
    Minimum & Maximum TIME, in seconds, for             []              #
      holding attribute cache after any modification
    The Maximum NUMBER of biod daemons allowed          [6]             #
      to work on this file system
  * Allow execution of SUID and sgid programs            yes            +
      in this file system?
  * Allow DEVICE access via this mount?                  yes            +
  * Server supports long DEVICE NUMBERS?                 yes            +
  [BOTTOM]
```

Figure 5.20   SMIT screen to mount NFS filesystems (*cont.*)

specifying the same mount options. The results are written to the /etc/filesystems
file. If you wish, you could edit the file directly and then mount the filesystem after sav-
ing /etc/filesystems. Figure 5.21 shows the results of the SMIT execution.

```
/mnt:
        dev             = "/work"
        vfs             = nfs
        nodename        = philly
        mount           = true
        options         = ro,bg,hard,intr,acregmin=60,
                          acregmax=120,acdirmin=60,acdirmax=120,biods=4
        account         = false
```

Figure 5.21   Except of /etc/filesystems file showing NFS mount

5.3   Summary

The most important points in this chapter are:

1. AIX tools, such as netstat, netpmon, nfsstat, and tcpdump, give you
    insight into how heavily the network is being stressed.

2. The most effective configurations to change for efficient TCP/IP are network device transmit queue, network memory limits, such as `thewall`, and TCP and UDP spaces.

3. The most frequent cause of poor NFS performance is retransmissions due to packet loss.

4. The most expedient remedies to packet loss are to reduce `biods` on the client and to increase the `nfsd` socket-receive buffer on the server.

6

Programming Tools

The discussion of programming tools in this chapter is oriented toward programmers rather than system administrators. Programmers have access to source code and have the ability to change their applications to perform more optimally.

6.1   Compiler

The first step in the conversion of program source code to running object code is the compilation step. There are many computer programming languages that can run on AIX, but I discuss only FORTRAN, C, and C++.

Since compilers are not statistics gathering tools, it is probably not appropriate to draw an analogy between compilers and optical instruments. A compiler doesn't help you to see more clearly; a compiler is more like a screwdriver that allows you to twist the "go faster" screw. In other words, compilers are tools that help you to affect remedies.

I will discuss compiler flags that affect some aspect of performance. The discussion applies to the following compilers:

C for AIX Version 3

C Set ++ for AIX Version 3

XL Fortran for AIX Version 3

6.1.1   XL Compiler Flags Common to All Languages

Most of the performance flags are common to all languages and have the most performance impact.

6.1.1.1 Standard Optimization

On	Off	Default
O	qnooptimize	qnooptimize
qoptimize		

The single most important compiler flag with respect to performance is the optimize flag. Standard optimization can improve performance of certain floating-point-intensive programs tenfold. I can recall the incident of a database program that was compiled entirely unoptimized because the developer discovered a compiler optimizer bug. Rather than take the time to isolate the bug to a certain module, the developer took the easy approach and compiled everything unoptimized. When customers complained of poor database performance, my support team identified lack of optimization as a potential culprit. The developer did recompile the entire database application optimized. By this time, the bug had been fixed, and the application passed its quality-assurance testing. The customer experienced a doubling of transaction throughput by using the new, optimized version of the database management application.

Optimized code runs so much better than unoptimized code because the unoptimized code is truly inefficient. Several factors contribute to this inefficiency. First, all local variables are stored into memory, as are all function arguments. Optimization avoids storing results into local variables; the values are kept in registers instead. When optimized, the first five arguments are kept in registers and are not redundantly stored on the stack. Second, optimization performs common techniques such as code hoisting and subexpression elimination. Third, unoptimized code makes no attempt at performing instruction scheduling; optimized code does take into account optimum placement of loads, stores, and branches so that the processor pipeline does not stall unnecessarily. Fourth, unoptimized code does not attempt to use floating-point, multiply-add instructions. Optimized code does use multiply-add instructions capable of executing in one clock cycle.

The moral of the story is to use the optimizer to get full benefit of the PowerPC superscalar hardware. If you encounter a bug that is uncovered with optimization, don't be tempted simply to turn off optimization for the entire program. Take the time to isolate the bug to at least a single compilation unit so that only that unit can be compiled unoptimized.

6.1.1.2 Intensive Optimization

On	Off	Default
O3	qnooptimize	qnooptimize
qoptimize=3		

There are three different levels of optimization. No optimization could be thought of as level 0. Level 1 optimization is identical to level 2 optimization, corresponding to standard optimization, which I just discussed. Level 3 intensive optimization, denoted by the

O3 option, tends to be more aggressive in optimizations and the amount of compile time to complete these optimizations. Furthermore, such aggressive optimization might cause the behavior of the program to change. An example of such an optimization would be motion of a loop-invariant floating-point subexpression outside the loop. Since any floating-point calculation could cause an exception, motion of the calculation might cause the program to behave differently. Level 2 optimization would not perform the code motion; level 3 optimization would. The probability of such code motion causing a change in program semantics is quite low, but the probability exists, nonetheless.

Now that I have you so worried that you will never even try O3, let me show an example of a semantic error that level 3 optimization might cause:

```
int index;
float matrix[N], x,y;
for ( index = 0, index <N; index ++)
    if ( matrix[index] < MAX )
        matrix[index] = x+y;
}
```

Note that with level 3 optimization, the expression x+y would be hoisted out of the loop, while level 2 optimization would not move the calculation. If the addition caused an exception and you wrote a signal handler to handle the SIGFPE signal, that signal handler might assume that since the exception occurred, matrix[index] < MAX is true. However, this assumption would be false because the calculation of x+y that caused the exception happened before entry to the loop. If you have programs that rely on such an assumption, do not use level 3 optimization.

Practical experience with O3 shows that it does not yield smashingly fantastic results. The performance gains are usually in the single-digit percentage gains, if that. Sometimes level 3 optimization causes a slight drop in performance. If your program is not floating-point intensive, you are unlikely to see any performance gain. You will have to experiment to see what sort of gifts O3 optimization will bring to you.

6.1.1.3 Hardware Architecture Targeting

Option	Hardware Chipset	Default
qarch=com	All	Yes
qarch=pwr	Power	No
qarch=pwr2	Power2	No
qarch=ppc	PowerPC	No

The PowerPC architecture has some related predecessor architectures that are not totally compatible. See Figure 6.1 for an ancestry chart of the related architectures. The origin of the PowerPC architecture is the Power architecture; the Power2 architecture is a derivative of Power that enhanced floating-point performance with the addition of new instructions. The PowerPC architecture is a derivative of Power that streamlined the instruction set by omitting certain instructions in order to improve performance and reduce cost. To

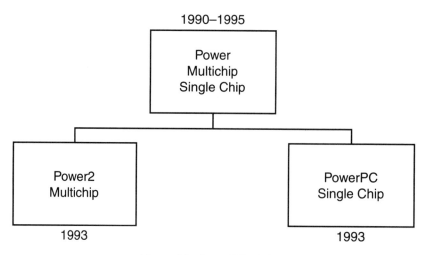

Figure 6.1   PowerPC origins

further complicate matters, different chipsets in the PowerPC architecture implement different instructions. The PowerPC 601 is a special case; it implements several instructions that are not strictly in the PowerPC architecture but are in the Power architecture. See Figure 6.2 for a Venn diagram of how the chipsets relate to one another with respect to implemented instructions. Set 1 is the instructions common to all the chipsets; Set 2 is the PowerPC instructions that are not in the Power instruction set; Set 3 is the Power2 instructions not in the Power instruction set; Set 4 is the Power instructions that are only in the PowerPC 601 instruction set, not in the instructions sets of the rest of the PowerPC family; and Set 5 is the Power instructions that are not in PowerPC.

All of this is interesting from a performance aspect because if your programs happen to take advantage of instructions on a particular chipset, the program has the potential to perform better while running on that chipset. The danger is that, if a program using unique instructions runs on a chip set that does not implement those instructions, the program may run more slowly or not at all.

Table 6.1 shows how programs targeted to specific chipsets behave on all the PowerPC-related chipsets. Note that common architecture mode programs can run on any chipset—that is why "common" is the default architecture setting. Also note that Power2-targeted programs can run only on Power2 chipsets. Power-targeted programs can run on any chipset, but performance can be an issue on PowerPC chipsets.

Since PowerPC architecture removed instructions from Power architecture, it is important to consider what happens to a program that contains some of these instructions. If a program tries to execute an instruction that the CPU does not implement, an instruction trap occurs. If the instruction was one of the Power-only instructions, the AIX kernel handles the trap and emulates the instruction with one or more equivalent instructions. This trap and emulation can take hundreds of cycles more than the instruction normally would take; the more "missing" instructions that are emulated, the worse the performance.

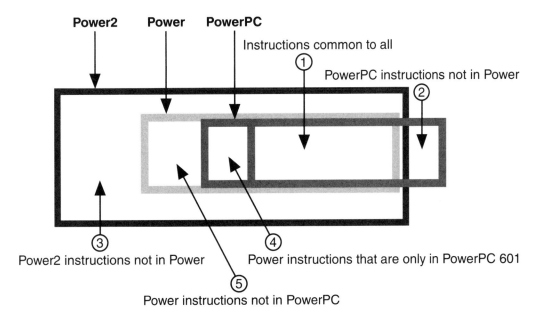

Figure 6.2 PowerPC instruction map

There are only two instructions in Set 5. These are emulated on a PowerPC 601. All the rest of the Power-only instructions, Set 4, are implemented in the 601 chipset. The two emulated instructions are data cache control instructions that the compiler does not emit, so it is unlikely that any of your programs would have them. The only way your programs would have either of those two instructions is for you to have coded them in machine assembly language. The 603 and 604 (and any future PowerPC chipsets) would have a much greater likelihood of emulation for Power-targeted architecture due to Set 5.

There are only three ways that your program could have Power-only instructions in it. The most obvious way is if you had compiled the code with qarch=power, and there is no reason to have done this, performance-related or otherwise. The second way is if the code had been compiled before the compiler default changed, which was in the August 1993 time frame. The third way is to have linked on an AIX 3.2.5 system.

Even though the rows in Table 6.1 that describe the characteristics of programs targeted for PowerPC and Power2 show they don't run completely on chipsets, there is motivation for such targeting. For instance, Set 3 has several instructions that would potentially speed up your code when run on a Power2 chipset. These instructions perform square root, float to integer conversion, and a quad work load and store. Quad load has the capability to load two immediately adjacent double-precision floating-point variables with one instruction. In FORTRAN or C programmers' terms, these instructions can improve the performance of floating-point-intensive applications that use double precision floating-point matrices, or square roots.

	Power	Power2	PowerPC 601	PowerPC 603	PowerPC 604
Common	Yes	Yes	Yes	Yes	Yes
Power	Yes	Yes	Yes	Emulation	Emulation
Power2	No	Yes	No	No	No
PowerPC	No	No	Yes	Yes	Yes

Table 6.1   Codeset comparison

Set 2 also contains float-to-integer and single-precision instructions. If your programs use single-precision or double-precision floating point, your programs may run faster on PowerPC when targeted for PowerPC.

6.1.1.4   Floating-Point Traps

On	Off	Default
qflttrap	qnoflttrap	qnoflttrap

If floating-point calculation exceptions are important to the results of your program, you need to investigate the use of the qflttrap, which can take several suboptions that can disable detection of certain exceptions. It is sufficient to say that without the suboptions, qflttrap enables extra code to check for overflow, underflow, division by zero, invalid operation, and inexact computation exceptions. If an exception is detected, then a trap is generated by signaling SIGFPE to your program. If you have a SIGTRAP handler function, it can take remedial action for the exception.

Please take note of the performance implication of this option. Specifying it will severely impact floating-point performance. Because the hardware floating-point units will operate in a nonpipelined mode, the exact point of exception is known. The default mode is to run in pipelined mode. If an exception occurs, that exception is simply noted by setting a bit in a floating-point status register.

If you must enable floating-point traps, you can do a compromise to detect exception and get reasonable performance at the same time. If you specify qflttrap=imprecise, the compiler will put exception check code only at the beginning and end of functions instead of after each floating-point operation. Furthermore, the hardware will run in pipelined mode and perform to its optimum. What you sacrifice in return is the ability to detect the exact instruction that caused the exception. Your trap handler will be able to conclude only that the exception occurred somewhere in that function.

I have not attempted to describe how to write trap handlers and recover from floating-point exceptions because my intent was only to inform you of the severe performance implications of the same. If you need more information, please consult *Optimization and Tuning Guide for Fortran, C, and C++*.

6.1.1.5 Compact Code Generation

On	Off	Default
qcompact	qnocompact	qnocompact

Optimization levels 2 and 3 both cause the object code to be larger than unoptimized object code. Such techniques such as loop unrolling, strength reduction, and branch optimization in loops can generate more instructions that actually execute more quickly. This code expansion can be noticeable but usually not more than 50%. If code expansion is a concern, you can still optimize, but tell the optimizer to prioritize code size over code speed by specifying qcompact. This option will surely not improve code speed, but it may not harm it significantly either. My experience has shown that this option is rarely useful because buying more RAM is cheaper than buying a faster CPU. However, if you have a special application that has some sort of tight loop, it is possible that specifying qcompact might cause a sufficient reduction in code size. In such a case, the code fits into the instruction cache better and thus performs faster. It is possible, but not probable—try it if you must.

6.1.1.6 General Function Inlining

On	Off	Default
qinline	qnoinline	qnoinline

Functions, if they are extremely short, can be dominated by the function linkage. It might be advantageous to eliminate the linkage instructions by putting the function inline at the point of call. A secondary benefit is the improvement of the instruction cache locality. Quite often programmers use preprocessor macros instead of functions so that the code is placed at the point of call rather than generating linkage to the function that resides elsewhere. It is possible to inline the function without having to resort to preprocessor macros.

C++ has a function modifier, called inline, that instructs the compiler to inline that particular function. Ordinary C does not have this language modifier. If you specify qinline, the compiler will inline C functions that are less than 20 executable statements. If you want to inline functions longer than 20 statements, you can specify that threshold with qinline=30, which would inline functions less than 30 statements.

Inlining has some negative aspects of which you should be aware. It requires that the function be included in the source of the compilation. You might have to change your program source to make this true. If the number of functions to be inlined is large, changing your source may be a big effort. If a function is called from many places in a program, inlining can cause object-code expansion that might offset any performance gained from omitting linkage code.

Be aware that in C inlining is not performed unless optimization is also specified. Also be aware that specifying `qinline` for a C++ program does not accomplish anything. The C++ compiler will inline only functions that are declared to be inline in the program source.

My experience shows that using qinline is an unknown proposition, similar to using O3. Sometimes it's good and sometimes it isn't. If it's good, do it.

6.1.1.7 Floating-Point Optimizations

There are several options that specify floating-point trade-offs between accuracy and speed. The qfloat options make the most sense when used in conjunction with O or O3. The on value tends to improve performance but in some way is not compliant with IEEE 754 floating-point standards. These on values tend to produce results that are more precise than IEEE 754 specifications dictate. Usually more precise is good, but sometimes you need to reproduce results to the same degree of accuracy calculated on a different system.

First, let me describe how some of these options can be used in different combinations to achieve certain performance and standards characteristics. Then I will describe what each option means when specified alone.

Be aware that the default float settings for the XL C and XL FORTRAN compilers do not conform to IEEE standards. The default setting produces results that are more accurate than IEEE standards dictate. This increased accuracy also produces greater performance, which is the main motivation for choosing them as defaults. To state this another way, if you require IEEE 754 standard conformant floating-point arithmetic, you should specify the following float options:

```
qfloat=norsqrt:nofold:nomaf
```

If you are using the O3 option and you want IEEE standard arithmetic, you should specify `qstrict`, in addition to the above qfloat options.

If you have any doubts as to whether you should turn any of these on, you shouldn't. In other words, these options are for numerical computation experts who have an intense understanding of their programs and the values of the computations. Discussion of floating-point standards is beyond the scope of this book. I suggest you read *Risc System/6000 NIC Tuning Guide for Fortran and C* to learn more about such topics.

On	Off	Default
qfloat=fltint	qfloat=nofltint	with O2, qfloat=nofltint
		with O3, qfloat=fltint

Float-to-integer conversion is performed inline rather than calling a library routine. This inline-conversion routine does not check the float variable to ensure that it is within the range of an integer. Usually an out-of-range conversion would cause an exception trap; it is the lack of exception checking that makes your code both potentially faster and IEEE nonconformant. Note that `qstrict` will turn off `fltint`.

On	Off	Default
qfloat=fold	qfloat=nofold	qfloat=fold

Floating-point constant expressions are calculated at compile time rather than at runtime. The expression would be saved in the program data and then simply loaded instead of being computed at program runtime. The more frequent the occurrence of expressions and the more complex the expression, the more the potential benefit.

On	Off	Default
qfloat=hsflt	qfloat=nohsflt	qfloat=nohsflt

Range checking is not done for single-precision calculations or for conversion from floating-point-to-integer values. This option is similar to `fltint` in that range checking is avoided, and, therefore, a potential program speedup is produced. It is one of those potentially "dangerous" options that can produce incorrect results. You should not use this option unless you can be sure of the ranges of the floating-point values.

On	Off	Default
qfloat=hssngl	qfloat=nohssngl	qfloat=nohssngl

Single-precision expressions are converted to double precision when the architecture option value is anything except `ppc`. The `hssngl` allows intermediate expressions to be kept in double precision and rounded only when the value is stored into a single-precision memory location. Avoiding rounding intermediate results to single precision is the potential performance payback. This option may achieve similar payback compared to `hsflt`, but `hssngl` is safer since range checking is done when single-precision to double-precision rounding occurs. Also note that if a single-precision variable is never changed, then operations on it are not affected by `hssngl`.

On	Off	Default
qfloat=maf	qfloat=nomaf	qfloat=maf

The multiply-add float (`maf`) instruction typifies the superscalar design of the PowerPC architecture. The `maf` instruction can multiply two floating-point values together and add the result to a third value—all in one processor cycle. The `maf` option is on by default and instructs the compiler to use `maf` instructions. I suggest leaving this option set because turning it off is likely to kill the floating-point performance of your program. Not only will the performance be slower, but the results are likely to be less accurate than those produced with maf.

On	Off	Default
qfloat=rndsngl	qfloat=norndsngl	qfloat=norndsngl

The rndsngl specifies that all single-precision variables are to be rounded after each operation; the default is to delay rounding until a full expression has been evaluated. Note that norndsngl is a more moderate attempt at avoiding single-precision rounding compared to hssngl. Hssngl says to round only when the variable must be stored to memory; norndsngl says to round only when a full expression has been evaluated. Expressions are evaluated much more frequently than variables are saved.

On	Off	Default
qfloat=nans	qfloat=nonans	qfloat=nonans

The nans option generates more instructions to detect not a number (NaN) values during single- to double-precision conversion. If your program does not generate NaNs, don't specify nans, since performance will be potentially slower.

On	Off	Default
qfloat=rsqrt	qfloat=nosqrt	qfloat=nosqrt

The rsqrt allows expressions that involve division by a square root to be replaced with a multiplication by a reciprocal square root. This substitution can potentially improve performance because division is a much costlier operation than multiplication. The speed improvement can be on the order of five to ten times. Since reciprocal square root can be calculated in a time similar to square root, avoiding division can make a noticeable speed improvement.

On	Off	Default
qstrict	qnostrict	qnostrict

The strict option is needed only in conjunction with O3 in order to achieve IEEE conformance when using O3 optimization. The qstrict option is simple shorthand for the following options:

    qfloat=nofltint:norsqrt

6.1.2   XL FORTRAN Unique Flags

The only performance-related option that is used exclusively with the XL FORTRAN compiler is the high-order transformation (hot) option.

On	Off	Default
qhot	qnohot	qnohot

Hot allows the compiler to perform complex matrix optimizations like loop interchange, loop unrolling, and loop blocking. These types of optimizations were formerly done by hand in order to increase the performance of applications that perform floating-point operations on large arrays. Descriptions of these techniques are outside the scope of this book. I suggest reading *Optimization and Tuning Guide for Fortran, C, and C++* and Kevin Dowd's *High Performance Computing*.

6.1.3   XL C Unique Flags

The only performance-related option that is used exclusively with the XL Cset++ compiler is the unroll option.

On	Off	Default
qunroll	qnounroll	qnounroll

It potentially performs loop unrolling in a manner similar to the hot option on the XL FORTRAN compiler.

6.2   Linker

The AIX linker is a remedy tool that helps your program to use virtual memory efficiently. Dynamically linked objects, or libraries, can be shared among several process address spaces, thus having the potential to reduce the amount of virtual memory used. The idea is to take from a static library a common chunk of code that would be copied several times into several different executables and create a single copy that could be shared among these same several executables. There is a small execution time price to pay for this flexibility; therefore, I will show you how to link with both static objects and dynamic objects.

First, let me define what a dynamic object is in terms of how to tell a dynamic object from a static object. If the object has a "loader section," then the object is dynamic; if the object does not have a loader section, it is static. The loader section is a part of the executable image that the kernel loader uses to determine which symbols need to be resolved.

For example, Figure 6.3 shows the loader section of a program I will use to illustrate dynamic objects. The dump command with the H option dumps the loader section header. Figure 6.4 shows the same command attempted on an object produced by the compiler. Note that the file command cannot distinguish shared objects from dynamic objects.

I do make a distinction between dynamic objects and shared objects. A dynamic object can be shared or nonshared, although it is usually shared because that is the primary

```
file hdump
hdump:              executable (RISC System/6000) or object module not stripped
dump -H hdump

hdump:

                        ***Loader Section***
                     Loader Header Information
VERSION#             #SYMtableENT      #RELOCent         LENidSTR
0x00000001          0x0000000b        0x00000013        0x00000020

#IMPfilID           OFFidSTR          LENstrTBL         OFFstrTBL
0x00000002          0x0000020c        0x00000018        0x0000022c


                     ***Import File Strings***
INDEX   PATH                        BASE              MEMBER
0       .:/usr/lib:/lib
1                                   libc.a            shr.o
```

Figure 6.3   Dump report of loader section

```
file hdump.o
hdump.o:            executable (RISC System/6000) or object module not stripped
dump -H hdump.o

hdump.o:

Loader Section is not available
```

Figure 6.4   Dump report of nonexistent loader section

advantage for creating dynamic objects. A static object is usually not considered to be either shared or nonshared. However, because the object code is copied into the text section, the code that is linked from a static object has a redundant copy for every unique executable. Therefore static objects are technically nonshared. Even though static objects within an executable may exist as multiple copies, the multiple processes invoking the same executable do share the text segment.

Figure 6.5 shows executable spreadsheet being run by several users. The user processes all share the same text for the spreadsheet executable. Figure 6.6 shows more executables being run by these same users. These three unique executables do not share the text portion among the user processes; the gui object is a part of each of the executables. There are three copies of this code. Figure 6.7 shows these executables changed by dynamically linking to the gui shared dynamic object. Only the text portion of the object is shared; each process receives its own copy of the data portion of gui. Figure 6.8 shows

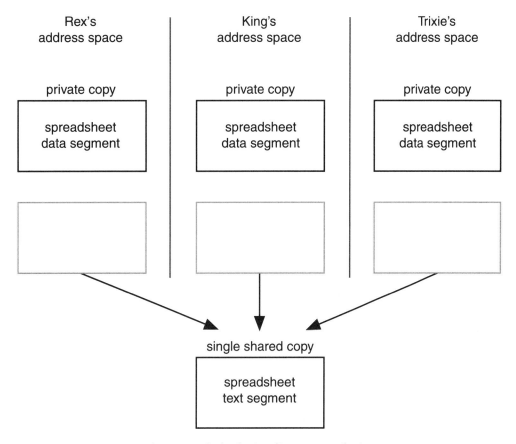

Figure 6.5   Code-sharing diagram—no sharing

these executables now changed again by linking them to gui as a nonshared dynamic object. Note that the text portion of gui is copied.

In order to calculate the potential virtual memory savings, you need to determine which objects are sharable and then the cumulative size of their text. The size command will report text sizes of compiler and linker objects. If the potential memory savings is not very large, it may be disadvantageous to create shared objects. The work in the creation may not be worth a minuscule memory payback, but there are other paybacks to creating dynamic objects that may affect your decision. Other reasons to create dynamic objects are faster linking of the main executable, ease in distributing code, and ease in manipulating code while in the development phase.

6.2.1   Dynamically Linked Objects

Since the compiler produces static objects, it is necessary to use the linker to produce dynamic objects. The idea is to collect one or more static objects and link them together to

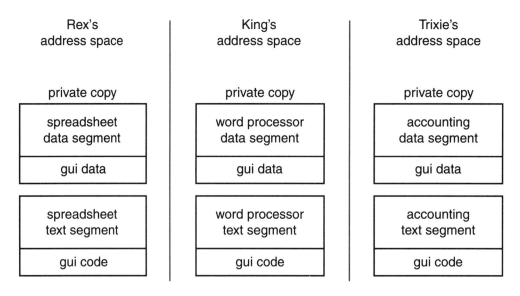

Figure 6.6   Code-sharing diagram—potential sharing opportunity

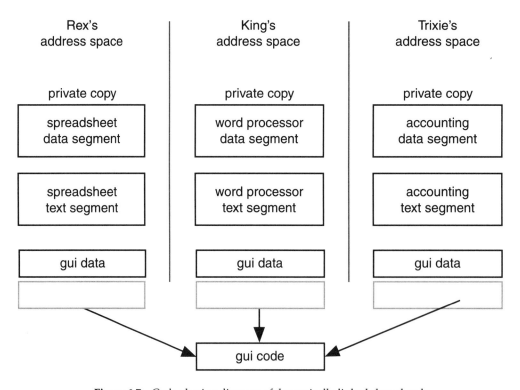

Figure 6.7   Code-sharing diagram of dynamically linked shared code

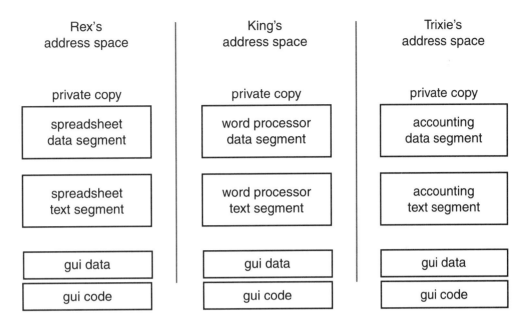

Rex's address space	King's address space	Trixie's address space
private copy	private copy	private copy
spreadsheet data segment	word processor data segment	accounting data segment
spreadsheet text segment	word processor text segment	accounting text segment
gui data	gui data	gui data
gui code	gui code	gui code

Figure 6.8   Shared code diagram—dynamically linked unshared code

produce a dynamic object that exports symbols to satisfy external symbol references from other objects. An object that uses an exported symbol imports that symbol. The loader section lists all the imported and exported symbols that an executable uses.

I'll use the hdump program as a simple example. The program consists of hdump.c, shown in Figure 6.9, and hexout.c, shown in Figure 6.10.

```
#include <stdio.h>
#include <fcntl.h>
main(argc, argv)
char *argv[];
int  argc;
{
FILE     *f1;
int      fd;
int      rc;
char     tbuf[BUFSIZ];
char     *fn;

if ( argc == 1 )
{
        fd = fileno(stdin) ;
        fn = "STDIN";
}
```

Figure 6.9   Example hdump.c (*continued on next page*)

```
else
{
        if((fd = open(argv[1],O_RDONLY,0)) == -1 )
            {
            perror(argv[1]);
            exit(1);
            }

        fn = argv[1];
}

printf("\ nFILE NAME: %s\ n\ n",fn );

while((rc = read(fd,tbuf,BUFSIZ)) == BUFSIZ)
    hexout(tbuf,rc);

if(rc)
    hexout(tbuf,rc);
}
```

Figure 6.9   Example hdump.c (*cont.*)

```
#include <stdio.h>
#include <string.h>
static long    aoff = 0;

hexout(cmd,cc)
char    *cmd;
int     cc;
{
int     i,j;
char    hstr[60];
char    astr[19];
char    tbuf[10];

while(cc)
    {
    strcpy(astr,"[................]");
    strcpy(hstr,"");

    for(i=0,j=1;i<16 && cc>0;i++,j++)
        {
        cc--;
        sprintf(tbuf,"%02X",*(cmd+i));
        strcat(hstr,tbuf);
        if(j==8)
            strcat(hstr," - ");
        else
            strcat(hstr," ");
```

```
        if(isprint(*(cmd+i)))
            {
            astr[j] = *(cmd+i);
            }
        }
    cmd+=16;
    printf("%08X: %-50s %s\ n",aoff,hstr,astr);
    aoff += 16;
    }
}
```

Figure 6.10   Example `hexout.c`

Figure 6.11 shows the makefile that builds `hdump`, a hex dump formatter. Since compiling is not of concern here, I just used the built-in rules for compiling `.c` files. `Hdump` is the main executable, and `dump.shr.o` is the shared object that contains only `hexout`. If this were a more realistic example, `dump.shr.o` would contain lots of functions made from lots of .o files. Hdump imports hexout from dump.shr.o automatically because dump.shr.o is a dynamic object and `hexout` is explicitly exported. The exports file, `dump.exp`, contains the single word `hexout`. If I had been building a larger dynamic object, the exports file would have more symbols listed, one per line. This exports file is mandatory for creating the dynamic object. If the object didn't export anything, it wouldn't be dynamic.

```
# You probably want to set the LIBS variable to something different
LIBS = -L.

hdump:      hdump.o dump.shr.o
            cc -o hdump $(LIBS) hdump.o dump.shr.o

dump.shr.o: hexout.o
            ld -H512 -T512 -o dump.shr.o -bE:dump.exp hexout.o -lc
            chmod 555 dump.shr.o
```

Figure 6.11   Dynamic linking makefile, method 1

Note the `chmod` command after the link of `dump.shr.o`. This ensures that the dynamic object is sharable. If the file permissions are readable for everyone, the object is sharable and is loaded in the system-shared text segment when the executable is run. If the file permissions are not readable for everyone, the object is not sharable and is loaded into the process private segment. This is the only time the system will map a code-persistent file into a working segment. If you happen to get the permission wrong, the object you intended to share may not be shared at all; make sure your makefile performs a `chmod` on any shared objects you create.

Please take note of the `L` option used to build the `hdump` command. It has nothing to do with performance, but its use is a common stumbling block. I set the `L` library search directory to the current directory in order to test the command. You would most likely set it to a full directory name of the eventual library path. See InfoExplorer for more details on how to use L and libpath options of the ld command. Also see information on the LIBPATH environment variable.

With the advent of AIX 4.2, the linker has acquired some new functions that make creating dynamic objects easier. In particular, you can dispense with creating the dreaded exports files. What other UNIX systems did, and what AIX now does, is to presume that every global symbol in an object be exported. This eliminates the burden of creating an exports file by hand, which is rarely done anyway. What had typically been done is to create an exports file mechanically with a shell script that used nm to dump the external symbol table. The linker will automatically create such an exports list, if you specify the bexpall option. Figure 6.12 shows the makefile that you would use on AIX 4.2 to create a shared object. Note that the -bnoentry prevents the warning message that the makefile Figure 6.11 would produce.

```
# You probably want to set the LIBS variable to something different
LIBS = -L.
hdump.new: hdump.o dump.shrn.o
            cc -o hdump.new $(LIBS) hdump.o dump.shrn.o

dump.shrn.o: hexout.o
            ld -H512 -T512 -o dump.shrn.o -bexpall -bnoentry hexout.o -lc
            chmod 555 dump.shrn.o
```

Figure 6.12   Dynamic linking makefile, method 2

Remember that the new link options don't mean that the old method has stopped working. If you have working makefiles that were developed on AIX 4.1 or earlier, these will still do the same thing they have always done.

If your shared object contains any C++ code, you must use the shell script /usr/lpp/xlC/bin/makeC++SharedLib to create your shared object. This script does all the things that I mention doing, and more, to accommodate C++ static constructors.

6.2.2   Statically Linked Objects

Now that you know how to create a dynamic object, you know how to link dynamically. Linking with a dynamic object automatically creates dynamic links to that object, but there is a way to override that behavior and link a dynamic object statically. The only performance-related reason for doing this is to avoid the external linkage penalty, which is only about 9 cycles, very small for a dynamically linked routine of any appreciable size. If you did call very short execution-time routines in a dynamic object very frequently, you might gain a small percent improvement in execution time. I statically linked hdump and was unable to measure any execution-time reduction even when repetitively looping hdump for several minutes.

Even though I could not improve hdump by linking statically, I will show you how to do it. The first approach is to link everything statically. Figure 6.13 shows the makefile that does the link. The important option that makes this link static is bnso, which means "no shared object." Here shared object is equivalent to dynamic object. I was also forced to add `bI:/lib/syscalls.exp` to the link options in order to make the system calls resolve. This is because `libc` is being linked statically. System calls are resolved through `libc.a`, which in turn resolves them through the AIX kernel, `/unix`. Since you specify `bnso`, the automatic import via `libc` is overridden. The `bI` option refers to an import file that imports the system calls directly from `/unix` rather than from `/usr/lib/libc.a`. This extra import is needed only when statically linking `libc.a`.

```
hdump.static: hdump.o libdump.a
              cc -o hdump.static $(LIBS) hdump.o -bI:/lib/syscalls.exp -bnso -ldump
libdump.a: hexout.o
              ld -H512 -T512 -o libdump.a -bE:dump.exp hexout.o -lc
              chmod 555 dump.shr.o
```

Figure 6.13   Static linking makefile, method 1

Also note I changed the name of the shared object, which I named `dump.shr.o` in Figure 6.11. I called the output file `libdump.a` so I could use `-ldump` shorthand on the link line. This has nothing to do with my wanting to link statically; I just wanted to show you that names of objects are completely arbitrary. This trick may sound odd to you, but I think it's cool. It's only an old naming convention that says that any file called `libxxx.a` is an archive created with the `ar` command. In this case, `libdump.a` is the direct output of the `ld` command. Subsequent links with a flat object (not an archive) are actually more efficient than if I had created an archive with `ar`. Remember that using `ar` was a handy way to package a bunch of `.o` files from the compiler in an easy-to-manipulate file. I use the past tense because using `ld` to do this packaging is even handier—just eliminate a redundant step of using `ar`.

Statically linking any system library is risky business. The risk has nothing to do with performance, but rather with incompatibility. The library implementation may change in future releases and possibly make your application incompatible with the new release. `Libc` is the riskiest library to link statically; I suggest never statically linking with it.

Figure 6.14 shows how statically to link `hdump` partially. I want to link only `libdump.a` statically, but link `libc.a` dynamically. This requires a two-pass link. The first link does a partial link, statically linking `hdump.o` (which is the main routine) and `libdump.a` (which contains `hexout`). The second link creates the executable that is dynamically linked to `libc.a`.

```
hdump.staticpx: hdump.o libdump.a
                ld -o hdump.temp.o -r -bnso hdump.o $(LIBS) -ldump
                cc -o hdump.staticpx $(LIBS) hdump.temp.o
                rm hdump.temp.o
```

Figure 6.14   Static link makefile, method 2

AIX 4.2 has added some shorthand to make static and dynamic linking much easier. Figure 6.15 shows how to use the `bstatic` and `bdynamic` options to switch between static and dynamic linking. The `bstatic` options turn on static linking for any libraries that follow, which, in this case, is only `libdump.a`. The `bdynamic` switches to dynamic linking for all the libraries that follow, which implicitly happens to be `libc.a`. You can switch between static and dynamic as many times as you wish.

```
hdump.staticp: hdump.o libdump.a
cc -o hdump.staticp $(LIBS) hdump.o -bstatic -ldump  -bdynamic
```

Figure 6.15   Static link makefile, AIX 4.2 method

6.3   Profilers

Profiling tools are used to isolate suboptimal code by identifying which portions of the code are executed the most. These frequently executed portions are known in the vernacular as hot spots. Profilers, a type of magnifying glass tool, are used after a more basic tool, such as `vmstat` or `tprof`, shows that a particular program has a CPU-performance bottleneck. A profiler will produce a list of program objects sorted in order of the most heavily executed. These program objects are either functions or source statements.

We will use `linpack` as a victim application program. `Linpack` performs many of the matrix calculations that are used in solving systems of linear equations; it is a good program to illustrate profiling because it has a very obvious hot spot. See Appendix A for locations to obtain `linpack` source code.

6.3.1   `Tprof` Revisited

Let's review how you use `tprof` because I'm now going to show you how to delve deeper into a process with the intent of possibly changing the program code.

The pertinent compile flags to use are

```
CFLAGS=-O -g
```

I emphasize compiling with the same optimization flags as you normally use to build your application. The debug flag (`-g`) may look odd for a profiling flag, but we will soon see why this is needed.

The `tprof` command that I used is

```
tprof -x linpack 100 2000 >lp.out
```

The `__prof.all` file shown in Figure 6.16 shows results similar to those in Chapter 3.

The `linpack` process takes the lion's share of the ticks, which is probably obvious if you know that `linpack` is a CPU-bound program. Since most of the time shows up under the user column, what kind of other detail can we see?

I now run `tprof` again and see some different reports. Note that I have to run `tprof` in the same directory as the source. If you cannot run it in the source directory, then use symbolic links to a different directory in order to make it appear that the source files are in the same directory. Use

```
tprof -p linpack
```

Process	FREQ	Total	Kernel	User	Shared	Other
linpack	**1**	**3648**	**6**	**3638**	**4**	**0**
gil	4	34	34	0	0	0
sh	2	14	5	6	3	0
init	1	10	1	9	0	0
X	1	9	7	2	0	0
tprof	3	7	3	4	0	0
swapper	1	4	4	0	0	0
xautolock	1	4	2	0	2	0
expr	1	2	2	0	0	0
afsd	1	1	1	0	0	0
xclock	1	1	1	0	0	0
XDiary-aix32bin	1	1	0	0	1	0
Total	18	3735	66	3659	10	0

Figure 6.16 Tprof report, linpack example

Note that this invocation does not run linpack again; only specification of the x option causes the program to be run. Omitting the x option tells tprof to use the existing raw data from a previous run. Now there are lots more files to examine.

First let's look at the __linpack.all file, shown in Figure 6.17. I have omitted the first part of __linpack.all because it looks identical to __prof.all. Skip down to the bottom section of the file, and you will see a list of linpack functions given in order of how many ticks they used. Also note that this section shows a percentage of the total time, so it is a lot easier to determine which functions to examine in greater detail.

```
Total Ticks For linpack(    USER) =    3638
```

Subroutine	Ticks	%	Source	Address	Bytes
.daxpy_ur	**1116**	**29.9**	linpackcalc.c	268438596	448
.matgen	**1000**	**26.8**	linpackcalc.c	268441924	340
.daxpy_r	**983**	**26.3**	linpackcalc.c	268439416	236
.dgefa	253	6.8	linpackcalc.c	268441008	916
.idamax	206	5.5	linpackcalc.c	268437400	304
.dscal_ur	27	0.7	linpackcalc.c	268437704	404
.dscal_r	26	0.7	linpackcalc.c	268439044	156
.dgesl	24	0.6	linpackcalc.c	268439652	1356
.second	2	0.1	second.c	268442376	136
.gettimeofday	1	0.0	glink.s	268442512	36

Figure 6.17 Tprof report of subroutine profile for linpack

Let's look at the top three functions. Because I compiled with debugging enabled, all the functions have their own "tick" files. Tprof uses the line number information in the debugger section of the executable to map addresses to line numbers. Let's look at __t.daxpy_r_linpackcalc.c, shown in Figure 6.18.

```
Line    Ticks   Source

  502      -    if (n <= 0)
  503      -        return;
  504     49    if (da == ZERO)
  505      -        return;
  506      -
  507     87    if (incx != 1 || incy != 1)
  508      -            {
  509      -
  510      -        /* code for unequal increments or equal increments != 1 */
  511      -
  512      -            ix = 1;
  513      -            iy = 1;
  514      -            if(incx < 0) ix = (-n+1)*incx + 1;
  515      -            if(incy < 0)iy = (-n+1)*incy + 1;
  516      -            for (i = 0;i < n; i++)
  517      -                {
  518      -                dy[iy] = dy[iy] + da*dx[ix];
  519      -                ix = ix + incx;
  520      -                iy = iy + incy;
  521      -                }
  522      8        return;
  523      -            }
  524      -
  525      -    /* code for both increments equal to 1 */
  526
  527      -    for (i = 0;i < n; i++)
  528    828        dy[i] = dy[i] + da*dx[i];
  529      -        }
972 Total Ticks for daxpy_r in linpackcalc.c
```

Figure 6.18   Tprof hotlist for linpack example

Note that line 528, which is the heart of the daxpy multiply loop, is the most heavily executed. I don't have any optimizations to recommend, because the code is so simple that it is
already optimal. However, this spot in the code is the hottest spot. All that tprof can do is to
lead you to the program hot spots; you have to figure out how to put out the fire yourself.

Let me show you another version of linpack. I compiled it in the same manner as
before, but I linked things differently. Instead of statically linking all the compiler objects,
I linked the routine containing daxpy_ur into a shared object. (Section 5.2.1 discusses
this method in detail.) There is no good reason to statically link other than I needed an
example to show how tprof profiles share object code. Figure 6.19 shows the
__prof.all file from this run:

```
tprof -x linpackmain 100 2000 >lp.out
```

When we look at this version of the __prof.all file, we see that the total ticks count is
about the same as that in Figure 6.16, but the ticks show up in the shared column instead
of the user column. Tprof treats shared objects differently than an ordinary executable.
To get more detail on a program that has a significant CPU percentage in the shared column, you must use the s option:

```
tprof -s
```

Process	FREQ	Total	Kernel	User	Shared	Other
linpackmain	1	3648	8	0	3640	0
gil	4	21	21	0	0	0
sh	2	14	4	6	4	0
X	1	11	9	1	1	0
wait	1	8	8	0	0	0
tprof	2	8	5	3	0	0
XDiary-aix32bin	1	2	0	1	1	0
expr	1	2	2	0	0	0
xautolock	1	1	1	0	0	0
trace	1	1	1	0	0	0
Total	15	3716	59	11	3646	0

Figure 6.19   Tprof report of dynamically linked linpack

Now when we look at the __prof.all file, we see a shared object report at the bottom, as shown in Figure 6.20. Note the same three routines show up in the hot list. Unfortunately there is no way to generate a statement-level hotlist as we could when using the -p flag. The linpack.sp.com object was indeed compiled with the O and g options, but tprof isn't smart enough to use this information.

Let's look at a more complex example just to illustrate the real world, which tends to be more complex than linpack. I chose to look at xrn, the X news reader, which does a little bit of a lot of things: It performs file I/O, X graphics, network I/O, and miscellaneous

Total Ticks For All Processes(SH-LIBs) =   3646

Shared Object	Ticks	%	Source	Address	Bytes
linpack/linpack.sp.com/	3635	97.8	/tools/SRC/BENCH	4747264	7449
libc.a/shr.o	10	0.3	/usr/lib	880	990393
libXm.a/shr4.o	1	0.0	/usr/lib	4870312	1785147

Profile: /tools/SRC/BENCH/linpack/linpack.sp.com

Total Ticks For All Processes(/tools/SRC/BENCH/linpack/linpack.sp.com) =   3635

Subroutine	Ticks	%	Source	Address	Bytes
.daxpy_ur	1108	29.8	linpackcalc.c	2484	448
.daxpy_r	1003	27.0	linpackcalc.c	3304	236
.matgen	967	26.0	linpackcalc.c	5812	340
.dgefa	272	7.3	linpackcalc.c	4896	916
.idamax	191	5.1	linpackcalc.c	1288	304
.dgesl	35	0.9	linpackcalc.c	3540	1356
.dscal_ur	32	0.9	linpackcalc.c	1592	404
.dscal_r	24	0.6	linpackcalc.c	2932	156
.second	2	0.1	second.c	6264	136
.linpack	1	0.0	linpackcalc.c	512	776

Figure 6.20   Tprof dynamic object report for linpack example

internal bookkeeping. I decided to look at reducing the start-up time from command invocation to the time the first screen is ready. I immediately hit quit to terminate xrn and ran tprof with more than one option, just to show that you can do this:

```
tprof -p xrn -s -x xrn
```

Note that because I specified the p option, no __prof.all file is created. Instead, everything is put into the __xrn.all file.

Figure 6.21 shows the first part of the report. Note that 11.94 seconds of a total of 24.11 seconds is spent in shared library code, while 6.54 seconds is spent in user code. Figure 6.22 shows the shared library report. This profile is fairly flat. The most frequent routine is called number; after searching the xrn code, that number is not called directly, so it must be called indirectly. Later we will try to use other tools to try to find out what the call hierarchy to number is.

Process	FREQ	Total	Kernel	User	Shared	Other
xrn	1	1932	84	654	**1194**	0
wait	1	236	236	0	0	0
X	1	91	37	26	28	0
jfsc	1	90	90	0	0	0
gil	4	23	23	0	0	0
sh	2	15	5	6	4	0
fvwm	1	10	2	6	2	0
tprof	2	6	4	2	0	0
xautolock	1	2	2	0	0	0
FvwmPager	1	2	2	0	0	0
aixterm	1	2	1	0	1	0
afsd	1	1	1	0	0	0
expr	1	1	1	0	0	0
Total	18	2411	488	694	1229	0

Figure 6.21   Tprof report for xrn example

Shared Object	Ticks	%	Source	Address	Bytes
libc.a/shr.o	1138	47.2	/usr/lib	880	990393
libXt.a/shr4.o	50	2.1	/usr/lib	4324608	324246
libX11.a/shr4.o	6	0.2	/usr/lib	2941096	639782

Profile: /usr/lib/libc.a shr.o

Total Ticks For xrn(/usr/lib/libc.a) =   1138

Subroutine	Ticks	%	Source	Address	Bytes
.number	171	7.1	../../../../../../../src/bos/usr/ccs/lib/libc/doscan.c	83720	3732
.$PTRGL	109	4.5	ptrgl.s	284332	64
.malloc_y	70	2.9	../../../../../../../src/bos/usr/ccs/lib/libc/malloc_y.c	14100	1288
.__wctomb_sb	69	2.9	../../../../../../../src/bos/usr/ccs/lib/libc/__wctomb_sb.c	216124	80
._doscan	65	2.7	../../../../../../../src/bos/usr/ccs/lib/libc/doscan.c	76936	2732
.wctomb	56	2.3	../../../../../../../src/bos/usr/ccs/lib/libc/wctomb.c	215548	112

Figure 6.22   Tprof report of dynamic objects for xrn example

The second most frequent routine is $PTRGL, which is an internal routine that is the "pointer glue" code that performs linkage to a shared library routine. This code is written in assembler, so I doubt if there is any way to improve it.

The third routine is malloc_y, which is one of the malloc worker routines in libc. We do have some suspicion that perhaps, at most, a 3% speedup could be achieved if calls to malloc were somehow reduced. Xrn does call XtMalloc, which calls malloc in libc. There are a lot of these calls that might be consolidated, but remember that, at most, you could gain only 3%. A gain of 3% is not sufficient payback in my opinion.

Figure 6.23 shows the user portion profile, which is also very flat. Here there are no obvious opportunities that would get more than a small percent improvement, but I will leave it as an exercise for the reader to discover if any other speed-up possibilities exist.

```
Total Ticks For xrn(    USER) =    647

        Subroutine   Ticks     %                                                    Source   Address   Bytes
      ==============  ======  ======                                               =======   =======   =====
        .anyIterator    111    4.6                                                buttons.c  268660488    596
   .adjustMinMaxLines    62    2.6                                                buttons.c  268664628    688
      .setTranslations   42    1.7                                                buttons.c  268661084    324
        .DumpChildren    30    1.2  ../../../../../../../src/gos/2d/XTOP/lib/Xmu/EditresCom.c  268446332    336
     .artNextFunction    28    1.2                                                 artMode.c  268659740    228
        .DumpWidgets     25    1.0  ../../../../../../../src/gos/2d/XTOP/lib/Xmu/EditresCom.c  268446140    192
         .readnewsrc     23    1.0                                              newsrcfile.c  268503128   1376
   ._XEditResGetString8  23    1.0  ../../../../../../../src/gos/2d/XTOP/lib/Xmu/EditresCom.c  268449944    260
```

Figure 6.23   Tprof report of subroutine profile of xrn example

6.3.2   Gprof

We saw that tprof showed where most of the time was spent in linpack, but it did not show any information about who calls whom. Call lineage is important where no one routine takes up a large proportion of time. If you could view how much time a routine and all its downstream children take, this might give you insight on avoiding those costly calls.

The gprof utility is a profiler that has one similarity to tprof; it samples the program counter to determine which parts of the program are spending the most time. The differences from tprof are greater than the similarities. The first difference you encounter is the way that the program must be compiled and linked. Shown here are the compile and link flags that you must use in order to have executables generate profiling data:

```
CFLAGS=-O -pg
LDFLAGS=-pg
```

Note how the compile flags (CFLAGS) are different from those used for tprof. I added the pg option to enable gprof profiling. Also note that pg is needed for the link-time flags (LDFLAGS). This is an important but often forgotten step. If gprof profiling fails to work, ensure that you have specified pg for both compile and link-time flags.

Another difference is that gprof can look at only one process, whereas tprof looks at the entire system. You use tprof to determine which program is giving you the most trouble and to examine detail about a particular program for which you don't happen to possess the source code. To get the greater detail that gprof affords requires recompiling the source in order to intercept subroutine calls and count them. Gprof will both count how many times a subroutine is called and remember which subroutine called it. Tprof can't perform this sort of counting and call hierarchy determination.

After rebuilding your application to enable gprof, the only thing left to do is to run it. First, you need to run the application in a writeable directory because the binary output file, gprof.out, is created there. Second, the application must exit before the gmon.out file is created. If the application runs as a daemon or is otherwise impossible to terminate, gprof will not work for you. Requiring the program to exit is another negative to using gprof that doesn't exist with tprof.

Once you run the application and create the gmon.out file, the only thing necessary is to run gprof with no arguments. Gprof puts its report on stdout, so you will probably want to redirect output to a file.

Figure 6.24 shows sample output of the linpack program. I have omitted the report prologue, which is a descriptive tutorial on what the various fields of the report mean, but I have included a section from the call graph profile. The index column is a routine number beginning with main. The last section of the report, which I have also omitted, is a list of routines sorted by name showing the index number. I skipped to routine number 4,

```
                                  called/total        parents
index  %time    self descendants  called+self         name       index
                                  called/total        children
       ------------------------------------------------------------------

               1.52      13.00      2000/2000          .linpack [1]
 [4]    56.2   1.52      13.00      2000               .dgefa [4]
               6.25       0.00   1225000/1324000       .daxpy_ur [5]
               5.47       0.00   1225000/1324000       .daxpy_r [6]
               0.96       0.00     98000/98000         .idamax [10]
               0.24       0.00     49000/49000         .dscal_ur [12]
               0.09       0.00     49000/49000         .dscal_r [15]

       ------------------------------------------------------------------

               0.50       0.00     99000/1324000       .dgesl [9]
               6.25       0.00   1225000/1324000       .dgefa [4]
 [5]    26.1   6.75       0.00   1324000               .daxpy_ur [5]

       ------------------------------------------------------------------

               0.44       0.00     99000/1324000       .dgesl [9]
               5.47       0.00   1225000/1324000       .dgefa [4]
 [6]    22.9   5.91       0.00   1324000               .daxpy_r [6]
       ------------------------------------------------------------------
                                                       <spontaneous>
 [8]    18.2   4.69       0.00                         .__mcount [8]
```

Figure 6.24   Gprof report for linpack example

the most interesting to examine. The routine dgefa is on the same line as the index number. The parent of the routine, linpack, is on the line right above. All of the children routines are listed on lines right below. The %time column tells you that dgefa and all of its progeny take 56% of the total CPU time, that is, 13 seconds. The self column means different things, depending on whether we are discussing the routine, the parent, or the children. Self for the routine is the CPU seconds in the routine only, but not in any of the progeny. Dgefa took 1.52 seconds, all of which is attributable from calls from linpack. Note that linpack is the only parent of dgefa, so that line also has 1.52 seconds.

Index 5 shows daxpy_ur, which has two parents, dgefa and dgesl. Daxpy_ur (it has no children) takes 26.1% of the total CPU time, 6.75 seconds. Of that, 6.25 seconds were from calls from dgefa and .50 seconds from calls from dgesl. All of these figures were obtained from the self column.

The descendants column for the routine dgefa (index 4) shows that 13 seconds were spent in all descendants of dgefa. You can verify this by adding 6.25 + 5.47 + .96 + .24 + .09, which is 13.01. The extra .01 is a round-off tax, which you should send to me in care of the publisher!

The called column is the total number of times the routine was called, which for dgefa is 2000. Daxpy_ur was called a total of 1,324,000 times; 99,000 of these were calls from dgesl, and 1,225,000 were calls from dgefa.

Look at mcount, which took up 18.2% of the total CPU time. Mcount is the routine that the compiler inserts into the code to count subroutine calls. Running a gprof-enabled application will typically take 10% to 25% more overhead compared to a normally linked application.

6.3.3 Xgprof

You have seen the useful information that gprof gave you about linpack. Recall that Performance Toolbox can let you visualize numerical data from reports such as vmstat and iostat; the xgprof tool lets you visualize numerical data from gprof in a graphical way similar to the Performance Toolbox.

Xgprof uses the same gmon.out file as does gprof. I kept the gmon.out file that was generated and ran xgprof with no arguments, as shown in Figure 6.25. Figure 6.26 shows the initial screen that appears.

Note that there are about five large boxes. I picked the largest of these and pulled down a menu with the left button. This square represents daxpy_ur, which showed up as index 5 both in gprof and xgprof. Note that the call count of 1,324,000 and the CPU usage of 6.75 seconds matches the gprof report. I selected "immed parents" and got the next screen, as shown in Figure 6.27.

This expansion of the immediate parents of daxpy_ur shows the familiar names of dgesl and dgefa and the number of calls made by each. Another way to zoom in is to set filters from the filter menu. Figure 6.28 shows a calls filter window set to select the five topmost call arcs. (An arc is a line from one node or box to another.)

If you like to see the gprof ASCII reports, there is no need to run gprof because xgprof will produce the call profile, flat profile, and index in scrollable and searchable windows. There is one feature in xgprof that doesn't exist in gprof, however. If you

```
xgprof
xgprof:  opening gmon.out
xgprof:  gathering load information
xgprof:      100001C8 linpack
xgprof:      D017CAE4 /lib/profiled/libc.a : meth.o
xgprof:      D046F4A0 /lib/profiled/libc.a : shr.o
xgprof:  reading executable and library symbol tables
xgprof:      linpack
xgprof:      /lib/profiled/libc.a : meth.o
xgprof:      /lib/profiled/libc.a : shr.o
xgprof:  gathering sampling data
xgprof:      100001C8-100028DC  linpack
xgprof:      D017CAE4-D017CAE8  /lib/profiled/libc.a : meth.o
xgprof:      D046F4A0-D0520EE0  /lib/profiled/libc.a : shr.o
xgprof:  gathering call graph data
xgprof:  performing statistical analysis
xgprof:  0 cycles
xgprof:  sorting
xgprof:  time 6 seconds
```

Figure 6.25   Xgprof initial ASCII output

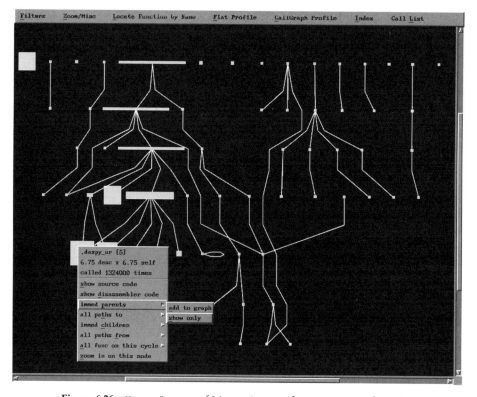

Figure 6.26   Xgprof screen of linpack example, daxpy_ur subroutine

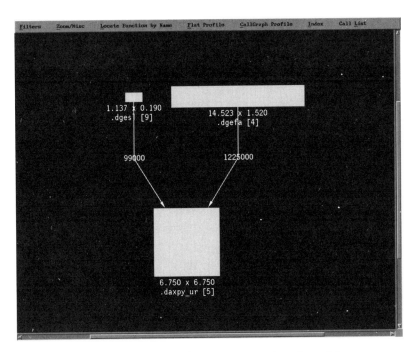

Figure 6.27 Xgprof screen of linpack example, callers of daxpy_ur

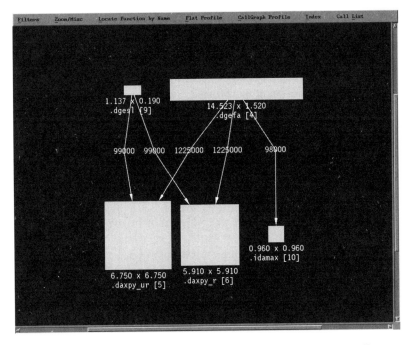

Figure 6.28 Xgprof screen of linpack example, five topmost calls

compile with the debug option (-g), gprof can produce a statement-level hotlist just like tprof does. If you select the "show source code" item, as shown in Figure 6.26, you will get the screen shown in Figure 6.29. Type daxpy_ur in the search line; hit return until the function body scrolls into view. Lines 649–652 are the busiest lines in daxpy_ur.

```
save      includes

line     no. ticks     source

603
604               /*
605               ** constant times a vector plus a vector.
606               ** Jack Dongarra, linpack, 3/11/78.
607               ** UNROLLED version
608               */
609               static void daxpy_ur(int n,REAL da,REAL *dx,int incx,REAL *dy,int incy)
610
611                   {
612                   int i,ix,iy,m;
613
614                   if (n <= 0)
615                       return;
616          15       if (da == ZERO)
617                       return;
618
619          51       if (incx != 1 || incy != 1)
620                       {
621
622                       /* code for unequal increments or equal increments != 1 */

Search:

daxpy_ur
```

Figure 6.29   Xgprof screen of linpack example, code hotlist

6.4   Debugging

The next group of tools would most properly be classified as debugging tools because the level of detail they uncover is at the program-event level. These tools can tell you which parts of the program were executed in which order. Since events are being recorded in their entirety, the amount of data that event-recording tools collect can be huge compared to the profiling tools. Debugging tools would also be classified as microscope tools because the data being gathered is very detailed and interesting to a small audience.

6.4.1   Trace

There are some questions that tprof cannot answer about xrn behavior. What contributes to the wait time as shown by the ticks on the wait process? Who are the callers to number? Let's tackle the first question by using a detailed AIX tools called trace, which traces kernel events. A process sleeping due to a system call causes wait, and a system call trace can show where the wait transitions are.

Figure 6.30 shows how you would capture a trace to examine details about xrn. Note that 20 seconds of real-time execution produces two files exceeding 13 megabytes in size. The size of the data files produced is a definite barrier to tracing programs for long periods of time.

```
trace -a -L10000000 -s -o trace.raw ;xrn; trcstop
trcrpt -o trace.report -Oexec=on,pid=on trace.raw
ls -l trace.*
-rw-rw-rw-   1 chukran   system     2189336 Apr   4 16:18 trace.raw
-rw-------   1 chukran   system    11962380 Apr   4 16:22 trace.report
```

Figure 6.30   Trace command example

Before we delve into the xrn trace, let me describe a representative section of the trace report so you can understand the meaning of the fields. Figure 6.31 shows a trace portion with all the interesting fields occupied. ID is the trace hook ID, which is interesting if you want to omit trace hooks from the report. Process name is the command name that you will get only if you specify Oexec=on in the trcrpt command. PID is the process ID that is helpful in keeping track of processes, if you have many with the same name. I is the interrupt indicator; a 1 in this column means the event is a hardware interrupt of some kind. The running time line in seconds is ELAPSED_SEC, and the delta time difference between the current event and the immediately previous event in units of milliseconds is DELTA_MSEC. The remaining four columns describe the event. If the description starts in the particular column, the event is one that occurs in the application, system call interface, intrakernel, or interrupt. The trace will have no application events unless someone writes trace calls in the application. InfoExplorer tells you how to do this. A SYSCALL event is either an entry into a system call or an exit out of a system call and back to the application. A trace will mostly have events internal to the AIX kernel, and these are often useful to examine. Note that the open-system call does not give any meaningful data, but the lookuppn call right after it gives the file name being opened. There are too many events to describe in this book what they mean. Unfortunately there is no AIX documentation that fully describes these events; you just have to use your AIX internal knowledge and general intuition to read traces.

```
ID  PROCESS NAME   PID       I    ELAPSED_SEC    DELTA_MSEC  APPL  SYSCALL KERNEL   INTERRUPT
101 xrn            22470          0.270383360     0.067584          open LR = D00009D8
107 xrn            22470          0.270383360*                              lookuppn: /usr/lib/X11/nls/nls.ldx
100 xrn            22470          0.270793216     0.409856                            I/O INTERRUPT
102 xrn            22470     1    0.270812416     0.019200                            slih clock [10004 usec]
234 xrn            22470     1    0.270835712     0.023296                   clock:   iar=9B00 lr=C8FD0 [10001 usec]
103 xrn            22470     1    0.270918912     0.083200                            return from slih [106 usec]
106 xrn            22470     1    0.270940672     0.021760                   dispatch:   cmd=xrn pid=22470 tid=22485
                                                                                                      priority=64 old
                                                                          _tid=22485 old_priority=64 CPUID=0 [3628 usec]
200 xrn            22470     1    0.270947584     0.006912                   resume   xrn
10D xrn            22470          0.271470848     0.523264                            vfs number=0006, inode number=2B830
```

Figure 6.31   Trace report

If we examine the trace.report file and search for the dispatch of the wait process, we find the lines shown in Figure 6.32. A page fault causes this particular idle event, although grep tells me there are more than 500 of these events, and you don't want to examine each one of these individually.

```
ID  PROCESS NAME    PID    I  ELAPSED_SEC  DELTA_MSEC  APPL  SYSCALL KERNEL  INTERRUPT

1B0 xrn             22470     0.082341120   0.045056         VMM page assign:        V.S=808F.0000 ppage=0A11
                                                               working_storage system_segment modified
1B9 xrn             22470     0.082348288   0.007168         VMM zero filled page: V.S=808F.0000 ppage=0A11
                                                               working_storage system_segment modified
200 xrn             22470     0.082362368   0.014080         resume   xrn
100 xrn             22470     0.082608640   0.246272                 DATA ACCESS PAGE FAULT
1B2 xrn             22470     0.082620928   0.012288         VMM pagefault:          V.S=03BC.280A
                                                               working_storage modified
1B0 xrn             22470     0.082670848   0.049920         VMM page assign:        V.S=03BC.280A ppage=0A33
                                                               working_storage modified
1BA xrn             22470     0.082721280   0.050432         VMM start io:           V.S=03BC.280A ppage=0A33
                                                               working_storage modified
                                                                 bp=7C710B0 B_READ
10B xrn             22470     0.082753280   0.032000         LVM lstart: rhd6 lbp=7C710B0 lblock=7710
                                                                             bcount=1000 B_READ opts:
10B xrn             22470     0.082808320   0.055040         LVM pstart: rhdisk0 pblock=8B910 (lbp,pbp)=
                                                                       (7C710B0,549 01E0) B_READ opts:
221 xrn             22470     0.082832128   0.023808         SCDISKDD strategy: bp=54901E0
221 xrn             22470     0.082897152   0.065024         SCDISKDD coalesce: (bp,sc_bp)=(0000,546E400)
221 xrn             22470     0.082908416   0.011264         SCDISKDD bstart: rhdisk0 bp=546E400 pblock=
                                                                       8B910 bcount=1000 B_READ
223 xrn             22470     0.082926848   0.018432         SCSIDD entry_strategy: errno: 00 devno:
                                                             00120000 bp: 0546E400 flags: 00048001 block: 571664 bcount: 4096
223 xrn             22470     0.082963712   0.036864         SCSIDD entry_bstart: errno: 00 devno:
                                                             00120000 bp=546E400 pblock=8B910 bcount=1000 B_READ
10C kproc           516       0.083162368   0.198656         dispatch:    idle process   pid=516 tid=517
                                                             priority=127 old_tid=22485 old_priority=63 CPUID=0
200 kproc           516       0.083174144   0.011776         resume    IDLE
```

Figure 6.32   `Trace` report, page fault

While we are looking at the `trace`, let's look at how the network I/O is done. Figure 6.33 shows a read on the network socket connection to the news server. Note two things of importance: The read has to block because there is no more data ready, and idle is dispatched. The reads are done in 4K buffer sizes (4K = 1000 hexadecimal), which is fairly large and efficient.

```
ID  PROCESS NAME    PID    I  . ELAPSED_SEC  DELTA_MSEC  APPL  SYSCALL KERNEL  INTERRUPT

104 xrn             22470     1.706632448    0.095232          return from 07EFD93C. error EACCES [125 usec]
101 xrn             22470     1.706671104    0.038656          kreadv LR = D0042D10
163 xrn             22470     1.706692864    0.021760          read(9,2003B1C0,1000) SOCKET
253 xrn             22470     1.706711808    0.018944              SOCK soreceive soaddr=05A3B400 paddr=
                                                                  00000000 uio=2FF3B240 mpo=0 contrl=00000000
460 xrn             22470     1.706744576    0.032768              e_assert_wait:    tid=22485 anchor=
                                                                              5A3B46C flag=1 lr=42684
462 xrn             22470     1.706776832    0.032256              e_block_thread:    tid=22485 anchor=
                                                                              5A3B46C t_flags=0020 lr=4280C
10C kproc           516       1.706816256    0.039424          dispatch:    idle process   pid=516
                                                                          tid=517 priority=127
                                                                        old_tid=22485 old_priority=72 CPUID=00
200 kproc           516       1.706825216    0.008960          resume    IDLE
```

Figure 6.33   `Trace` report, socket call

6.4.2   `Trace` **Postprocessing Tools**

Let's use the `trace` of xrn described in Section 6.4.1 and perform some data reduction on it with the `utld` tool. First reorder the binary trace with `trcrpt`, and then create a `namelist` file with `trcnm`, as shown in Figure 6.34. The `utld` command uses the `trace` and the `namelist` to produce two output files. Figure 6.35 shows the system summary

```
trcrpt -r trace.raw > trcrpt.r
trcnm >trcnm
utld -i trcrpt.r -o utld.out -n trcnm -d

ls -lt
-rw-------    1 chukran   system        13566 Apr  5 18:19 utld.out
-rw-------    1 chukran   system        35660 Apr  5 18:19 utld.out.details
-rw-------    1 chukran   system        71557 Apr  5 18:09 trcnm
-rw-------    1 chukran   system      2187976 Apr  5 18:09 trcrpt.r
```

Figure 6.34 Utld command example

```
                           SYSTEM SUMMARY

        processing          percent        percent
        total (msecs)       tot  time      busy time    processing category
        =============       ========       ========     ====================
          22515.114          77.363         87.838      APPLICATION
            833.159           2.863          3.250      KERNEL
           1389.989           4.776          5.423      FLIH
            860.906           2.958          3.359      SLIH
             33.261           0.114          0.130      DISPATCH
        -------------       --------       ---------
          25632.430          88.075        100.000      CPU(s) busy time
           3470.622          11.925                     WAIT
        -------------       --------
          29103.052         100.000                     TOTAL
```

Figure 6.35 Utld system summary report

section of the utld.out file. Figure 6.36 shows the application summary sorted by process using the most CPU time. This information is similar to that presented by tprof, but with one important difference: The tprof data is obtained by sampling 100 times per second and is subject to some error. The utld data is a data reduction of a trace, which captures all kernel events. The utld data would not have sampling error and would be more accurate than tprof. What's more, utld does a nice job of calculating percentages. Recall that you have to calculate most of these percentages by hand when using tprof. The downside to using utld is that you must run a full trace, which takes more data to guarantee accuracy.

```
             APPLICATION and KERNEL SUMMARY (Per Thread/Process)

--  processing total  (msecs) --   -- percent of total processing time --
   combined   application   kernel    combined      app    kernel   process name (proc id / thrd id)
   ========   ===========   ======    ========      ===    ======   ================================
 18286.732     17903.262   383.470     62.834    61.517    1.318    xrn   ( 22470  22485 )
  3390.254      3390.254     0.000     11.649    11.649    0.000    kproc ( 3506   4539 )
   954.308       643.769   310.540      3.279     2.212    1.067    X     ( 15410  15937 )
```

Figure 6.36 Utld application summary report

I find the most valuable part of the utld report is the detail report. Figure 6.37 shows the detailed system call report that is in the utld.out.details file. This report notes that read and write were the busiest system calls as far as xrn is concerned. You would have to produce a full trace report and examine the system calls in context to determine what the sequence and the arguments are. Often you will need to consult the program source code to find the system call invocation point and then determine if the code is optimal. You would normally not need to run trace and utld unless you needed more detail than tprof provides. In particular if the xrn tprof report had reported a high percentage of system ticks, you would probably want to rerun the scenario with trace and utld to get a system call breakdown.

Utld is not part of the AIX product and therefore may be difficult to obtain. See Appendix for sources for utld.

```
DETAILED PROCESS REPORT
SYSTEM CALLS AND APPLICATION TIMES PER PROCESS
**************************************************


                   PROCESS xrn ( thread 22485   proc id 22470 )

processing        percent              - path in msecs        -
total (msecs)    proc time    count     -min-     -avg-    -max-    system call
=============    =========    =====    =====     =====    =====    ============
   152.295         0.523    000000386    0.000     0.395    0.744    kreadv
   124.008         0.426    000000214    0.261     0.579    2.120    kwritev
    23.192         0.080    000000001   23.192    23.192   23.192    _exit
    16.075         0.055    000000019    0.295     0.846    2.070    open
    14.604         0.050    000000123    0.104     0.119    0.347    select
     6.284         0.022    000000042    0.025     0.150    0.221    smt_load
     5.845         0.020    000000002    2.047     2.923    3.798    unlink
     5.480         0.019    000000009    0.366     0.609    0.964    access
     4.318         0.015    000000009    0.291     0.480    1.321    statx
```

Figure 6.37   Utld detailed process report

6.4.3   Program Visualizer

You saw how difficult it was to read traces, but you can also see the valuable data they contain. Now we will examine a tool, Program Visualizer (pv), that takes a trace and lets you more easily visualize the meaning of the reams of text data with colored graphs. The trace data is collected with a script that calls trace and omits lots of unnecessary trace hooks; consequently it produces a much smaller trace file.

The following shows how to trace xrn; it is similar to using trace directly:

```
pvtrace xrn
ls -l *.trc
-rw------- 1 chukran system 1622516 Apr 5 10:38 xrn.trc
```

Start pv with no arguments, and you get the screen shown in Figure 6.38. Select the tracefile menu and the xrn.trc file in the dialog. Then select the Configuration pulldown menu as shown in Figure 6.39, and choose the `system.cfg` configuration. Punch the forward-play arrow button in the main window, and let the tracefile play back. I let the playback run for about ten seconds and hit the pause button; the resulting screen is shown in Figure 6.40.

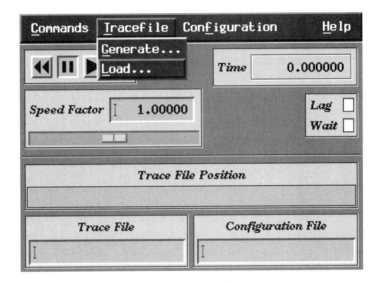

Figure 6.38   Pv initial screen

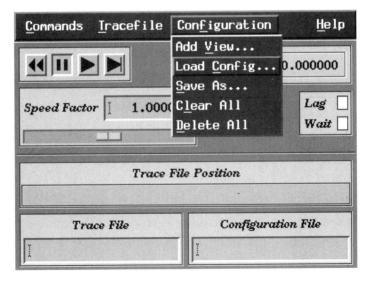

Figure 6.39   Pv screen, step 2

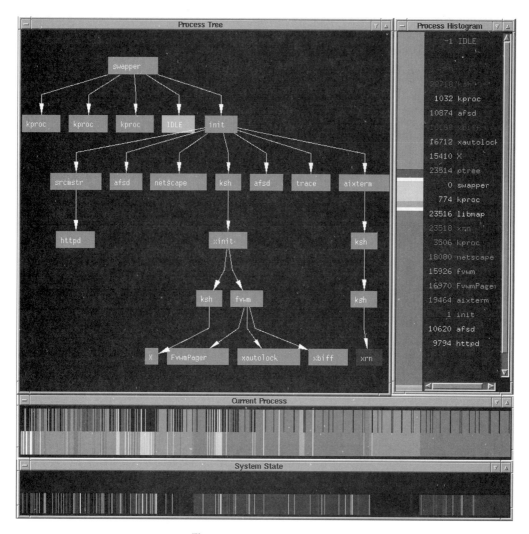

Figure 6.40   Pv screen, step 3

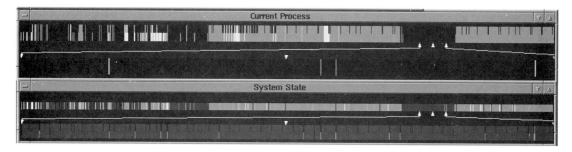

Figure 6.41   Pv screen, step 4

Figure 6.41 shows the current process menu after you select zoom with the menu that is activated by mouse button 3. This zoom feature allows you to look for obvious things like idle time, which shows up in the process window as dark blue and in the system-state window as red.

The `pv` documentation has an excellent tutorial that walks you through all the fine points of operating `pv`. It uses a real example of a research project whose performance was improved significantly by use of `pv`. The real trace data for this exercise is provided, and you can use these tutorials as a real-life example of features that can be used to solve real problems.

Since `pv` is not part of the AIX product, you may have trouble obtaining it. See Appendix for information on obtaining `pv`.

6.5   Summary

The most important points in this chapter are:

1. Optimum use of compiler flags has the potential to speed up CPU-bound applications. The most effective flag that you should use is the optimization (`-O`) flag.

2. The AIX linker and kernel loader have the capability of sharing common code among related processes, and they consequently use less virtual memory.

3. Profilers such as `tprof`, `gprof`, and `xgprof` provide a look into where the most time is being spent in CPU-bound applications.

4. Debugging-level tools such as `trace` and `pv` allow programmers to examine detailed sequences of system events that may enable you to determine suboptimal behavior.

7

Remedies for Programmers

This chapter addresses what a programmer should change once the programmer's tools identify bottlenecks.

7.1 System Calls

If your system CPU percentage is predominantly system CPU-bound, it would be wise for you to understand which system calls are most heavily used. Smart choices regarding system calls can make the difference between programs that lumber and those that fly. Profiling techniques discussed in Chapter 6 enable you to determine which and how many system calls your program executes. You can then use your code optimization skills to eliminate unnecessary system calls.

Knowing which system calls to use when there is a choice is difficult. This section will concentrate on how to make choices for system calls that have significant performance implications.

7.1.1 Read and Write

The most commonly used system calls are `read` and `write`. These can be called either directly or indirectly via `fread`, `printf`, `putc`, and other similar higher-level I/O functions. Programmers should be concerned about the buffer size when coding `read` and `write` calls. If the program is reading or writing a file on the filesystem, the minimum buffer size that should be used should match the filesystem page size, 4K for AIX. This size is not a coincidence; the VMM performs I/O to the filesystem in units of pages.

Therefore a program that tries to get or put data into smaller pieces is bound to perform suboptimally, especially in sequential I/O.

If you recall the description of read-ahead in Chapter 2, performing I/O in buffer sizes smaller than the page size will delay the engagement of read-ahead and, therefore, will decrease throughput. It would even be preferable to read or write in units of 4 to 16 pages. I can't give you a single optimal value to use, because the buffer size depends on several factors such as CPU speed, disk speed, disk controller type, striping factor, and so on. You will have to experiment with buffer size to find an optimum, but a general rule of thumb is: larger is faster, to a point. The size of diminishing returns will probably be less than 128K.

If you are concerned about portability and do not wish to experiment to find the optimum buffer size, I suggest you set your I/O buffer size to match the MAXBUF definition in stdio.h. Each UNIX vendor chooses this value to be an optimum for the platform. MAXBUF is 4096 on AIX. Following is an example of how you would code this:

```
#include <stdio.h>
#define MYIOBUFFERSIZE MAXBUF
read(fd,buffer,MYIOBUFFERSIZE);
```

7.1.2   Interprocess Communication

The issue of interprocess communication is second only to I/O system calls in popularity and confusion. You can make several choices from among system calls that cause processes, or threads, to communicate or synchronize. There are two major types of synchronization calls. One is a simple, mutual exclusion lock that protects a critical section of code from having more than one process executing in the critical section. These types of calls are

```
_check_lock / _clear_lock
msem_lock / msem_unlock pair
pthread_mutex_lock / pthread_mutex_unlock
semop
cs
```

The second type of synchronizing call signifies an event with perhaps some transfer of data. The data transfer calls are

```
msgsnd / msgrcv
socket send and receive calls
kill (signal)
```

These choices present varying degrees of speed, portability, and difficulty of debugging. Table 7.1 summarizes the speed of choices in interprocess calls. (These calls were measured on AIX 4.1, running on a PowerPC 604 CPU.) The programs that exercised these calls were designed to use a blocking call. The second column represents the overhead per call that involves a process block and subsequent task switch. The third column represents the overhead of a call that does not involve a task switch.

System call	Blocking overhead	Nonblocking overhead us
_check_lock	N/A	00.22
_clear_lock	N/A	00.04
cs	N/A	00.30
msem_lock msem_unlock	20.17	00.34
FAST pthread_mutex_lock pthread_mutex_unlock	12.08	00.48
pthread_mutex_lock pthread_mutex_unlock	01.56	01.10
semop	21.02	05.36
msgsnd/msgrcv	27.34	N/A
pipe	36.24	N/A
socket	48.24	N/A
kill (signals)	69.29	N/A

Table 7.1 Synchronization call overhead

It is interesting to note that the slowest calls happen to be the most mature UNIX system calls. Because System V semaphores, message queues, sockets, pipes, and signals are so pervasive in the UNIX domain, I won't go into details on how to use them. Instead, I suggest you consult *Advanced Programming in the UNIX Environment* by Stevens on the use of these system calls. Suffice it to say that these calls are portable but slow. If you value performance, don't rely on them, for they will certainly become a performance bottleneck. I will discuss the remaining interprocess calls in detail. These remaining calls are not yet standard and present some portability concerns. In other words, these AIX calls do not exist on all UNIX platforms. You would choose these if you are concerned more about speed than portability.

7.1.2.1   PowerPC Weak Memory Ordering

One of the characteristics of superscalar RISC architectures is the instruction unit or units that execute instructions "out of order." It is possible for instruction N, in a sequence of linear instructions with no branches, to complete after instruction N+1. See Figure 7.1 for a simple example of a pseudo assembler language to understand why out-of-order execution is useful.

```
C code fragment
b++;
c=a++;

Psuedo machine assembler language
1          load      r1,a
2          load      r2,b
3          inc       r1,1
4          inc       r2,1
5          store     r1,c
6          store     r1,a
7          store     r2,b
```

Figure 7.1   Pseudo assembler code for execution ordering

This is a seven-instruction fragment that might possibly represent code for the C language fragment. Note that, for this fragment, c depends on a, a depends on a, and b depends on b. Let's assume that b is in the processor cache and takes one cycle to access. Note that neither a nor c is in the cache, and both take ten cycles to access.

While the data fetch unit is loading a, the instruction decode unit has already decoded instruction 2. This load does not depend on anything; therefore the load can be done in parallel with instruction 1. In fact, the memory fetch will complete faster because of the location being cached. The decode unit will decode instruction 3 and discover that it depends on instruction 1, which is not yet complete. Instruction 2 will proceed with instruction 4 and decode it on "speculation" that it will eventually have to be executed. Once it is decoded and discovered that the instruction is not conditional, it can be executed by the fixed-point unit, since that instruction doesn't depend on anything. Instruction 5 is next; it involves r1, which can't go until instruction 3 is done. So the instruction stream will stall and wait for a to be fetched; then instructions 3 and 5 can complete.

Instruction 6 can't proceed until 3 and 5 are done, but instruction 7 can proceed if instructions 2 and 4 are done. Instruction 7 would probably execute far ahead of instruction 5. Since b was cached, its memory access was very short, as is the register increment time (probably one cycle also). The data is stored into a small store buffer, and the memory subsystem will take care of updating cache and memory.

The important part of this scenario is not the exact order of when instructions complete; the order is not deterministic. That is, the order might change depending on the location and corresponding speed of access of the data, which PowerPC processor is running, and how many internal units it has that can operate in parallel. The instruction order may vary, but only if the interdependencies of the data permit it. More important, the order of memory update is not dictated by the order of instruction stream.

This concept of storing memory locations out of order is called a *weakly ordered memory system.* The PowerPC architecture permits this and gains performance as a result. Oddly enough this order is not important as long as your program is running on a uniprocessor; the CPU will ensure that the instruction stream correctly accesses data for that processor.

On a multiprocessor system, however, you must take some additional care when multiple threads attempt to access and update the same variable in memory. Your program must use a mutual exclusion lock to ensure that concurrent threads, or processes, don't erroneously update data while another thread is using it. If you don't know exactly how mutual exclusion locks work, I suggest you consult *Unix Systems for Modern Architectures* by Curt Schimmel.

Figure 7.2 is a simple illustration that builds on the example presented in Figure 7.1. Suppose that you want to consider the update of a few counters as a critical code section and surround it by a mutual exclusion lock. The update of the variables a, b, and c in memory must be complete before the unlock occurs. Otherwise, the variables could potentially end up with the wrong values because a C language increment operation cannot be done as an atomic operation. We will establish a convention that a mutual exclusion lock must also act as an instruction fence. That is, the instruction stream pipeline must be purged before the lock takes effect. Likewise, a mutual exclusion unlock must ensure that all pending memory updates are completed before the unlock takes effect. All of the system calls that AIX provides for mutual exclusion locking ensure that this convention is followed; therefore the mutual exclusion locks ensure correct operation on PowerPC hardware.

```
SETLOCK;
b++;  c=a++;
UNLOCK;
```

Figure 7.2 Instruction fence example

7.1.2.2 _check_lock **and** _clear_lock

The following system calls comprise a locking primitive pair that does not block:

```
boolean_t _check_lock( lock_word atomic_p , compare int, value
int )
void _clear_lock(destination atomic_p, value int )
```

Check_lock interrogates a full word lock and atomically sets it to a new value if the original value compares to a known value. (Note that I refer to the calls without the proper leading underscore in order to preserve the pleasant demeanor of my editor, who gets palpitations when sentences begin with underscores. Programmers should code with the underscore as shown in the examples.) In practicality, the scenario tests if the lock is unlocked and then sets its locked value. The programmer can assign any value to mean locked and unlocked. If the lock is already locked, check_lock returns false; that is, check_lock will not block the processes or act as a blocking semaphore. Both check_lock and clear_lock use memory-ordering fences to ensure they work as mutual exclusion locks on SMP systems.

The lock word can reside in any part of memory, but in reality the word must be sharable among several threads of execution. This means that the lock word can reside in the data static area or data heap for cooperating threads, or it can reside in a shared memory region for cooperating processes.

As Table 7.1 shows, check_lock has the lowest overhead of all the locking calls, but it does not block. I recommend you use check_lock with an optional spin loop and a way to block the process upon failure to obtain the lock. The spin loop would not be used on a uniprocessor, but on a multiprocessor, the spin count would ideally be externally tunable by the user. Figure 7.3 shows an example code fragment implementing my suggestions. Since check_lock does not block when the lock is not free, you must devise a means to have the thread sleep, once it becomes apparent that the lock will not be freed soon. The WAIT_FOR_LOCK routine will do just that.

```
#include <sys/atomic_op.h>
struct   lock_str
{
        atomic_p lockword;
        unsigned int waiters;
}  ;

struct lock_str *lockp;
struct lock_str lock1;    /* a typical lock in static storage */
unsigned int looplimit=100;
unsigned int num_processors;
#define BUSY 1
#define FREE 0

Mutex_example()
{
        int i;
        num_processors = sysconf(_SC_NPROCESSORS_ONLN);
        if ( !_check_lock( &lockp->lockword, FREE, BUSY) )
        {  /* if first try for lock fails, keep trying for a while    */
             while ( !_check_lock( &lockp->lockword, FREE, BUSY) )
             {
             /* loop only on a multiprocessor */
                  if (num_processors >= 1 )
                  {
```

```
                              for ( i=0; i< looplimit  ; i++)
                          /* at this point we must wait for lock to be freed() */
                                if ( _check_lock( &lockp->lockword, FREE, BUSY) )
                                {
                                        goto gotlock; /* Forgive me for my sin */
                                }
                          }
                          WAIT_FOR_LOCK();
                          /* at this point the lock owner has given it up
                          and we must try again and maybe compete with other
                          threads */


                      }
              }
              /* at this point we have the lock and can proceed */
gotlock:
              /* This is the critical section code */

/* time to unlock critical section here */

              _clear_lock(&lockp->lockword,FREE);
              WAKEUP_LOCK_WAITERS();
}
```

Figure 7.3   `Check_lock` code example

Figure 7.4 illustrates using System V semaphores to put the process to sleep. The
WAIT_FOR_LOCK routine is called only after several attempts at trying the lock with
check_lock. Note that repetitive lock attempts, called *spinlocks*, are avoided when the
system is a uniprocessor. A lock miss on a uniprocessor means that the lock holder is
either asleep or on the run queue, so continuing to spin will only delay releasing the lock.
Since waiting or sleeping involves a high overhead kernel call, it would be advantageous
to avoid them if possible. When the semaphore is used, a flag is set to denote that there
are threads waiting on the lock. This flag is used by the lock release notification routine,
WAKE_UP_LOCK_WAITERS, to reset the semaphore conditionally. Note that there are


```
#include <sys/ipc.h>
#include <sys/sem.h>
struct sembuf semwait = {  0,0,0} ;
int semid;


WAIT_FOR_LOCK()
{
        int rc;
        fetch_and_add(&(lockp->waiters),1); /* this is an atomic version of waiters++ */
        rc = semop( semid, &semwait , 1);
        semctl( semid, 0, SETVAL, 1);     /* put sem back the way we found it*/
        fetch_and_add(&(lockp->waiters),-1); /* this is an atomic version of waiters++ */
}
```

Figure 7.4   Locking code example (*continued on next page*)

```
WAKEUP_LOCK_WAITERS()
{
        if (lockp->waiters > 0)
        {
            /* wake up all waiters by clearing semaphore */
            semctl( semid, 0, SETVAL, 0);
        }

}
```

Figure 7.4   Locking code example (*cont.*)

three semaphore calls used, which makes for a fairly high-overhead means to suspend the thread. This would make for a high penalty for heavily contended locks.

7.1.2.3 Cs

The following call is obsolete:

```
int cs( destination *int , compare int, value int )
```

It does not implement memory-ordering fences and therefore will not work properly on an SMP system as a mutual exclusion lock. The problem is that the cs call is insufficiently designed and can be implemented using a fence. Here is how the cs call was to be used in AIX Version 3:

```
cs( lock, UNLOCKED, LOCKED)
..... critical code section ....
lock = UNLOCKED
```

Note that the lock call does not have a corresponding unlock call. The program must unlock the lock by simply storing the UNLOCKED value in it. If the AIX designers had created some sort of unlock call, they could have implemented memory fences for both, and both would continue to work today. Since there was no unlock call, there was no way to add the fence to the unlock sequence. However, the designers felt that it was best to declare that the cs call was obsolete and force programmers to use check_lock and clear_lock instead. If your application program uses cs, it will continue to work correctly on a uniprocessor system, but it will not work correctly on an SMP system.

7.1.2.4 Msem_lock **and** msem_unlock

Section 7.1.2.2 showed how to create your own complex locks using check_lock and clear_lock. Check_lock does not have the ability to sleep if the lock is already taken; msemaphores do. Figure 7.5 shows a code fragment using a msemaphore allocated in shared memory. In this particular case, the shared memory is allocated with the shmat call, but I could just as well have used the mmap call.

   The motivation for using the msemaphore instead of a System V semaphore (semop) is that the overhead for the uncontended, or nonblocking, case is 30 times less, as Table 7.1 shows. The design is such that the uncontended lock scenario is more prevalent than the

```
#include <sys/mman.h>
msemaphore *msem;
#define SOURCE_DONE    &msem[0]
/* code omitted */
    if ((shmad = shmat(shmid,0,0)) == (char *)-1) {
        perror("shmat");
        exit(errno);
    }
        /* allocate 2 msems at top of shared memory */
        msem= (msemaphore *)shmad;
        msem_init(SOURCE_DONE,MSEM_UNLOCKED);
/* more code omitted */
        msem_lock(SOURCE_DONE,0);
/*  critical code section here */
        msem_unlock(SOURCE_DONE,0);
```

Figure 7.5   Msemaphore code example

contended case. If this is so, then msemaphore msem_lock and msem_unlock will offer a performance advantage over semop.

Msemaphores are restricted; they must be allocated inside a shared memory segment. This is not too significant since they are intended to be used for synchronizing cooperating processes and somehow must be accessed in a shared, writeable region of virtual memory.

7.1.2.5 `Pthread_mutex_lock` and `pthread_mutex_unlock`

If your program uses pthreads interfaces, you must use the locking protocol pthread_mutex_lock and pthread_mutex_unlock. Pthread_mutex_lock behaves in much the same manner as msem_lock; they both block if the lock is already taken. The major difference between them is that a msemaphore must be allocated in shared memory, while a pthread_mutex must be allocated in the process private data segment, that is, either the static data area or the dynamic heap. A pthread_mutex will not work when shared between different processes.

Figure 7.6 gives an example of how to code using a pthread_mutex_lock. Note the pthread_mutexattr_setkind_np call, which makes the mutex a "FAST" mutex. Table 7.1 shows that FAST mutexes are about half the overhead of ordinary mutexes for the uncontended case. Unfortunately the contended case is about nine times the overhead of the "ordinary" mutex. You can't blindly choose to use FAST mutexes because of the very high contention overhead. There is a small limitation with a FAST mutex; it is "fast" because there is no checking to see if the mutex is already locked by the same thread. If you can be sure that your threads do not attempt to double lock a mutex, then you can use FAST mutexes. It would be nice if AIX provided some middle ground between a FAST mutex and a normal mutex; perhaps such a compromise mutex might be called a "HALF FAST" mutex, or FAST mutexes might improve over time for the contended case. For now, however, I suggest trying both kinds and running a representative test of your application to see which kind produces the better performance for your unique situation.

```
#include <pthread.h>
pthread_mutex_t *mutex;
#define PARENT_DONE    &mutex[0]
pthread_mutexattr_init(&ptmattr);
pthread_mutexattr_setkind_np(&ptmattr,MUTEX_FAST_NP);
pthread_mutex_init(PARENT_DONE, &ptmattr);
/* code omitted */
pthread_mutex_lock(PARENT_DONE);
/* critical code section here */
pthread_mutex_unlock(PARENT_DONE);
```

Figure 7.6 Pthread mutex code example

7.1.2.6   Atomic Arithmetic and Boolean Primitives

Figure 7.7 shows a very simple example of a common occurrence where a single value has to be atomically updated. I'll even presume that the unbounded while loop on lock success is acceptable, in which case this short critical section is as simple as possible.

```
while ( ! _check_lock( &lockword, FREE, BUSY); /* null while body */
counter ++;
clear_lock(&lockword, FREE);
```

Figure 7.7 Check_lock code example

By using an atomic call, as shown in Figure 7.8, the critical section becomes much simpler. The fetch_and_add call is implemented in assembler language and is truly able to perform an atomic increment. Not only is the code simpler, but it is also faster. Following is the list of atomic system calls that are available on AIX:

fetch_and_add

fetch_and_and

fetch_and_or

compare_and_swap

Fetch_and_and and fetch_and_or would be useful in atomically turning bits on or off in a status word. Compare_and_swap would be useful in inserting or deleting nodes in a linked list. Consult InfoExplorer for details on how to use them.

```
fetch_and_add(&counter, 1);
```

Figure 7.8 Fetch_and_add code example

7.1.3   Mapped File I/O

Performing I/O on a mapped file instead of on an ordinary file speeds up file I/O. The major distinction of a memory-mapped file is that the I/O can be made by simple access values from or to an array instead of accessing values in a buffer, which are subsequently copied with a `read` or `write` system call. Since the `read` or `write` is avoided, the extra data copy is avoided, thus reducing the amount of CPU time required. Table 7.2 shows the comparison between the AIX `cp` command and the `mcopy` program, illustrated in *Advanced Programming in the UNIX Environment* by W. Richard Stevens. Stevens did such an admirable job with the `mcopy` program that it compiled and ran on AIX without change, which is how porting UNIX programs should be—painless. Figure 7.9 illustrates the source code for `mcopy`. The `mcopy` program copies a source file to a destination file sequentially. The test I tried involved copying an 8MB file using both `cp` and `mcopy`. Note that the CPU time used for `mcopy` was about 50% less than that for `cp`. This example involved sequential I/O of two files, both of which fit entirely in the filesystem cache. The real-time benefit would tend to diminish as the files got larger and physical I/O was required. However, the CPU time benefit of mapped files would still be apparent. Mapped I/O to sparsely written files in a random fashion would benefit more than traditional I/O compared to sequential I/O. Updating a few variables in each file page of a mapped file would avoid the overhead of reading and writing bytes that do not change.

	User	System	User+system	Real
cp	0.12	1.45	1.57	1.57
mcopy	0.98	0.09	1.07	1.07

Table 7.2   Mapped file I/O overhead

The code in Figure 7.9 is taken from W.R. Stevens, *Advanced Programming in the UNIX Environment*, pages 411 and 412. © 1992 by Addison-Wesley Publishing Company, Inc. Reprinted by permission of Addison Wesley Longman.

```
#include <sys/types.h>
#include <sys/stat.h>
#include <sys/mman.h>  /* mmap() */
#include <fcntl.h>
#include "ourhdr.h"

#ifndef  MAP_FILE     /* 44BSD defines this & requires it to mmap files */
#define  MAP_FILE   0    /* to compile under systems other than 44BSD */
#endif
```

Figure 7.9   Mcopy code example (*continued on next page*)

```
int
main(int argc, char *argv[])
{
        int             fdin,  fdout;
        char            *src,  *dst;
        struct stat     statbuf;

        if (argc != 3)
                err_quit("usage: a.out <fromfile> <tofile>");

        if ( (fdin = open(argv[1], O_RDONLY)) < 0)
                err_sys("can't open %s for reading", argv[1]);

        if ( (fdout = open(argv[2], O_RDWR | O_CREAT | O_TRUNC,
                                                FILE_MODE)) < 0)
                err_sys("can't creat %s for writing", argv[1]);

        if (fstat(fdin, &statbuf) < 0)     /* need size of input file */
                err_sys("fstat error");

                        /* set size of output file */
        if (lseek(fdout, statbuf.st_size - 1, SEEK_SET) == -1)
                err_sys("lseek error");
        if (write(fdout, "", 1) != 1)
                err_sys("write error");

        if ( (src = mmap(0, statbuf.st_size, PROT_READ,
                        MAP_FILE | MAP_SHARED, fdin, 0)) == (caddr_t) -1)
                err_sys("mmap error for input");

        if ( (dst = mmap(0, statbuf.st_size, PROT_READ | PROT_WRITE,
                        MAP_FILE | MAP_SHARED, fdout, 0)) == (caddr_t) -1)
                err_sys("mmap error for output");

        memcpy(dst, src, statbuf.st_size);        /* does the file copy */

        exit(0);
}
```

Figure 7.9   Mcopy code example (*cont.*)

7.1.4 Network Socket Options

Chapter 6 discussed how to use the no command to change the default socket buffer sizes systemwide. The setsockopt call changes these buffer sizes on a socket basis. Figure 7.10 is a code fragment showing how to set the send buffer size for a socket; Figure 7.11 shows how to set the receive buffer size. Remember that the buffer size cannot be set larger than sb_max, which cannot be set by program control. This must be set with the no command as described in Chapter 5.

```
sendsize=32000;
setsockopt(socketfd,SOL_SOCKET, SO_SNDBUF, (char *) &sendsize, sizeof(sendsize) );
```

Figure 7.10 Setsockopt send buffer example

```
rcvsize=32000;
setsockopt(socketfd,SOL_SOCKET, SO_RCVBUF, (char *) &rcvsize, sizeof(rcvsize) );
```

Figure 7.11 Setsockopt receive buffer example

7.1.5   Dynamic Module Loading

In Chapter 6 I discussed the qarch compiler flag. I noted that setting the qarch value to anything other than common has the potential advantage of running a faster application and the definite disadvantage of the code not being able to run on any chipset but the one specified. One way to solve this problem is to create multiple versions of the application compiled with a different qarch option setting. There are disadvantages to this straight-forward technique: First, the physical media size goes up with more versions, as do support complications. Second, the correct version has to be installed on the system. It is possible to find out the architecture type at install time and install the right one, although this doesn't work for applications from a network server unless the server has some means at runtime to select different binaries based on the architecture of the client. There are network operating systems, such as Transarc AFS, that can determine architecture type, but it would be more flexible to have the program itself perform this determination.

Figure 7.12 shows an example of such a technique. I used the linpack program, one of those programs that performs better when compiled for a specific architecture than for a common architecture mode. The idea is to have the main program inquire of the architecture type and then load the appropriate module. The load system call is used to do the module load. Load is similar to exec in that a new program file is loaded into the address space. There are two major differences, though: First, the loaded program does not wipe out the program space of the program that did the loading. Second, no transfer of control is made to the loaded program. After loading, the main program is free to call one or more functions in the loaded module.

```
#include <stdio.h>
#include <stdlib.h>
#include <math.h>
#include <time.h>
#include <float.h>
#include <sys/systemcfg.h>

#ifndef PRECISION
#define PRECISION 1
/* 2 means double precision, 1 means single precision */
#endif
```

Figure 7.12 Dynamic loading code example (*continued on next page*)

```
#if !(PRECISION - 1)
#define ZERO        0.0
#define ONE         1.0
#define PREC        "Single"
#define BASE10DIG   FLT_DIG

typedef float    REAL;
#else

#define ZERO        0.0e0
#define ONE         1.0e0
#define PREC        "Double"
#define BASE10DIG   DBL_DIG
typedef double  REAL;
#endif

extern REAL linpack  (long nreps,int arsize, void *mempool);

struct cputab{
        int model_type;
        char *filename;
        } ;

#define LOADTABSIZE  3
#define DEFAULTFILE "linpack.sp.com"
struct cputab load_table[LOADTABSIZE] =
        {
                {  POWER_RS2, "linpack.sp.power2"} ,
                {  POWER_601, "linpack.sp.ppc"} ,
                {  POWER_604, "linpack.sp.ppc"}
        } ;

void main(int argc, char **argv )
{
    int     i, arsize;
    int lptr;
    int cpu_model;
    int rc;
    char *filetoload;
    long    arsize2d,memreq,nreps;
    size_t  malloc_arg;
            void *mempool;

/* load proper linpack module */
        cpu_model = _system_configuration.implementation;

        filetoload = DEFAULTFILE;            /* if no match , use default */

        for ( i=0; i< LOADTABSIZE; i++)
        {
                if ( load_table[i].model_type == cpu_model)
                    {
                            filetoload = load_table[i].filename;
```

Figure 7.12   Dynamic loading code example (*cont.*)

```
                              {
                                      filetoload = load_table[i].filename;
                                      break;
                              }
              }

        if ( !  (lptr = load( filetoload, 1, ".:/usr/lib" ) ))
/*      if filetoload is fully qualified pathname, 3rd arg can be null */
        {
                perror ("load failed ");
                exit (1);
        }
/* end load module */




              arsize=atoi(argv[1]);
        arsize/=2;
        arsize*=2;
        if (arsize<10)
              {
                      arsize=10;
              }
        arsize2d = (long)arsize*(long)arsize;
        nreps=atoi(argv[2]);

        memreq=arsize2d*sizeof(REAL)+(long)arsize*sizeof(REAL)+(long)arsize*sizeof(int);
        printf("Memory required:  %ldK.\ n",(memreq+512L)>>10);
        malloc_arg=(size_t)memreq;
        if (malloc_arg!=memreq || (mempool=malloc(malloc_arg))==NULL)
              {
              printf("Not enough memory available for given array size.\ n\ n");
                  exit(1);
              }
        printf("\ n\ nLINPACK benchmark, %s precision.\ n",PREC);
        printf("Machine precision:  %d digits.\ n",BASE10DIG);
        printf("Array size %d X %d.\ n",arsize,arsize);
        printf("Average rolled and unrolled performance:\ n\ n");
        printf("    Reps Time(s) DGEFA   DGESL  OVERHEAD    KFLOPS\ n");
        printf("----------------------------------------------\ n");
        while (linpack(nreps,arsize,mempool)<10.)
              nreps*=2;
        free(mempool);
            unload(lptr);
        printf("\ n");
```

Figure 7.12   Dynamic loading code example (*cont.*)

The example loads one of three architecture types. If the AIX system is running on a 601 or 604 chipset, a module compiled for PowerPC is loaded. If the system is a Power2 chipset, the Power2 module is loaded. If the chipset type is anything else, a common architecture mode module is loaded.

Figure 7.13 shows the makefile that compiles and links the linpack program. Figure 7.14 shows the contents of the import file, linpack.imp, that is used to link the main program, `linpackmain`. The contents of the file contains only one symbol, the `linpack` function. If main called more functions in the loaded module, then the import file should list each function name.

```
CFLAGS=-O -g

OBJS=linpackmain.o linpackcalc.com.o second.o linpackcalc.ppc.o linpackcalc.power2.o linpack linpackmain
linpack.sp.power2 linpack.sp.ppc linpack.sp.com linpackmain.1.o

all: linpackmain linpack.sp.power2 linpack.sp.ppc linpack.sp.com

# The main program is compiled for common and linked here
linpack: linpackmain.o linpackcalc.com.o second.o
        cc $(CFLAGS) -o linpack linpackmain.o  linpackcalc.com.o second.o

linpackmain.o: linpackcalc.c
        $(CC) -qarch=com $(CFLAGS) -DPRECISION=2 -o linpackmain.o -c linpackmain.c

# The different calculation modules are compiled here
linpackcalc.power2.o: linpackcalc.c
        $(CC) -qarch=pwr2 $(CFLAGS)   -DPRECISION=2 -o linpackcalc.power2.o -c linpackcalc.c

linpackcalc.ppc.o: linpackcalc.c
        $(CC) -qarch=ppc $(CFLAGS) -DPRECISION=2 -o linpackcalc.ppc.o -c linpackcalc.c

linpackcalc.com.o: linpackcalc.c
        $(CC) -qarch=com $(CFLAGS) -DPRECISION=2 -o linpackcalc.com.o -c linpackcalc.c
# The different module types are linked here

linpack.sp.power2: linpackcalc.power2.o second.o
        ld -e linpack -H512 -T512 -bE:linpack.imp -o linpack.sp.power2 linpackcalc.power2.o second.o -lc -lm

linpack.sp.ppc: linpackcalc.ppc.o second.o
        ld -e linpack -H512 -T512 -bE:linpack.imp -o linpack.sp.ppc linpackcalc.ppc.o second.o -lc -lm

linpack.sp.com: linpackcalc.com.o second.o
        ld -e linpack -H512 -T512 -bE:linpack.imp -o linpack.sp.com linpackcalc.com.o second.o -lc -lm
```

Figure 7.13   Dynamic loading makefile example

```
#!
linpack
```

Figure 7.14   Example import file, `linpack.imp`

Note that the `linpackcalc.c` file is not modified in any way for the different modules. There is only one function name, `linpack`, that is consistent for all the different load modules. Contrast this with an alternate method that does not use load. The architecture determination code would be the same, but instead of loading one module, the different modules are all linked statically into the main program. Each `linpack` routine would have to have a unique name. This is easy where there is only one function to call, but it would get out of hand if you had hundreds of different functions.

7.2   Hardware Type Inquiry

Until now I have not made any assumptions about the specific hardware that is running your application program, but there is an important trade-off to consider. The less your program knows about its environment, the more portable it will be. The more your program knows about its environment, the greater the opportunity to optimize for speed. Your program can intelligently inquire about the underlying hardware and use this information to make decisions about how to perform optimally.

Figure 7.15 shows an example of how to inquire about the hardware characteristics of your AIX system. You probably would not want to test every one of the features that the sample program tests, but you might want to inquire of the processor type so that you could call subroutines compiled with compiler flags that target a specific hardware architecture. You might also want to inquire whether the system is a multiprocessor system, that is, with the number of CPUs greater than one. This information would tell you whether it is useful to perform spin locks to lock program resources. You might also want to inquire about the level 1 cache size in order to perform blocking techniques in your matrix multiplication routines.

```
#include <sys/systemcfg.h>
/* purpose: to format contents of _system_configuration structure */

main()

{
        char **tempbuf;
/* architecture */
        if ( __power_rs() )
                tempbuf = "Power Classic";
        else
        if ( __power_pc() )
                tempbuf = "PowerPC";
        else
                tempbuf = "UNKNOWN";
        printf( " Architecture = %d = %s \ n",
                _system_configuration.architecture, tempbuf);

/* implementation */

        if ( __power_rs1() )
                tempbuf = "Multichip Power";
        else
        if ( __power_rsc() )
                tempbuf = "Single chip Power";
        else
        if ( __power_rs2() )
                tempbuf = "Power 2";
        else
        if ( __power_601() )
                tempbuf = "PowerPC 601";
        else
        if ( __power_603() )
                tempbuf = "PowerPC 603";
```

Figure 7.15   System configuration example code (*continued on next page*)

```
        else
        if ( __power_604() )
                tempbuf = "PowerPC 604";
        else
        if ( __power_620() )
                tempbuf = "PowerPC 620";
        else
                tempbuf = "UNKNOWN";
        printf( " implementation = %d == %s \ n",
                _system_configuration.implementation, tempbuf);

/* processor version */
        printf( " Processor version = %d \ n",
                _system_configuration.version );

/* processor word width in bits */
        printf( " Processor word width = %d \ n",
                _system_configuration.width );

/* number of CPUs */
        printf( " Number of CPUs = %d \ n",
                _system_configuration.ncpus );

/* cache attributes */
        printf( " cache attributes = %08X \ n",
                _system_configuration.cache_attrib );

        if ( _system_configuration.cache_attrib & 0x00000001 )

        {       /* cache detected */

                if ( _system_configuration.cache_attrib & 0x00000002 )
                {
                        printf ("\ tCombined instruction and data cache\ n");
                        printf ("\ t\ t size = %dK block = %d, line = %d,
                                            associativity = %d \ n",
                                _system_configuration.icache_size/1024,
                                _system_configuration.icache_block,
                                _system_configuration.icache_line,
                                _system_configuration.icache_asc);
                }
                else
                {
                        printf ("\ tSplit instruction and data cache\ n");
                        printf ("\ tIcache \ n");
                        printf ("\ t\ t size = %dK block = %d, line = %d,
                                            associativity = %d \ n",
                                _system_configuration.icache_size/1024,
                                _system_configuration.icache_block,
                                _system_configuration.icache_line,
                                _system_configuration.icache_asc);
```

Figure 7.15 System configuration example code (*cont.*)

```
                        }

                }
                else
                        printf ("\ tNo cache detected \ n") ;

        /* L2 cache */

                printf( "L2 cache size = %dK\ n", _system_configuration.L2_
                                                cache_size/1024);

                if ( _system_configuration.L2_cache_size )
                        printf( "L2 cache associativity = %d\ n", _system_
                                        configuration.L2_cache_asc);

        /* TLB */
                printf( " TLB attributes = %08X \ n", _system_
                                configuration.tlb_attrib );

                if ( _system_configuration.tlb_attrib & 0x00000001 )

                {       /* tlb detected */

                        if ( _system_configuration.tlb_attrib & 0x00000002 )
                        {
                                printf ("\ tCombined instruction and data TLB\ n");
                                printf ("\ tITLB \ n");
                                printf ("\ t\ t size = %d , associativity = %d \ n",
                                        _system_configuration.itlb_size,
                                        _system_configuration.itlb_asc);
                        }
                        else
                        {
                                printf (" Split TLB\ n");
                                printf ("\ tITLB \ n");
                                printf ("\ t\ t size = %d , associativity = %d \ n",
                                        _system_configuration.itlb_size,
                                        _system_configuration.itlb_asc);
                                printf ("\ tDTLB \ n");
                                printf ("\ t\ t size = %d , associativity = %d \ n",
                                        _system_configuration.dtlb_size,
                                        _system_configuration.dtlb_asc);
                        }
                }

        }
```

Figure 7.15   System configuration example code (*cont.*)

7.3   Hardware Optimization

So far, I have talked about avoiding time-expensive system calls to the kernel; they are expensive simply because they execute lots of instructions. As far as the high-level language programmer is concerned, each instruction takes the same amount of time as any other, but the machine language programmer knows better—there are cheap instructions, and there are expensive instructions. I hope to give you a sense of which operations are the more expensive ones without resorting to coding in machine language.

7.3.1   Matrix Access Optimization

Most RISC-based processors, including the PowerPC, use memory cache to make the memory system appear faster than it really is. Ideally all memory accesses would be from the cache, which effectively has an access time four times faster than from main RAM. Typically the processor first-level cache is only tens or hundreds of kilobytes large, whereas main memory is hundreds of megabytes large. Since 100% cache utilization is impossible, the goal is to maximize cache utilization. This maximization translates into a simple axiom: Once a data item reference causes a cache miss, that data item should be referenced as many times as possible in short succession. This reuse of data items is handled quite well by the compiler optimizer that loads a data item from memory once and keeps it in a register for as long as necessary to perform adjacent computations. When it is necessary, the register is stored to memory. This cache reference axiom has a corollary, which is, perhaps, even more important than the axiom: Data items in the same cache line should be accessed in short succession. The goal is to access each data item serially.

For examples that illustrate data cache utilization, I will assume a cache line size of 64 bytes, and a total size of 32K, the cache size of the PowerPC 601 processor. For 8-byte double-precision floating-point values, a cache line will hold eight array elements. I will also assume that the cache miss overhead to reload the cache line is nine cycles. Other processors in the PowerPC family, particularly Power and Power2, have longer cache lines of 128 and 256 bytes and have cache sizes varying from 32K to 128K.

Figure 7.16 shows a simple FORTRAN code example of two vectors being added together. Vectors, or single-dimension arrays, are laid out linearly in memory such that a(2) is in the word address following a(1). Vectors a, b, and c are probably immediately adjacent, but the FORTRAN language does not guarantee that. I will also assume that the arrays I am describing start on a cache line boundary. This assumption makes the description of the start-up conditions easier. Eliminating this assumption does not affect the average calculations of cache miss penalties when the arrays are very large.

When the example begins executing, the first time through the loop will cause a cache miss for the references to a(1), b(1), and c(1). When the cache is reloaded, values

```
real(8)  a(10000), b(10000), c(10000)
do j=1,10000
                c(j)=a(j)+b(j)
enddo
```

Figure 7.16   Stride 1 example

for a(1) to a(8) will be loaded into one cache line, b(1) to b(8) into another, and c(1) to c(8) into another. For the next seven loops there will be cache hits for references to a(j), b(j), and c(j). When j reaches 8, the array elements are now in a new cache line, so we encounter three misses again. The cache miss ratio is 1 miss per 8 accesses. If every array element is referenced once and only once, as in this example, then 1 miss per 8 is the best that can be achieved. The program is accessing each array in increasing memory order with a one element increment. This term of one element increments is called *stride one* access, which is optimal and the nirvana that numerical coders seek to attain.

You might ask how anyone could concoct a program that accesses vectors in anything but a stride one pattern. Figure 7.17 shows a ludicrous example of a stride 8 access pattern. The inner loop causes the a, b, and c arrays to be accessed by skipping eight elements. This contrived program has a cache miss on every access and has the minimum performance. I had to write a lot of extra obtuse code to get anything but stride one access. We will see shortly how easy it is to get large strides when the code accesses two-dimensional arrays.

```
real(8)   a(10000), b(10000), c(10000)
do i=0,7
          do j=1,10000,8
              c(j+i)=a(j+i)+b(j+i)
          enddo
enddo
```

Figure 7.17   Stride 8 example

Table 7.3 shows the theoretical performance impact due to cache miss overhead compared to various strides. I show the cycle cost for 8 accesses for the various stride values.

Stride Length	Cycle Penalty	Cycle Penalty Total	Speed Penalty
fully cached	8	= 8	100%
stride 1	9+7	= 16	50%
stride 2	2*(3+9)	= 24	33%
stride 4	4*(1+9)	=40	20%
stride 8	8 * 9	=72	11%
stride 1024	8*(36+9)	360	2%

Table 7.3   Data cache miss penalties

Increasing the stride beyond 8 can't get any worse, or can it? When an access crosses a page boundary, there is another possible penalty due to translation lookaside buffer (TLB) misses. The TLB caches recently translated virtual page addresses. If that page has not been recently accessed, it is likely that the TLB does not have the address cached, and the page frame table must be searched for a match. This address table lookup takes about 36 cycles. As the stride approaches 4K, TLB miss overhead begins to overshadow cache miss overhead. For stride 1024 (one page), there is a TLB miss per access, which gives an overhead of 36 cycles for the TLB miss and 9 cycles for the cache miss, or 45 cycles per access. For 8 accesses this means 360 cycles, or 2% of the theoretical maximum. Even though this book is being written in Texas, I contend that bigger is not better—when it comes to stride.

Figure 7.18 shows a FORTRAN program, and Figure 7.19 shows a C program that accesses two-dimensional arrays. Both programs look identical, except for the different language implementation. In Figure 7.18, array c is accessed in order of elements c(1,1), c(1,2), c(1,3), and so on. Unfortunately the FORTRAN language specifies that the array is arranged in memory in order c(1,1), c(2,1), c(3,1), and so on. The stride for arrays a, b, and c are all stride 100. Since the arrays are all too big to fit in a 32K-cache, the cache miss penalties start to add up. The code can be easily fixed by switching the inner and outer loops as shown in Figure 7.20. The C program is already stride 1 because C arranges matrices in the opposite memory order.

```
real(8) a(100,100), b(100,100), c(100,100)
do m=1,100
        do n=1,100
            c(m,n) = c(m,n) + a(m,n) * b(m,n)
        enddo
enddo
```

Figure 7.18   Optimal stride example

```
double x[100,100], y[100,100], z[100,100]
 for ( m=0;m<100; m++)
        for ( n=0; n<100; n++)
            z[m,n] = z[m,n] + x[m,n] * y[m,n]
```

Figure 7.19   Nonoptimal stride example

```
real(8) a(100,100), b(100,100), c(100,100)
do n=1,100
        do m=1,100
            c(m,n) = c(m,n) + a(m,n) * b(m,n)
        enddo
enddo
```

Figure 7.20   Improved stride example

The rule to remember is that FORTRAN arrays should be accessed so that the leftmost subscript varies most frequently, that is, the subscript should vary in the innermost loop. C arrays should be accessed so that the rightmost subscript varies most frequently.

There are many other techniques to improve the performance of programs that calculate with arrays of floating-point numbers. The example of stride minimization has the most impact for the least hand tuning. These techniques are described in several other publications. Kevin Dowd's *High Performance Computing* covers these techniques as they apply to the general class of high-performance workstations. *Optimization and Tuning Guide for Fortran, C, and C++* and *Rise System/600 NIC Tuning Guide for Fortran and C* cover these topics with specific examples pertaining to the Power architecture.

7.3.2   Lock Access Optimization

So far, the examples of locking have considered contention among competing threads for only one lock. There is another type of contention that occurs only on multiprocessor systems in which different threads running concurrently on different processors are accessing different locks. Considering the program, the locks are independent and uncontended, but considering the multiprocessor system, the locks are contended because they both reside in the same cache line. Figure 7.21 shows the situation. Thread A is accessing lock 1, while thread B is accessing lock 2. Lock 1 and lock 2 are adjacent in memory so they are in the same cache line. Because the system has to maintain cache coherency of all of the processor L2 caches, anytime a lock changes state, the cache line that contains that lock is written to memory and the caches of every other processor are invalidated. For the simple two-processor example, lock 1 changes state in the cache of processor A. The cache line is written to memory, and the same cache line in processor B is invalidated. When B accesses lock 2, the access must come from memory instead of cache, which is two to four times slower. When access to lock 2 completes, the cache line in processor A will be invalidated, causing the next reference to lock 1 to come from memory.

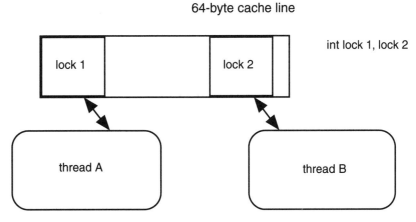

Figure 7.21   False sharing example

All this cache invalidation can be avoided simply by ensuring that lock 1 and lock 2 are in separate cache lines. Figure 7.22 shows how to remedy the situation. Instead of accidentally allowing the compiler to place two independent locks adjacent to one another in memory, you place the lock in a structure followed by padding. The structure and padding ensure that the locks will not end up in the same cache line. Data cache line sizes for PowerPC is 64 bytes. You should make sure that your lock words are spaced at least 64 bytes apart. Even if you have to supply padding, the cost is well worth the increase in performance. A simple test of programs that repetitively test locks in the same cache line and different cache lines shows a sixfold speedup for locks in different cache lines.

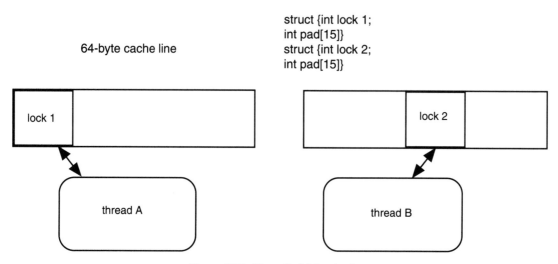

Figure 7.22   Remedied false sharing

7.3.3   Word Alignment

RISC processors tend to be sensitive to how integers are aligned in memory, and the PowerPC is no exception. The processor can access an integer that is aligned on a word boundary (addressed by an address that is evenly divisible by 4) much faster than it can address one that is not aligned on a word boundary. Normally the compiler and linker properly align integers and floats at their optimal address alignment. However, programmers playing with pointers can cause major disruption. A loaded pointer in the wrong hands can be a dangerous weapon. Figure 7.23 shows an example of how a pointer can point to a misaligned data word. The address 20000102 is a misaligned word because the address is not divisible by 4. However, 20000100 is divisible by 4 and is, therefore, properly aligned.

Figure 7.24 shows a program that contrasts correctly aligned words with incorrectly aligned words. Notice the (int *) cast that tips you off that something is fishy. This sort of pointer manipulation usually happens by accident with FORTRAN programs that call C programs. The C programmer can quite easily forget what the data arrays contain, or this kind of alignment mistake can happen without pointers in FORTRAN by using the dreaded EQUIVALENCE statement.

Unaligned word access

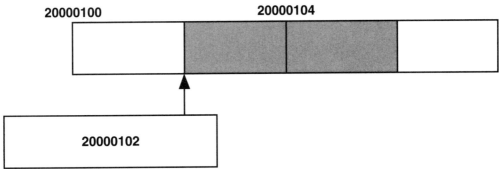

Properly aligned access

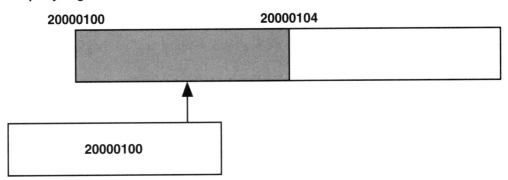

Figure 7.23   Illustration of pointer misalignment

```
int *p, a[100],i;
short *q;
p=a;

for ( i = 0; i< 10000000;i++)
        *p = 0;
q=a;  q++;
p=(int *)q; /* note that you really have to want this badly */
for ( i = 0; i< 10000000;i++)
        *p = 0;
```

Figure 7.24   Code example of misaligned data

The final misbegotten moral to the story is: Loaded pointers don't kill data—loaded programmers kill data.

7.4   Summary

The important points to remember from this chapter are:

1. Applications should perform file I/O with a minimum of 4K buffer size and a maximum on the order of 128K.

2. AIX has several unique interprocess synchronization programming interfaces that can speed up applications that have a heavy reliance on process synchronization. `Msem_lock` and `check_lock` are two interfaces that exist only on AIX.

3. Mapped file I/O can speed up an I/O intensive program by eliminating `read` and `write` calls and reducing the overall system CPU percentage.

4. Programs that compute with very large matrices of data should attempt to access these matrices in stride-one fashion in order to minimize hardware cache miss penalties.

5. Programs that run on SMP systems should avoid placing unrelated locks in the same cache line to avoid unnecessary cache updates.

8

Putting It All Together

The previous chapters have described individual tools and how to use and interpret their reports. I want to discuss how to use these tools to work together efficiently. A lot of what I have to say in this chapter is common sense that is not specific to AIX. Hopefully generic common sense is always in demand. Let me pose this statement of common sense in the form of a question: What really is the problem? You need to know where to start once you are convinced you have a valid problem that you are capable of solving. Then you need to know in which direction to proceed once you have analyzed initial data, and you need to know when you are done.

8.1   What Is the Problem—Really?

I usually get involved in solving a performance problem when someone approaches me with a complaint. The complainer has expectations that his AIX system should be faster than it really is. Perhaps a similar system performs better. Or perhaps a deadline will not be met if the system doesn't speed up and finish the job. Or perhaps if the system does not perform fast enough, a multithousand dollar sale will be lost, and the complainer will not be able to make his boat loan payment next month. All of these expectations can be legitimate, but they can also be bogus if some of the underlying assumptions are wrong.

The expectation of a similar system being faster is one that I can relate to objectively. The faster system can be measured and proven to run the assigned task in the claimed time. It can also be examined to see if it is inherently faster. We want to avoid what I call the "racing Volkswagens against Ferraris" (RVAF for short) syndrome. It is ludicrous to put a Volkswagen on the racetrack with a Ferrari and expect the Volkswagen to win (barring a jet engine under the Volkswagen's hood).

The primary way to avoid the RVAF syndrome is to determine the configuration of the problem system. Before you spend a lot of time gathering data to determine the bottleneck, you should understand two of the most important configuration items. Determine the processor type and its speed rating and the amount of RAM in the system. If either of these is underpowered in comparison to another system that seems to perform fine, then fix the hardware before trying to tune the system. We want to avoid racing Volkswagens against Ferraris and then complaining that the Volkswagen is too slow.

Comparing the CPU power of two systems with different processors is difficult. The simplest and least time-consuming approach is to compare the SPEC ratings of the two systems to see how similar they are. I was involved in a situation a few years ago when a customer complained that his system was performing poorly. The time to compile and link was taking twice as long as he expected. What was the rationale for his expectation? He was comparing the speed of compilation to his other system (made by a competitor of the company I work for). The other system was a brand new one whose SPECint95 rating was about double that of the five-year-old slow system. The solution to the performance problem was to get a faster system. There was no way that I could make up the difference of the processor speed by some magic system tuning. I saved a lot of time by determining that the race between the Volkswagen and the Ferrari was mismatched from the start.

SPEC ratings may not be the proper metric with which to compare systems. I used SPECint95 because compiling programs is largely integer computing, but you could just as well use some other metric that is published for both systems. The choice is yours based on the type of work load that is problematic and which metrics are available to you.

Be aware that comparing performance metrics is merely a sanity check for your expectations. If the SPEC numbers of two systems are evenly matched, but the actual performance running the same application differs markedly, then it should be possible to correct the performance of the slower system. There may be factors beyond CPU speed that affect performance.

This brings me to the next point: You should check memory configurations right after you check processor speed. A system with half the memory of another could be at a disadvantage if the memory were overcommitted enough to cause paging. For example, most people know that AIX running the Common Desktop Environment (CDE) should have at least 32MB of RAM. If someone complained to you that CDE was slow, you might ask how much RAM there was. If the answer was 16MB, you would immediately say "Take a 16MB pill, and call me in the morning." Likewise, if a customer called you complaining of poor AIX performance while trying to design an airplane wing using a CAD-CAM application, you would immediately ask how much RAM he was using. If the answer is 128MB, you should suspect a potential memory shortage. If the answer is 64MB, you definitely know that memory is inadequate. With application experience, you get a feeling for inadequate memory resources.

8.2   Where Do I Start?

If you ask, "Where do I start?" then I must answer a question with a question. What is the predominant system bottleneck? Is it CPU-bound, disk I/O bound, or memory-bound?

The starting place is a reading glass tool—namely, `vmstat`. `Vmstat` produces a compact report that identifies the three most important bottlenecks. The sum of the user (`us`) plus system (`sy`) approaching 100% tells you the system is CPU-bound. The I/O wait percentage (`wa`) far exceeding 10% indicates the system is disk I/O bound. And, the paging rate (sum of `po` plus `pi`) far exceeding 10 pages per second indicates the system is memory-bound. In addition, `vmstat` is free (it comes with AIX), its report can be sent by e-mail, and it can be run in the background with a shell script.

You can certainly answer the predominant bottleneck question with the Performance Toolbox also. Its primary advantage is that the output is easy to read, but don't assume every system administrator has it. If you are in the business of troubleshooting performance problems on systems other than your own, you can't rely on the Performance Toolbox being there for you.

8.3   Where Do I Go Next?

Once you have determined the primary bottleneck, you can gather more details. A CPU-bound problem would indicate running `tprof` next to determine which process is using the most CPU time. Once the offending process is discovered you have a choice to make. If you have capability to take remedies (namely changing source code) on the application that seems to be the CPU culprit, then additional profiling is in order. Run `tprof` again, specifying the program file name to get a subroutine breakdown, or recompile and relink the application to run `gprof`.

Memory-bound situations would indicate running `svmon` to determine which program is using the most memory. And disk I/O bound situations would indicate running `filemon` to get more details on which files and disks are taking the worst I/O beating.

8.4   Take Some Remedy

Remedies are the really hard part of this business, although they are more easily described than done. I discussed system administrative remedies in Chapters 3 and 4, but I can't really describe how to make program remedies since this requires application domain knowledge.

The first rule of thumb for remedies is to attack the top bottleneck; determining it is sometimes obvious. A profiling report for a 100% CPU-bound system readily illustrates this example: the top subroutine on the list is the top bottleneck. But what if the system is only 60% CPU-bound and 20% I/O wait, and the profile report says subroutine B is taking 30% of the time? At first glance, it is not clear which is predominant, but if you estimate the upper bound of the improvement if the bottleneck is entirely eliminated, then you have the best guess you can get. If subroutine B were infinitely speeded up (its time goes to zero), then the total speedup is 30% of 60% which equals 18%. If the I/O wait could be entirely eliminated, then the speedup is 20%. The numbers tell you to work on remedying the I/O wait.

Another rule of thumb is to make one remedy at a time. After making the remedy, run the work load again and see if the remedy had an effect on the performance of the work. If the effect was positive, gather more statistics to determine if the bottleneck was diminished to the point where another bottleneck now predominates. The main problem with trying more than one remedy is that the negative effect of one remedy can cancel the positive effect of another. The result looks as if both remedies are useless, but in reality one remedy has a positive effect.

8.5   When to Stop

The decision when to stop trying performance remedies depends on how tenacious you are—or how much free time you have on your hands—it's very subjective. The complainers may think that the time you spend to improve performance a small percent is time well spent, but you may have a different opinion. And remember that you can rarely eliminate bottlenecks entirely; therefore your expectation for improvements is really much less than the upper bound you estimated.

Quite often you stop trying remedies when you run out of time. In customer-oriented situations, the sales team has a completion deadline to meet. On race day, the pit crew has to have the car ready at start time. The crew can't ask to delay the race because the car isn't running at top form. Likewise, a race is sometimes not won by the fastest but by the car that runs the longest. Sometimes the fastest car crashes and does not finish the race, but don't take my analogy too literally. My point is that the winner of a computer competition is not necessarily the fastest—the system has to be only fast enough. Other factors like price and sexy-colored covers may sway a buy decision.

8.6   Summary of Tools

Let me present a final summary of which tools to use for which situations. Table 8.1 lists the reading glass tools that you should use first to gain a systemwide view of performance. Once you get a systemwide view from the reading glass tools, you should collect more detailed data by using the magnifying glass tools to get a process-level view. You would use the specific tools indicated by the predominant bottleneck. Table 8.2 lists the magnifying glass tools. If the magnifying glass tools are unable to provide sufficient insight, you might need to use some of the microscope tools to deduce what is happening. Table 8.3 lists the microscope tools.

Command Name	Primary Use
vmstat	CPU utilization
iostat	disk I/O utilization
sar	CPU utilization
ps	process status
xmperf	all statistics
monitor	all statistics
netstat	network utilization
nfsstat	NFS utilization

Table 8.1   Reading glass tools

Command	Primary Use
tprof	CPU-bound
filemon	disk I/O bound
svmon	memory-bound
rmss	memory-bound
netpmon	network-bound

Table 8.2   Magnifying glass tools

Command	Primary Use
gprof	program detailed profiling
xgprof	program detailed profiling
trace	detailed event sequences
pv	detailed event sequences

Table 8.3   Microscope tools

Appendix

A.1 References

A.1.1 IBM Publications

The following publications can be ordered through IBM by calling (800) 879-2755 or by accessing the IBM Direct online catalog at http://www.elink.ibmlink.ibm.com/pbl/pbl

AIX 4.1 Performance Tuning Guide: SC23-2365
Cset++ for AIX User's Guide: SC09-1968
Optimization and Tuning Guide for Fortran, C, and C++: SC09-1705
Performance Toolbox for AIX—Guide and Reference: SC23-2625
Risc System/6000 NIC Tuning Guide for Fortran and C: GG24-3611
XL Fortran User's Guide: SC09-1610

A.1.2 External Publications

The following publications can be obtained in bookstores or through the publishers:

Comer, Douglas E. *Internetworking with TCP/IP.* vol. 1. Englewood Cliffs, NJ: Prentice-Hall, 1991.
Dowd, Kevin. *High Performance Computing.* Sebastapol, CA: O'Reilly and Associates, Inc., 1993.
Loukides, Mike. *System Performance Tuning.* Sebastapol, CA: O'Reilly and Associates, Inc., 1991.

Nichols, Bradford et al. *Pthreads Programming.* Sebastapol, CA: O'Reilly and Associates, Inc., 1996.

Schimmel, Curt. *UNIX Systems for Modern Architectures.* Reading, MA: Addison-Wesley, 1994.

Stern, Hal. *Managing NFS and NIS.* Sebastapol, CA: O'Reilly and Associates, Inc., 1991.

Siegert, Andreas. *The AIX Survival Guide.* Harlow, England: Addison-Wesley, 1996.

Stevens, W. Richard. *Advanced Programming in the UNIX Environment.* Reading, MA: Addison-Wesley, 1992.

Stevens, W. Richard. *TCP/IP Illustrated.* vol. 1, Reading, MA: Addison-Wesley, 1994.

A.2   Sources for AIX Software

This section tells how to obtain the software packages referred to in the text.

A.2.1   IBM Sources

One of the common problems is finding the location of tools. Since so much of AIX is optionally installed, often the tool you want isn't installed. Most of the software is licensed by the system supplier from IBM, so I refer to these sources as IBM sources. The actual order numbers and prices must be obtained from your software supplier. Once you have the proper software media in hand, the following tables will help you to determine what to install.

A.2.1.1   Base AIX

The following tools, shown in Table A.1, are packaged in the base operating system (bos).

Tool	Fileset
vmstat	bos.acct
iostat	bos.acct
sar	bos.acct
netstat	bos.net.tcp.client
ps	bos.rte.control

Tool	Fileset
pdt_config	bos.perf.diag_tool
tcpdump	bos.net.tcp.server
no	bos.net.tcp.client
nfsstat	bos.net.nfs.client
nfso	bos.net.nfs.client
gprof	bos.adt.prof
trace	bos.sysmgt.trace

Table A.1   Base AIX tools

A.2.1.2   Performance Toolbox

Several of the tools mentioned in Chapter 2 are not found in the base operating system. Instead, they are packaged in the optional Performance Toolbox software package. The tools are outlined in Table A.2.

Tool	Fileset
tprof	perfagent.tools
svmon	perfagent.tools
rmss	perfagent.tools
filemon	perfagent.tools
perfmgr	perfmgr

Table A.2   Performance toolbox

A.2.1.3 Pv and Xgprof

Pv and xgprof can be obtained from the IBM AIX Developers Connection CD-ROM distribution. In the United States call (800) 633-8266 or FAX (303-330-7655) for information on subscriptions. The WWW URL is http://www.developer.ibm.com/devcon/index.html.

A.2.1.4 Utld

Utld can be obtained from the World Wide Web at the following address:

ftp://ftp.software.ibm.com/aix/tools/perftools/utld/utld.obj

A.3   Sources for Free Software for AIX on the Net

Sources for monitor (the AIX version of the top monitor) and the xrn newsreader can be obtained at the WWW addresses that follow. Not only is monitor found here, but a lot of other useful free software is available, too.

Bull Worldwide Information Systems has a download page of precompiled packages that are installed via SMIT. The Bull site seems to have the most up-to-date packages.

http://www-frec.bull.com/download/out/

The University of California at Los Angeles has the oldest archive site for AIX software, but just because it's the oldest doesn't mean it's the best. Some of the packages here tend to be rather out-of-date, but there are more packages listed here than at the Bull site.

http://aixpdslib.seas.ucla.edu/aixpdslib.html/

Linpack sources can be found at the following netlib site:

http://www.netlib.org

A.4   Performance Toolbox Metrics

The Performance Toolbox graphical interface (xmperf) allows you to monitor a mind-numbing assortment of system statistics. Most of the time, these statistics are not useful. However, I have compiled a list of my favorite system statistics to make your job of configuring your own toolbox consoles a bit easier. The following list was created by editing the full list of statistics, which I created by running xmpeek -l. Try this on your system, and you should get at least 500 statistics. I have condensed them into just a couple of pages of statistics that really matter. These measure the most common system resource bottlenecks. I have also included network error counters. When network error counts become significant, they imply the network subsystem is possibly retransmitting data and impacting performance.

CPU/	Central processor statistics
CPU/gluser	System-wide time executing in user mode (percent)
CPU/glkern	System-wide time executing in kernel mode (percent)
CPU/glwait	System-wide time waiting for IO (percent)
CPU/glidle	System-wide time CPU is idle (percent)
Mem/	Memory statistics
Mem/Real/	Physical memory statistics
Mem/Real/size	Size of physical memory (4K pages)
Mem/Real/numfrb	Number of pages on free list
Mem/Real/noncomp	Number of non-computational pages resident in memory
Mem/Real/comp	Number of computational pages resident in memory
Mem/Real/numlocal memory	Number of local pages resident in
Mem/Real/numclient	Number of client pages resident in memory
Mem/Real/maxclient	Maximum number of client pages allowed
Mem/Real/pdecay	Decay rate for repaging values
Mem/Real/sysrepag	Global repaging rate
Mem/Real/%free	% memory which is free
Mem/Real/%pinned	% memory which is pinned
Mem/Real/%comp	% memory allocated to computational segments
Mem/Real/%noncomp	% memory allocated to non-computational segments
Mem/Real/%local	% memory allocated to local segments
Mem/Real/%clnt	% memory allocated to client segments
Mem/Virt/	Virtual memory management statistics
Mem/Virt/pagein	4K pages read by VMM
Mem/Virt/pageout	4K pages written by VMM
Mem/Virt/pgspgin	4K pages read from paging space by VMM
Mem/Virt/pgspgout	4K pages written to paging space by VMM
Mem/Virt/comrepag	Repage rate to computational segments
Mem/Virt/%comrepag	% of repage requests coming from computational segments
Mem/Virt/ncomrepag	Repage rate to non-computational segments
Mem/Virt/%ncomrepag	% of repage requests coming from non-computational segments
Mem/Virt/comrepl	Page replace rate in computational segments
Mem/Virt/%comrepl	% of page replace requests coming from computational segments
Mem/Virt/ncomrepl	Page replace rate in non-computational segments

Mem/Virt/%ncomrepl   % of page replace requests coming from
                                non-comp segments

PagSp/   Paging space statistics
PagSp/%totalfree   Total free disk paging space (percent)
PagSp/%totalused   Total used disk paging space (percent)
PagSp/pgspgin   4K pages read from paging space by VMM
PagSp/pgspgout   4K pages written to paging space by VMM

Disk/   Disk and CD ROM statistics
Disk/hdisk0/   Statistics for disk hdisk0
Disk/hdisk0/busy   Time disk is busy (percent)
Disk/hdisk0/xfer   Transfers to/from disk
Disk/hdisk0/rblk   512 byte blocks read from disk
Disk/hdisk0/wblk   512 byte blocks written to disk

Proc/   Process statistics
Proc/pswitch   Process context switches
Proc/runque   Average count of processes that are
                              waiting for the cpu
Proc/runocc   Number of samplings of runque
Proc/swpque   Average count of processes waiting to be
                              paged in
Proc/swpocc   Number of samplings of swpque

Syscall/   System call statistics
Syscall/total   Total system calls
Syscall/read   Read system calls
Syscall/write   Write system calls
Syscall/fork   Fork system calls
Syscall/exec   Exec system calls

FS/   File system statistics
FS/rootvg/   Statistics for volume group rootvg
[00008920c6715e2d]
FS/rootvg/free   Free space in volume group, MB
FS/rootvg/hd4/   /
FS/rootvg/hd4/size   File system size in KB
FS/rootvg/hd4/%totfree   Free space in percent
FS/rootvg/hd4/%totused   Used space in percent

LAN/   LAN Interfaces
LAN/ent0/   Statistics for network interface ent0
LAN/ent0/bytesout   Count of bytes transmitted correctly
LAN/ent0/bytesin   Count of bytes received correctly
LAN/ent0/framesout   Count of frames transmitted correctly
LAN/ent0/framesin   Count of frames received correctly
LAN/ent0/xmiterrors   Count of frame transmit errors at
                                 adapter level

LAN/ent0/rcverrors	Count of frame receive errors at adapter level
LAN/ent0/highxmitq	Maximum transmits ever queued for this device
LAN/ent0/recvintr	Receive data interrupts for this device
LAN/ent0/xmitovfl	Count of transmit queue overflows
LAN/ent0/xmitdrops	Count of transmit packets dropped at device driver level
LAN/ent0/recvdrops	Count of receive packets dropped at device driver level
IP/	Internet Protocol statistics
IP/rcvtotal	Total IP packets received
IP/rcvfrag	IP fragments received
IP/forward	IP packets forwarded
IP/rcvdgrm	Successfully received IP datagrams
IP/snddgrm	Transmitted IP datagrams

A.5   Source Examples

A.5.1 Sieve of Erosthenes—`sieve.c`

```
#include <stdio.h>

#define ARGS "spdh?"
#define USAGE "[ARGS] filename"
#define MAIN 1
#define TRUE 1
#define FALSE 0

int print=0;
int debug=0;
int syscall=0;

int *prime,*start,*end;

main(int argc,char **argv)
{
  int c;
          extern int optind;
          extern char *optarg;
          register int x;
          double sqrt();
          int last;

/* parse command line arguments */
          while ((c = getopt(argc, argv,ARGS)) != EOF){
```

```
        switch (c) {
                case 'p':
                        print=1;
                        break;
                case 's':
                        syscall = 1;
                        break;
                case 'd':
                        debug = 1;
                        setbuf(stdout,0);
                        break;
                case 'h':
                case '?':
                default:
                        usage();
                        exit(1);
        }
    }

if    (optind>=argc){
        usage();
        exit(1);
    }
    last=atoi(argv[optind]);

        prime=malloc(sizeof(int *)*(int)(last));

    start=prime; *prime=2;
    prime++;
    end=prime;
    *end=0;

    for(x=3;x<last; x++){
        if (primecheck(x)){
                *end = x;
                end++;
                *end=(0);
        }
    }
    if (print){
        for(prime=start;*prime!=*end;prime++){
                fprintf(stdout,"%7d\n",*prime);
        }
    }
    free(prime);
    exit(0);
}

primecheck(int x)
```

```
{
        int isprime=TRUE;

        for(prime=start;*prime<=(int)sqrt((double)x); prime++){
            if (*prime == *end)
                    break;
            if (debug) { printf ("testing factors %d and
              %d\n",x,*prime);}
            if (syscall) { getpid(); }
            if ((x % *prime)==0){
                    isprime=FALSE;
                    break;
            }
        }
            return(isprime);
}

int usage()
{
            fprintf(stderr,"sieve -[p][s][d][h]#\n");
            return(0);
}
```

Index